Sovereign Individuals
of
Capitalism

By the same authors

THE DOMINANT IDEOLOGY THESIS
THE PENGUIN DICTIONARY OF SOCIOLOGY

Sovereign Individuals of Capitalism

NICHOLAS ABERCROMBIE

STEPHEN HILL

BRYAN S. TURNER

London
ALLEN & UNWIN
Boston   Sydney

Allen & Unwin (Publishers) Ltd,
40 Museum Street, London WC1A 1LU, UK

Allen & Unwin (Publishers) Ltd,
Park Lane, Hemel Hempstead, Herts HP2 4TE, UK

Allen & Unwin, Inc.,
8 Winchester Place, Winchester, Mass. 01890, USA

Allen & Unwin (Australia) Ltd,
8 Napier Street, North Sydney, NSW 2060, Australia

First published in 1986

British Library Cataloguing in Publication Data

Abercrombie, Nicholas
    Sovereign individuals of capitalism.
1. Capitalism 2. Individualism – Political aspects
I. Title II. Hill, Stephen, 1946–   III. Turner, Bryan S.
330.12′2   HB501
ISBN 0-04-301230-2
ISBN 0-04-301231-0 Pbk

Library of Congress Cataloging-in-Publication Data

Abercrombie, Nicholas.
    Sovereign individuals of capitalism.
Bibliography: p.
Includes index.
1. Capitalism. 2. Individualism. I. Hill, Stephen.
II. Turner, Bryan S. III. Title.
HB501.A23 1986   330.12′2   86-1122
ISBN 0-04-301230-2 (alk. paper)
ISBN 0-04-301231-0 (pbk.: alk. paper)

Set in 10 on 12 point Sabon by
Computape (Pickering) Limited, North Yorkshire
and printed in Great Britain by
Billing & Sons Ltd
Worcester

For
Bren, Jane and Karen

Over himself, over his own body and
mind, the individual is sovereign.
J. S. Mill,
On Liberty

Contents

Acknowledgements

We wish to acknowledge the helpful comments made by participants at seminars where we have read various versions of parts of this book: at the Universities of Lancaster, Essex, Birmingham, New South Wales, Monash and Tasmania. Our very grateful thanks also go to Pam Ebdon who typed the manuscript.

September 1985

Prologue

This book is about individualism and capitalism, and their relationship. The conviction that individualism and capitalism are related has proved pervasive, powerful and persistent. It is to be found in contemporary social and economic thought, and among those nineteenth-century commentators who shared a concern to describe and explain industrial capitalism. Indeed, classical sociology was largely formed in reaction to, and in order to understand, the changes that embryonic industrial capitalism brought about in society. These changes were seen as transforming traditional society and the place of individuals. The rise of individualism as a novel conception of the sovereignty of individuals, and as a new pattern of individual behaviour, appeared to be corrosive of existing social arrangements. Individualism was in turn seen to be a defining feature of capitalism. Individualism and capitalism have remained indissolubly linked in subsequent sociological and economic theory. The relationship, however, has been subjected to remarkably little systematic analysis. How and why it holds, and whether it will continue to hold, are questions that rarely get asked.

Several commentators have seen flaws in the purported linkage. These include the problem of periodization, namely that individualism and capitalism do not correspond in time, and the problem that some societies are capitalist but do not appear to give much weight to the individual. But such specific insights have not been developed into any more general position. We notice also that capitalism has been widely scrutinized and discussed in the literature, with some clarification of the concept and the phenomena to which it refers. Individualism, however, has not been examined in the same way; indeed, the term has largely been taken for granted as something whose meaning is both commonplace and common sense. In point of fact, current usages refer to several quite different things. These flaws indicate that there is a need to revisit individualism and

1

capitalism. In this book, we subject both, and their relationships, to systematic historical and conceptual investigation. We find that there is no necessary or inevitable linkage: they simply relate to each other contingently.

We can identify a number of different definitions of 'individualism'. These include the social recognition that individuals differ among themselves and that individuals should be given importance as against collectivities. This for us is the simplest and least developed social conception of the individual, and one that lies behind more elaborated cultural representations. We refer to this as the Discovery of the Individual. We also find individualism, individuality, individuation. Individualism, properly so called, was in origin mainly a political and subsidiarily an economic doctrine relating to the rights and obligations of persons that was associated with the English political theory of the seventeenth century, which later heavily influenced British and American culture. Individuality is concerned with the education of inner feeling and subjectivity. By contrast, individuation is a bureaucratic procedure that uniquely identifies individuals for the purpose of social administration and control.

These conceptual and terminological distinctions enable us to resolve a number of puzzling features about the relationship of capitalism and individualism. One is the connection between long-run and short-run accounts of what has loosely been called 'individualism'. On the one hand, Christianity is often seen as an individualistic religion that has shaped the cultural history of Western societies, while, on the other, individualism is seen to be a specifically modern ideology. Our argument is that, through Christianity, there has been in the West a long-term emphasis on the individual, but that Christianity is not an individualistic ideology or a version of individualism, because it gives prominence to collectivist norms (such as the Church as the body of Christ) and emphasizes altruistic morality. Individualism was a new system of belief and practice emerging in the seventeenth century and was classically formulated as a secular view of the political and economic rights of the propertied.

Discourses of the individual and capitalism have a certain historical and sociological autonomy. However, in the early modern period they collide and for a while shape each other. English agrarian capitalism took a particular shape under the influence of

2

individualism as a specific set of doctrines and institutions surrounding property and representation. But both phenomena are autonomous, have their own processes of development, and develop separately. Thus, with the changes of late capitalism and with shifts among discourses of the individual, capitalism and individualism diverge and cease to be related in modern times. Capitalism becomes collectivist and bureaucratic, and the discourse of individualism loses its prominence. Therefore, we claim that the capitalism–individualism relation is contingent, theoretically and substantively: capitalism and individualism are related only in one historical epoch and only in the West. We suggest that the capitalism of the Orient that has developed in Japan differs from early Western capitalism, while all forms of late capitalism also differ from early capitalism.

Just as Max Weber said that Protestantism did not cause capitalism, so we do not argue that any of the different forms of 'individualism' were causally important for capitalism either. More generally, we do not suggest that ideology or culture determine the economy or vice versa. But we do accept the relevance of cultural analysis to the sociological enterprise. We resolve the puzzle of belief and economic structure in our claim that capitalism and individualism can best be seen as being locked into a functional circle in a particular period, and that individualism defines the *form* that capitalism took.

We illustrate these arguments with historical and comparative analysis of Britain, America and Japan. Britain and America have conventionally been seen as examples of individualistic capitalism, Japan as the obverse, with Germany and France in between. We suggest that early British capitalism was not in fact unalloyed individualistic capitalism, there being a continual pressure towards non-individualistic forms. We further argue that the highly individualistic culture found in contemporary America is not compatible with an effective capitalist economy.

Modern liberals of the New Right postulate that capitalism and individualism are intimately connected. They suggest that capitalism promotes the economic and political freedom of persons, and so defends the individual against the state. They claim as their prerogative the championing of individualism against all the forces of collectivism. With the exception of F. A. Hayek, however, modern liberals rarely confront those changes which, in modern times, have dissolved the linkage between capitalism and individualism: namely, the dominance of non-individualistic, corporate capitalism, and autonomous developments within individualism. In this book we provide the necessary background against which the claims of neo-classical liberalism can be viewed.

In the process of such an investigation as this, one inevitably encounters a number of philosophical and methodological issues in the sociology of knowledge and ideology. We delineate a theoretical argument about the relation of ideology and economy, knowledge and society, which attempts to provide an understanding of the notion of the relative autonomy of discourse.

This book is a continuation of a study of the relationships among ideology, economy and society that we started in *The Dominant Ideology Thesis* (1980). There, we showed that subordinate classes cannot be regarded as being incorporated by a dominant ideology in Britain, whereas the proper functioning of the economy required the dominant class to accept the dominant ideology. In this study we are less concerned with subordinate individuals and the issue of incorporation, but we do consider the relation between the discourse or ideology of the dominant class and the way individualistic beliefs and practices provide a shape to economic activity.

The structure of this book is as follows. Chapter 1 investigates how classical sociology treated the subject of the individual and the link between capitalism and individualism. Chapter 2 takes up the long-run history of conceptions that ascribe importance to the individual, without necessarily relating these conceptions to particular societies. In Chapter 3, we argue that there are many different ways of ascribing importance to the individual and we separate individualism from individuality and from the views of the individual that obtain in anarchism and socialism. In Chapters 4 and 5, we show how individualism, considered both as a particular conception of the individual and as the actual practices that people engage in, functions in relation to capitalism both in its origin and in the contemporary world. In Chapter 6, we draw the various threads together and present an overall account of the relationship between social forms and conceptions of the individual.

4

CHAPTER

1

The Sociological Tradition

The sociological use of the term individualism derives from Alexis de Tocqueville's writings on American democracy. De Tocqueville saw American individualism as verging on egoism, which elevated private self-interest and selfishness above all other values, in the long run sapping all forms of public life and communal relationships. The classical sociological tradition had an ambiguous attitude towards this increasingly dominant system of beliefs and behaviour, as it did toward the new social order of capitalism which accompanied individualism. Classical sociology recognized the emancipation of individuals from the incubus of traditionalism, but was critical of many of the implications of individualism and capitalism.

Classical Sociological Views

The nineteenth-century view of the relationship between individuals and society was often summed up in the term individualism. However, as K. W. Swart argues, this term was used to designate three quite different clusters of ideas: 'first, the idealistic doctrine with equalitarian implications of the rights of man, or what may be called political liberalism; secondly, the anti-statist, largely utilitarian doctrine of laissez-faire, or economic liberalism; thirdly, the aristocratic cult of individuality, or Romantic individualism' (Swart, 1962, p. 77). To add further to the complexity, there have been clear national variations in doctrines of individualism. In nineteenth-century Germany, the stress on the individual meant the importance

5

of the development of individual talents and personalities. In France, individualism was frequently construed as a menace to social order, while in Britain the protection of individual rights was an important political good. A final source of confusion is the very widespread use of individualistic doctrines in quite different cultural spheres. It is this feature that makes this such an intriguing problem in sociology. Thus individualism is said to characterize political theories, religious beliefs, literature, painting and economic theory, all apparently different fields with different cognitive requirements.

Besides these diverse views surrounding the term individualism and the discussion of the relationship between individuals and societies in the nineteenth century, a number of *analytical* issues were jumbled together. The term individualism is a nineteenth-century invention. Most nineteenth-century social theorists discussed the actual relationship of individuals and society, the pictures of that relationship adopted in their societies, the desirable relationships, and the methodological issues of whether to explain social phenomena in individualistic or social structural terms. The discussion was largely organized in terms of the desirability of individualism, the vices or virtues of individualistic doctrines or ways of behaving. Accounts of the vices were prominent, particularly in France. Reactions to the Revolution from Catholic conservatives like de Maistre and de Bonald conceived of individualism as the destroyer of religion, law and social order generally; individualism was anarchy. The views of Saint-Simon were also influential, though rather different. He combined a progressive, rather than reactionary, view of history with a concern for social order and a dislike of the Enlightenment's respect for the individual. It is, however, probably Alexis de Tocqueville's views that are best known to sociologists. For him, individualism, which was produced by democracy, involved a withdrawal of individuals from public life into a private sphere, a development which severed social ties and left people at the mercy of a strong state. As an antidote, he gave a special emphasis to localism, regionalism and the social importance of voluntary associations. Intrinsic to most of these accounts was a moral reaction to the appearance of capitalism.

Social theorists were not all anti-individualists, of course. Most notably, Herbert Spencer argued that individuals should be set free from the tyranny of the state and other repressive social institutions – a view that led him to propose extreme laissez-faire doctrines. It is

6

true that, in Spencer's case, there is at least a potential discord between his individualism and his organicism (Peel, 1971). This is not the case with those German writers who cultivated individuality as 'a cult of individual genius and originality, especially as applied to the artist, stressing the conflict between individual and society and the supreme value of subjectivity, solitude and introspection' (Lukes, 1973, p. 19). It received its highest expression in the work of Stirner 'whose individualism amounted to an amoral and anti-intellectualistic vision of freely cooperating and self-assertive egoists' (Lukes, 1973, p. 19).

We turn now to the four major figures in the classical sociological tradition. They all formulated views about the relationship of individuals and society, and were impressed by the specific ways in which capitalist society constructed the individual. These formulations integrated methodological and substantive levels of analysis.

Karl Marx

In the Paris Manuscripts Marx put emphasis on the active, sensuous and practical aspect of human nature under the general notion of *praxis*. Against idealism, Marx modified Feuerbachian anthropology to give prominence to the sensuous character of human embodiment. Human beings are defined by their active appropriation and transformation of nature through their labour. At the ontological level, therefore, Marx saw human individuals as agents who, in transforming their environment, necessarily transform themselves. But this individual development as conscious and practical agents is set in the context of the *social* character of human reality. Marx argued, therefore, that before the development of private property, the division of labour and alienation, the utilitarian/liberal opposition between 'individual' and 'society' did not exist, at least as a meaningful opposition. The bare individual of bourgeois culture is a historical and social product of a particular type of society.

Marx's emphasis on the social/historical constitution of the separate individual became the basis for his opposition to utilitarian philosophers such as Jeremy Bentham and J. S. Mill. Bentham's account of human beings as dominated by anti-social instincts (such as greed and envy) was rejected by Marx on the grounds that 'economic man' in capitalism was not a universal statement of the human essence, but on the contrary a specific, time-bound commentary on free-market capitalism. Marx's philosophical anthropology involved the notion that to satisfy our individual needs we have to be social beings. It was this anthropology of the social individual that provided Marx with what he took to be a factual and moral critique of contemporary society. In particular, it is the division of labour under capitalist conditions of production that transforms complete or 'full' individuals into specialized bare individuals, whose 'personality' is distorted by the narrow, constrained circumstances of their labour and life-world.

These themes were important in Marx's early work (especially in the critique of Feuerbach and the *The German Ideology*), but they assumed a prominent place in the *Grundrisse*:

> A presupposition of wage labour, and one of the historic preconditions for capital, is free labour and the exchange of this free labour for money, in order to reproduce and to realize money, to consume the use value of labour not for individual consumption, but as use value for money. Another presupposition is the separation of free labour from the objective conditions of its realization – from the means of labour and the material for labour. The individual relates to himself as proprietor, as master of the conditions of his reality.
>
> (Marx, 1973, p. 471)

For Marx, the capitalist mode of production is an economic system in which commodities are produced for exchange rather than use. One of its most important preconditions is the existence of free labour, that is, of labourers who are able to sell their labour power in free markets to whomsoever offers the highest price. For capitalism to work effectively, labourers cannot be involved in feudal relations, being tied to particular landowners or to their parcels of land. Individuals have to be defined as *barely* as possible so that all their characteristics, skills or capacities are potentially saleable. In pre-capitalist societies people might be defined by their land, place or residence or particular skills. In classical Athens, for example, a person, together with his land, constituted the individual. In capitalism, however, these characteristics have to be separated from persons so that they can be sold. The relation between an individual and his or her characteristics is therefore one of *possession* not identity. What is required is for the individual to be isolated, bare and separable from social ties.

The requirement for the isolated or bare individual (adjectives that Marx often uses) is reflected in law and property relations. In pre-capitalist society, Marx believed that the basic unit of ownership was not the individual but the household. In capitalist society, however, the individual became the legal subject with the guaranteed freedom to dispose of property or skills as appropriate. The restrictive medieval guilds were abolished, as were customary and traditional restrictions on property, leaving the individual as the absolute proprietor of property.

At one further remove, the creation of the isolated individual was also reflected in the realm of ideas. As Marx says of notions of bourgeois freedom in the *Communist Manifesto*: 'Your very ideas are but the outgrowth of the conditions of your bourgeois production and bourgeois property, just as your jurisprudence is but the will of your class made into a law for all, a will, whose essential character and direction are determined by the economical conditions of existence of your class' (Marx and Engels, 1970, p. 49). More precisely, in the *Grundrisse*, he discusses the relationship of the doctrines of individual freedom and equality that were popular in the eighteenth century to the requirements of the capitalist mode of production. Exchange of commodities is the crucial feature of capitalism and such exchanges require equality and freedom; individuals must not only be able freely to exchange, the exchange is treated as one between people equal for the purpose of the exchange. The real basis of the ideas of freedom and equality is the economic system of commodity exchange, and at the same time the exchanges demonstrate the ideas. Doctrines of liberty and equality are enshrined in legal, social and political practices that make the exchanges possible. Marx expresses the idea in the following manner: 'Equality and freeom are thus not only respected in exchange based on exchange values but also, the exchange of exchange values is the productive real basis of all equality and freedom. As pure ideas they are merely the idealized expressions of this basis; as developed in juridical, political, social relations, they are merely this basis to a higher power' (Marx, 1973, p. 245).

If the bourgeois social theory and capitalist economic and legal practice contain a definition of the individual in the barest possible terms, as a proprietor of capacities from which he or she can easily be parted, the problem remains: what features are *essential* to the individual in capitalist society, characteristics from which a person cannot be parted? Some writers have suggested that the isolated individual has will and choice, that is, the will to act and the capacity to choose courses of action. This makes the individual a creature who intervenes in the world and has to take responsibility for his or her choices (Parekh, 1982).

The concepts of will and choice were important for the eighteenth-century social theorists whom Marx saw as a reflection of capitalist economic practice. These theorists argued that capitalist society did *in fact* allow individuals to be truly unfettered, independent and free. Marx poured scorn on these arguments. 'In this society of free competition, the individual *appears* detached from the natural bonds, etc., which in earlier historical periods make him the accessory of a definite and limited human conglomerate . . . But the epoch which produces this standpoint, that of the isolated individual, is also precisely that of the hitherto most developed social relations' (Marx, 1973, pp. 83–4, our emphasis). Capitalism, ironically, therefore made individuals more interdependent because of its *social* method of production and, above all, because of its reliance on continued economic exchange between individuals.

Marx's more abstract views about methods of analysing social phenomena are related to his arguments against Adam Smith and David Ricardo, whom he saw as standing 'with both feet on the shoulders of the eighteenth century prophets'. One of the vices of bourgeois social theory was that it produced a methodological individualism in which social analysis was based on individual characteristics. Marx, on the contrary, takes the view that individuals do not have any essential characteristics abstracted from the society in which they find themselves. 'Society does not consist of individuals; it expresses the sum of connections and relationships in which individuals find themselves' (McLellan, 1971, p. 77). There is no natural individual; individuality and what constitutes an individual vary from society to society. Each society constructs the individual in its own particular way.

Marx's notion that each society constructs individuals in different ways is clearly connected to his ethical theory. The construction of individuals may also be their constraint. Marx's aim was the creation of social arrangements – socialism – which encouraged the full development and exercise of human capacities. Capitalism was, to some extent, a stage on the road to the liberation of these capacities, because its greater productive abilities encouraged a greater diversity of needs. However, since it depended so crucially on market relations, it was still constraining: it represented *having* rather than *being*. Consequently, the capitalist bare individual promoted only a partial human individuality, which could only be fully developed in socialism.

Emile Durkheim

In *The Division of Labor in Society (1893)*, Durkheim powerfully rejected the utilitarian individualism of Herbert Spencer. The thrust of his rejection was the impossibility of explaining economic relations by reference simply to economic self-interest. For Durkheim, the problem was how one should explain the binding nature of economic contracts, that is, the 'non-contractual element in contract'. The economic system would not work, Durkheim argued, if economic relations were not enforced and enforceable by appeals to general legal norms; these legal institutions must exist prior to economic contracts and cannot be explained in terms of self-interest. In general, this element of social solidarity in society is to be explained by social facts and not by inappropriate explanations of a psychologistic character. It was in this theoretical context that Durkheim produced the famous distinction between mechanical and organic solidarity. In pre-modern societies, the main root of social solidarity is to be found in the *conscience collective*, the absence of individualism and the low level of the division of labour. With the development of social specialization and the division of labour, the conscience collective becomes vaguer, weaker and less intense. Organic solidarity thus comes to rest primarily on the reciprocal obligations and relations that emerge as an effect of the division of labour.

Durkheim's position has often been taken to be a form of radical sociologism which treats the 'individual' as simply an effect of social relations. However, Durkheim's analysis of the individual is both more complex and more interesting than this conventional view would suggest. Individualism, and especially moral individualism rather than economic individualism, remained the abiding focus of Durkheim's sociology and of his political philosophy.

The problem of individualism does not emerge significantly in *The Elementary Forms of the Religious Life* (Durkheim, 1912), because there Durkheim was primarily concerned with societies based on mechanical solidarity, that is, with societies where the 'individual'

11

was yet to be developed. He acknowledged, however, that with the growing division of labour there would be a specialization of the individual, which would in turn give rise to a greater sense of religious individualism. In a similar fashion, Durkheim argued that the differentiation of society and the individuation of the person in Western societies had an effect on the educational system which, with the Renaissance and the Reformation, gave rise to an emphasis on the individual in educational theory and practice. In his study of the development of educational practice in France, Durkheim is perfectly aware of this growing emphasis on the subjectivity of the individual and the need to direct educational interests towards the developing person:

> With the Renaissance, by contrast, the individual began to acquire self-consciousness. He was no longer, at least in enlightenment circles, merely an undifferentiated fraction of the whole; he was himself already, in a sense a whole, he was a person with his own physiognomy who had and who experienced at least the need to fashion for himself his own way of thinking and feeling. We know that at this period there occurred, as it were, a sudden blossoming of great personalities.
>
> (Durkheim, 1977, p. 263)

Although Durkheim is often regarded as the sociologist of the social *sui generis*, he was also the sociologist of the moral individual as the product of long-term structural changes in the nature of Western societies, which gave rise to individualism and the individual.

The crucial element in Durkheim's commentary on individualism is the essay 'Individualism and the intellectuals' which was published in *La Revue Bleue* in 1898 (Durkheim, 1969). It is this short essay which perhaps best expresses the relationship between moral individualism and sociologism in Durkheim's thought. He starts with a central conceptual distinction between the utilitarian egoism of Herbert Spencer's sociology and the individualism that is associated with the moral philosophy of Kant and Rousseau. Whereas utilitarianism commends actions that are in accordance with our personal needs and interests, Kantianism applauds actions that are compatible with some universalistic standard of moral value. Kant's moral philosophy specifically condemns actions that are merely in conformity with our personal wishes. The categorical imperative urges us to do unto others as we would have them do unto us. The point about this moral form of individualism is that it glorifies the individual in general, not the self in particular. But

Durkheim also wanted to go beyond these philosophical distinctions to a more sociological interpretation of the 'individual' as a social institution, that is, as a social fact, which has binding consequences for modern societies.

Durkheim argued that individualism, rather than representing a form of anarchy, was actually essential for the re-integration of contemporary society around a new secular religion, namely the religion of humanity in general as represented in the notion of the general individual. Durkheim's explanation of the rise of individualism is not particularly clear, but it is interesting and bears directly on the problem of this study. He argued that as society becomes more 'voluminous', there is less social resistance to individual variations and individuals are more able to follow their own interests:

> At the same time, as a consequence of a more advanced division of labour, each mind finds itself directed towards a different point on the horizon, reflects a different aspect of the world and as a result the contents of men's minds differ from one subject to another. One is thus proceeding to a state of affairs, now almost attained, in which the members of a single group will no longer have anything in common other than their humanity.
>
> (Durkheim, 1969, p. 26)

Durkheim does not see individualism in its moral form as incompatible with social stability; on the contrary, the social order actually requires a religion of the individual, that is, of humanity.

The causes of the emergence of the social institution of the individual are clearly located in the division of labour. Durkheim also acknowledged that Christianity contributed to the growth of an individualistic 'spirit', because it encouraged an appreciation of the importance of individual judgement, personal conviction and conscience in moral life. Christianity also paved the way for the eventual arrival of scientific thought, which requires freedom of thought. However, individualism in modern societies does not require Christianity to legitimate it.

There are several features, characteristic of Durkheim's sociology as a whole, which we should note carefully in this argument. He wants to deny philosophy and psychology any role in sociological explanation and, as a result, treats 'individuals' as social facts, in the sense that individualism is now a moral institution that is general, common, external and constraining on the behaviour of individual persons. At the same time, he ends up with a special view of human

13

beings that, in its own way, is equally psychologistic (Turner, 1984). Durkheim pictures people in terms of a perpetual war between desires (which are to some extent pre-social and anti-social) and rationality (which is communal and binding). Social institutions, primarily 'religion' in the generic sense, are required to counteract the anti-social drives and to promote the social dimension of morality. Egoistic utilitarianism is a dangerous doctrine because it encourages dangerous anti-social forces and thus needs the counter-weight of moral individualism, which is a modern religion. The causes and origins of the 'individual' are somewhat vague. The origins of social change in Durkheim's theory of the social division of labour are ultimately demographic. Population pressures make society more 'voluminous' and this creates a requirement for an increase in the division of labour; in turn, this brings about a specialization of the individual and the emergence of new doctrines of individualism. The evidence for these changes can be found in the suicide rate, and in changes in the type of suicide, which is characteristic of different forms of society. For example, egoistic suicides are characteristic of modern society.

We might rephrase the overall sense of Durkheim's argument on the following lines. The individual can only develop with the emergence of the division of labour which, out of the undifferentiated mass of the social group, begins to form the individual as a specialized, separate and distinctive phenomenon. The individual is simultaneously separate from the 'social' and the product of the social. This change in status tends to accompany the development of new doctrines in society – both moral individualism and economic utilitarianism – which give cultural and ideological expression to the individual. It would seem unlikely that the doctrine of individualism would emerge in a society where the individual did not yet exist. Finally, Durkheim wanted to refer to the individual as a form of institution in the same way that religion might be defined as a social institution. As an institution, the individual can be viewed as a set of beliefs and practices, the effect of which is to bind persons together. The individual is a feature of the modern religion of humanity which, for Durkheim, can overcome the false religion of egoism. By a rather major extension of Durkheim's arguments, we might argue that economic man (that is, the egoistic personality of utilitarian thought) is the product of the capitalist economy (especially the capitalistic market), while Kantian man (that is, the moral personal-

14

ity of reciprocal relationships which are characteristic of the organic solidarity of modern society) is the product of social solidarity in civil society. In this Durkheimian world, the economic and the social order stand in a relationship of contradiction, a contradiction that is equally reflected in Durkheim's special view of human beings.

One other feature of Durkheim's argument deserves attention. He provides a short-run argument about the development of the individual and the growth of the division of labour in modern, urban and complex society. He also has a long-run argument about the effects of Christianity in fostering beliefs about the moral value of the autonomous individual. Christianity appears to set the stage for profound developments in the notion of 'personality' and distinguishes Western cultures from those where individualism is relatively unimportant. Durkheim produces both types of argument, yet does not appear to be aware that he has two and not one causal explanation for the predominance of individualistic beliefs and practices in modern society. The relationship between short-run and long-run arguments about individualism forms an important basis for our argument in Chapter 2.

There is a further tension in Durkheim's view of Christianity as one source of moral individualism. In general, Durkheim wants to argue that Christianity is irrelevant as a suitable religion for modern societies, and yet he ends up by noting that moral individualism is not only compatible with Christian morality but is an outcome of religious evolution. In particular, Durkheim wanted to commend Kant's moral philosophy as the basis of the religion of humanity, and yet Kant's philosophy is only a method of getting Christian morals into society via the back door. Kant's moral system is simply the ethical code of the New Testament dressed up in the language of philosophy. The sociological problem in Durkheim's dependence on Kant's theology is that Christian individualism may just as easily point towards an antinomian anarchy as towards the integrative universalism of shared standards based on a notion of humanity in general. The Christian answer to this dilemma has been that, provided we act as moral individuals and choose courses of action in good faith, we will always choose exactly what God wants. Our particular will thus blends with God's universal will, just as in Rousseau the particular will of individuals is merged into the General Will. Durkheim's moral philosophy is based on precisely the same assumptions. Individualism is not a threat to the community, so long as institutions can direct personal wishes into a general consciousness, which is humanity-in-general. The antinomian potential of individualism for social disruption was either submerged or disregarded as Spencerian utilitarianism. Thus Durkheim reminded us that the terms 'individual' and 'individualism' have no necessary relationship, since individualism, once properly understood, was not in fact about the isolated self but about the moral whole.

Max Weber

A similar range of questions confronted Max Weber. Formally, as expressed in his methodological writings, Weber's views on the methodology and philosophy of social science are the reverse of Durkheim's. In crude terms, whereas Durkheim adopted Cartesian positivism, Weber belonged to the neo-Kantian movement in German thought, which drew a sharp distinction between the methods of natural and social science. These differences of scientific orientation were combined with radically different views of the individual/society relationship. While Durkheim treated the individual as an institution and based his sociological approach on the causal primacy of the social over the individual, Weber denied the existence of collectivist or supra-individual actors and wanted to develop a theory of social action that involved individual meaning and choice. He asserted that all statements referring to 'collective conceptions' had ultimately to be broken down into statements about *individual* action and interaction. However, although Weber was formally committed to methodological individualism and interpretive sociology, and to a distinctive ethical approach to the individual, much of his substantive work appeared to diverge significantly from his philosophical position. Not only did he commonly fail to follow his own methodological procedures, but typically he emphasized the irony and fatefulness of human history, which negates and undermines human agency and intentionality. The unintended negative consequences of actions, rather than action as such, are what so often dominate his image of the world. The fatalism characteristic of Weber's historical sociology coloured his treatment of the history of individualism and the individual.

Like Durkheim, Weber also had long-run and short-run models of the history of the individual. First, Christianity as such was more conducive to the rise of the individual than were other religions. Weber's views on the impact of Christianity on city life are important in this respect (Weber, 1958). Because Christianity was a social movement in which communal ties were based on faith rather than on blood and kinship, Weber argued that Christianity had the effect of de-tribalizing urban space. It created an environment in which the individual could ultimately flourish untrammelled by the particularistic ties of family and kin. In addition, Christianity gave a clear emphasis to the soul and the cultivation of conscience in the confessional. Weber had, in addition, a short-run argument which provided the classic theme of *The Protestant Ethic and the Spirit of Capitalism* (Weber, 1930). The Reformation liquidated the institutional links between the individual and God; in particular, the whole sacramental system was virtually demolished leaving the individual 'naked' before God. Weber wrote eloquently about the results and implications of this great psychic transformation:

> In its extreme inhumanity this doctrine must above all have had one consequence for the life of a generation which surrendered to its magnificent consistency. That was a feeling of unprecedented inner loneliness of the single individual.
>
> (Weber, 1930, p. 104)

Religious individualism was associated with the rise of a new mode of consciousness, free from the confines of the confessional but subordinated to an interior court of conscience. It was this individualism which paved the way to the mentality of *homo economicus* and possessive individualism with the growth of capitalism.

Both Weber and Durkheim believed that individualism had novel characteristics in modern capitalist society, and recognized that, from a longer perspective, individualism had its roots in the Judaic-Christian inheritance. It was thus peculiar to the West. Weber, however, was essentially pessimistic and argued the paradox that, although capitalism had called forth individualism, it would also destroy it. More precisely, both capitalism and individualism may be seen as features of a more significant social process, namely the rationalization of culture.

Rationalization has a number of components (Brubaker, 1984). They include standardization, which makes rational measurement and assessment possible, and intellectualization, whereby the whole of life is subordinated to rational, scientific inquiry. There is correspondingly the elimination of magic, superstitution and religion as means of predicting the future, making moral judgements or conducting personal life. Rationalization thus involves secularization; this is not simply a decline of the social importance of the church, but a radical destruction of supernatural values, standards and meanings. An important part of this process, for Weber, was the undermining of natural law. Rationalization is thus a bundle of changes, which together make life subject to calculation.

Rationalization is two-edged. On the one hand, it has de-mystified the world, allowing the individual to emerge from the thrall of collectivist conceptions. On the other, it has made the individual a target of such calculative procedures. Weber came to see the individual as dominated by the products of rationalization: the rise of bureaucratic organizations, the centralized state and the modern civil service. The growth of prediction and calculation embodied in the bureaucratization of modern life tended to conflict with the moral principle, which is crucial to Weber's whole philosophy, of the moral autonomy of the individual. Although Weber saw the importance of charisma in the modern world as an antidote to these processes of administrative uniformity, he also recognized that charismatic transformations were unlikely, unstable and ephemeral (Hepworth and Turner, 1982). We also know that Weber treated socialism, not as an alternative to rationalization but as its enhancement and apogee. It was because rationalization appeared to Weber as an ineluctable force in modern world history that his metaphors of modern life tend to be bleak and deterministic; they are metaphors of cogs, cages, railway tracks, switches, engines and machines.

The administered society, in Weber's pessimistic view of the fatalism of historical processes, is consequently incompatible with the autonomy of the moral (and therefore free) agent. Weber's view is thus unlike Durkheim's, since he believed that moral individualism will be undermined by the forces of social control and calculation that are embedded in modern bureaucracy. In this respect, Weber's world has more in common with Foucault's panopticism, in which the body of the individual and the body of populations become the object and target of new disciplines and combinations of knowledge/power (Turner, 1984). This vision of stultifying uniformity and calculation as an outcome of rationalized bureaucracy is absent in Durkheim's relatively optimistic view of the liberating potential of Cartesian rationalism. For Weber, although science offers to make us free by liberating us from the garden of magic and the limited horizons of traditional societies, it also ultimately destroys meaning and renders ends vague and contradictory. Science as part of a rationalization process that includes and embraces bureacracy becomes incompatible with the autonomy of the moral individual.

Weber's analysis of individualism was complex, and this complexity was in part a consequence of the very diverse nature of the influences bearing upon his sociology. Weber was influenced by the Kantian division of the world into the noumenal and the phenomenal. Understanding human action would require hermeneutic interpretations of the meaningfulness and intentionality of human action and interaction. In some respects, however, Weber had more in common with Nietzsche and with a moral tradition which emphasized autonomy over the rationality of the subject, that is, with existentialism (Brubaker, 1984). Because there are no common or absolute standards of behaviour, we live in a polytheistic world of competing values where no resolution between alternative value-systems is possible. Hence, the autonomous moral individual is forced to choose between the ends of life, and this choice cannot be guided by magic, by institutionalized grace or by any force outside the individual. The weak individual is thus tempted to fly back into the arms of the church, but real moral value will be found in the individual who commits himself to a cause (to science or to politics) in the face of such moral chaos and uncertainty. The ethic of responsibility was Weber's answer to the realm of moral chaos proclaimed originally by the madman in Nietzsche's *Zarathustra* of 1883–5.

We know from Marianne Weber's (1975) biography of her husband that Weber was also deeply influenced by the Old Testament prophets, by the Reformation theologians and finally by evangelical Protestantism as represented by such writers as W. E. Channing. A particular view of individualism emerges from this religious perspective on the relationship between faith and 'the world'. True individualism does not follow the dictates of fashion, or immediate need, or pragmatism, but seeks to change the world and impose individual will upon it.

For Weber, individuality is not something individuals possess simply because they are persons, but something they achieve as a result of an inner struggle for personal coherence and unity. Personality is a condition we have to create (against the odds) rather than a status we acquire by virtue of our membership of the human species. This position on the ethics of virtuosity was a moral argument, which Weber had elaborated from Nietzsche. It was also closely connected to Weber's hostility to the German bureaucracy, to the absence of political leadership from the German middle class and to the cowardice of the political leadership in the aftermath of the First World War. There is consequently an important relationship between Weber's notion of 'personality' – a person whose inner being is coherent and self-consciously developed – and the definition of 'social action'. Personalities are capable of social action on the grand scale when they impose their meaning and will on the flux of the world. Their life is not mere behaviour, but a unified system of action that is organized around a value that is deliberately chosen. The problem for Weber was that this choice had itself to be ultimately irrational, because there could not be clear scientific guidelines for such ultimate choices.

Another influence on Weber was Georg Simmel, but the nature of that influence has been disputed (Frisby, 1981, 1984). The nature of this influence is not important for our present discussion: we simply wish to note that Simmel and Weber shared similar assumptions about the nature of modern culture. Modern capitalist societies both produce the isolated individual and the doctrine of individualism, and at the same time undermine the autonomous individual as a consequence of rationalization and standardization.

Georg Simmel

Georg Simmel contrasts the conceptions of individualism found in the eighteenth and nineteenth centuries (Simmel, 1950). In the eighteenth century, social theorists argued for the severance of the ties between individuals and society and the freedom of the individual from constraints. Freedom meant that the natural, essential qualities of mankind could be released. Only in absolute freedom could individuals behave as moral entities. Such a notion of freedom is highly congruent with equality, because the natural or essential core of every person is the same for all people. Differences between people are then purely accidental characteristics imposed by external social forces.

20

According to Simmel, the nineteenth-century conception *did* separate freedom and equality. In this view of individualism, the stress was not on free individuals as such, but on irreplaceable individuals whose individuality lay in their differences from others. Individuals, far from being essentially similar, were unique, and a high moral task, in Romanticism for example, was the realization of this uniqueness. This was an individualism of inequality that stressed the separate uniqueness of each person in place of the commonality of humankind. Simmel puts the difference between the two centuries as follows: 'the first is the ideal of fundamentally equal, even if wholly free and self-responsible, personalities. The other is that of the individuality which, precisely in its innermost nature, is incomparable and which is called upon to play an irreplaceable role' (1950, p. 79). And again: 'The new individualism might be called qualitative, in contrast with the quantitative individualism of the eighteenth century' (1950, p. 81).

Simmel's explanation of the different conceptions of individualism is ingenious. They each correspond to different *economic* forms: 'In terms of intellectual history, the doctrine of freedom and equality is the foundation of free competition; while the doctrine of differentiated personality is the basis of the division of labour' (1950, p. 83). The eighteenth-century doctrine was used to justify free competition, on the grounds that freedom of this kind permitted the optimum welfare of the whole. The nineteenth-century notion, on the other hand, encouraged the division of labour because, as every individual was different and unique, a specialization of function was possible.

We cannot fully appreciate Simmel's commentary on individualism without a consideration of his analysis of sociation. Simmel's exploration of this concept was an attempt to avoid any reification of the idea of society and any atomization of the individual. As an alternative, he sought to discover the forms of sociation which were simultaneously the outcome of human purposes and which constituted and channelled such purposes. The content of sociation was the creative intentionality of human actions and the form of interaction was, so to speak, the sedimentation of human actions. Simmel's thought as a result exhibited a fundamental dualism. There is the permanent opposition between form and content in human association, in which everything that is vital and creative (content) is in opposition to everything that is shaped and static (form). At the

21

same time, all human interaction requires form in order to give a structure to intentionality.

Like Weber, Simmel thought that the modern emphasis on the individual, the isolated nature of the individual and the individualization of personality were all fundamentally products of modern society. The individual and the individualization of the person are effects of the extension of social relations. The wider the social circles in which the individual is located, the more liberated the individual becomes from localized and restricted viewpoints and commitments. It is social expansion that produces an enlargement of the individual, who as a result becomes increasingly cosmopolitan. The increasing scope of social diversity creates the conditions for an increasing scope of individual differences.

It was in *The Philosophy of Money* (1978) that Simmel attempted to provide a systematic account of the rise of individualism in relation to the growing differentiation and complexity of social structures. The history of money as a medium of exchange provides us with the history of society as the growing abstraction and rationalization of social relations. When societies are relatively undifferentiated and relatively small in scale, there is comparatively little trade and exchange, because the household is self-sufficient economically. Money begins to develop with the growing complexity of exchange and with the growing density of social relations; at first, money takes the form of real value (gold, silver, shells, pigs) but it rapidly becomes separated from value and assumes a symbolic form (leather money, bank notes, cheques and then credit cards). Money reflects a society in which social relations become increasingly universalistic and abstract.

The increasing use of money in exchange and the gradual disappearance of barter also point to the emergence of the individual from the group and the development of the specialized personality. Money makes exchange between strangers possible; it provides for the emergence of greater cosmopolitanism; it liberates people from the narrow confines of rural life, the guild system and the local economy. The historical unfolding of money is the historical unfolding of individual freedoms.

At this point, Simmel's argument about the modern individual begins to bear a close family resemblance to the position taken by Durkheim. The growth of money becomes the medium by which individuals become increasingly interdependent and hence submerged in a network of social functions. The growth of the division of labour and its expression in money both separates the individual from the collectivity but, through reification, our personalities become less distinctive. In short, money creates both autonomy and reciprocity in a network of extensive exchange relationships under the general guidance of the state. The development of a society regulated by the state would be the logical outcome of a process of individualization via a rational division of labour and specialization of functions, but it would also be the logical outcome of a process of individuation whereby individuals can be regulated, measured, quantified and controlled.

We can now summarize the arguments of the classical sociologists. In Marx we find a critique of Bentham's political economy, on the grounds that he elevated economic man into a universalistic definition of humanity as such. Furthermore, Marx saw the ideology of individualism as a thin disguise for the naked self-interests of individuals and a legitimation of private property. Individualism as an ideology had legitimized the property rights of the bourgeoisie as against the landowning interest of the traditional aristocracy. In addition, Marx saw the capitalist division of labour as producing a highly specialized person. Marx was not, however, unambiguously critical of individualism, since he recognized that the working class could use individualistic ideology to legitimize its claims against the bourgeoisie. That is, a radical working class would appeal to the rights of free individuals as the medium for a critique of the sham democracy of capitalism. Marx's own view of human beings in a non-alienated or de-alienated state also drew upon a form of moral individualism, since a society which was no longer alienated would produce individuals who were rounded out and not over-specialized. In attempting to conceptualize this society, Marx, in a strange and paradoxical fashion, reproduced the moral discourse of much liberal and Christian thought by suggesting that in the absence of egoism individuals would be reconciled with the community.

This argument appears in an even more definite and clear fashion in the work of Emile Durkheim, whose sociology can be seen as a sustained critique of traditional political economy. His response can be seen to take shape under two separate issues. First, he rejected the idea that a laissez-faire society would lead to greater human happiness. On the contrary, he suggested that human beings would be increasingly subject to the forces of anomie in a situation where their desires and needs were untramelled and unshaped by normative restraint. That is, Durkheim saw moral control as an essential element of personal stability and happiness. Then he argued that there is a non-contractual element to contract, and this element of economic relations had its roots in moral facts which could not be reduced to the individual psychology of the persons making such contracts. We can encapsulate these arguments by saying that Durkheim made an important distinction between moral and economic individualism. He saw economic individualism as it emerged in Spencerianism and social Darwinism as the major cause of anomie and suicide. Against this, he argued the importance of moral integrity and moral regulation for human development and autonomy. His argument is a sociological Kantianism, in that individuals can only be free and happy in so far as they follow the imperatives of the social order, where this order is essentially moral.

Max Weber's position on individualism is more complex than those of Marx and Durkheim. Weber was distinctively a German liberal, who acquired the culture of Kantian German thought as a taken-for-granted legacy. This importance of individualism was expressed in Weber's methodology, that is, methodological individualism. It also finds expression in his research on religions, where Weber implicitly gives greater importance to religions such as Calvinism and treats Confucianism as a form of collective conformity and adjustment to social relations. Weber saw individualism as the product of Calvinism and capitalism, but also argued that individualism would gradually disappear with the evolution of late capitalist society. The main cause of this disappearance would be the spread of bureaucracy and rational forms of capitalism. Capitalism and bureaucracy are themselves in many ways simply phenomena of the more general process of rationalization. It was rationalization that would gradually undermine the autonomy of the individual in modern society, and this was the basis of Weber's view of the iron cage of capitalism.

Weber also noted important differences between America, Germany and Britain with respect to individualism. For example, writing about American sects, Weber perceived the quintessential form of individualism in the USA. By contrast, in Germany, he thought that the growing dominance of the state would eventually undermine the German cultural tradition of liberalism and, in combination with bureaucracy, would reduce people to mere elements within a massive machine of modern society. His work contains the paradox that, while capitalism has promoted the individual, the development of modern forms of capitalism would erode the spiritual autonomy of the individual and of individualism as an ideology. The future, in the form of socialism, would be even more antithetical to individualism.

We can see how these classical sociologists were critical of economic individualism but had a distinctive position on moral individualism. The restoration of the individual to the community in Marx was associated with the decline of alienation in the future socialist society. For Durkheim, professional ethics and nationalism might provide the sort of moral individualism that was a necessary antidote to the egoistic form of individualism. Weber sought to reconcile individual choice and interests with the wider needs of modern society. In his ethic of responsibility, we see this moral imperative at work, namely that individuals have to choose sensibly and honestly in a world without absolute guidelines and values.

Later Accounts

Social theorists of the nineteenth and early twentieth centuries were clearly concerned with the relationship between individualism and capitalism. In political and social theory since then, this relationship has been frequently assumed, though less often discussed in any detail. One of the more sociological accounts, in the sense of trying to *explain* individualism socially, is that offered by Lucien Goldmann (1973). His overall aim is to provide an account of what he regards as the seven basic categories of Enlightenment thought: the autonomy of the individual, contract, equality, universality, toleration, freedom and property.

Goldmann seeks to show that the development of these categories of thought, in particular individualism, is associated with the growth of the capitalist economy. A dominant feature of capitalism in Goldmann's analysis is the market for goods and services; in emphasizing this, Goldmann believes that he is following Marx's treatment of the commodity form in *Capital*, where it was stated that in the capitalist economy, commodities are produced for their exchange-value and not for use. Such an economy depends on markets to realize the exchange-value of commodities through unlimited exchanges. It is this root fact of exchange of goods within the market that provides Goldmann with his starting-point for the explanation of Enlightenment beliefs. For example, in order for freedom of exchange to exist, it is important that there are no impediments to economic exchanges from racial or religious considerations. Exchange, therefore, tends to promote religious tolerance. This feature of Goldmann's argument is vividly illustrated by Andrew Marvell's 'Character of Holland', which is frequently quoted in studies of the Dutch economy (Boxer, 1965; Smith, 1973):

> Hence Amsterdam, Turk, Christian, Pagan, Jew,
> Staple of sects and mint of schisms grew:
> That bank of conscience, where not one so strange
> Opinion but finds credit and exchange.

However, what market exchanges require above all else is that 'every individual appears as the autonomous source of his decisions and actions' (Goldman, 1973, p. 20). *Individuals* are recognized as free, equal and autonomous agents entering into unfettered contracts to exchange. Indeed, society itself is a consequence of:

> The action of countless autonomous individuals on each other and in response to each other, behaving as rationally as possible for the protection of their private interests and basing their actions on their knowledge of the market with no regard for any trans-individual authority or values.
>
> (Goldmann, 1973, p. 18)

Goldmann has elaborated this analysis in his study of the classical European novel (1975). He suggests that the eighteenth- and nineteenth-century novel was concerned with the question of the adaptation of the individual (the hero) to a social world that was being transformed by the revolutionary impact of competitive capitalism. The autonomous individual was the literary counterpart of laissez-faire economics, free trade and the minimalist state. As capitalism develops, however, the relationship between the individual and society becomes increasingly problematic. A meaningful adaptation to the social world is difficult because the rationality and meaningfulness of capitalist society itself become progressively uncertain and unclear. Capitalist society after the First World War was transformed from competitive capitalism, based on family ownership, into a new form that was increasingly dominated by large monopolies, multinational corporations, bureaucratic unions, mass parties and the interventionist state. While the novel and the author continued to extol the virtues of the autonomous individual in the shape of the hero, the possibilities of individualism in reality continued to diminish. Nevertheless, the ideology of individual freedoms remained dominant, according to Goldmann.

There is an interesting convergence between Simmel, Weber and Goldmann on the problem of the individual in capitalism, which is not surprising given Goldmann's dependence on Georg Lukács, who was part of the Simmel–Weber group. The convergence is familiar, namely that capitalism produces the individual as the natural counterpart of private property and exchange, but eventually undermines the individual as an effect of capitalist rationalization of production and exchange. Goldmann, like Lukács, was concerned to discover this history in the evolution of the novel.

Weber, Simmel and Lukács shared a common pessimism, because their argument was that capitalist rationalization undermines the autonomy of the individual will by subordinating people to bureaucratic regulation. The individual becomes a mere cog in the iron cage of capitalism. In somewhat different terminology, while capitalism may give a special emphasis to the individual by destroying traditional forms of constraint, as Simmel suggested, it also creates the apparatus whereby the individuation of populations enhances control, surveillance and regulation. Goldmann's treatment of the history of the individual through the history of the novel is thus one particular illustration of a more general social development. His critique of capitalist society also has a lot in common with traditional liberalism, since, by emphasizing individual freedoms, it denigrates a society which was becoming dominated by bureaucracy, the state and mass society.

Other writers have tried to link various aspects of individualism to the requirements of capitalist society. C. B. Macpherson offers an influential account of individualism as the cornerstone of seventeenth-century political theory. Its crucial assumption was possessive individualism, the doctrine that 'every man is naturally the sole proprietor of his own person and capacities (the absolute proprietor in that he owes nothing to society for them)' (Macpherson, 1962, p. 270). For Macpherson, the significance of possessive individualism is that it both underpinned a variety of philosophies and also matched the realities of seventeenth-century English society. A theory that depicts society as essentially a set of relations of exchange between individual proprietors, each of whom owns his own capacities, will be effective and powerful in a capitalist society dominated by markets in which such exchanges really do happen. It is not so effective, Macpherson argues, in contemporary society, where reality no longer matches theory so closely.

Ian Watt has discovered individualism in the eighteenth-century English novel. The essence of the novel is 'truth to individual experience – individual experience which is always unique and therefore new' (Watt, 1957, p. 15). The novel claims to be a plausible account of individual experiences. Plots, like those used by Defoe, departed from the literary conventions of their day in not using mythology, legend or history as their basis. They also had a new sense of character. While traditional plots took general human types as central characters, the new convention was for particular people to act out the plot in particular circumstances. Similarly, particularization of time and space became important. Causally significant events in the story were placed in a sequence instead of being timeless or included in an artificial twenty-four-hour period. *Robinson Crusoe*, for example, is set in a particular period and has a clearly developed sense of the passage of time. The net effect of the eighteenth-century novel's departure from older literary conventions is to emphasize the *reality* of *individual* experience. The novel incorporates a world-vision which 'presents us, essentially, with a developing but unplanned aggregate of particular individuals having particular experiences at particular times and at particular places' (Watt, 1957, p. 32). A novel of this kind could only have made sense to readers who also took individual experience seriously. Watt maintains that capitalism was one factor that contributed to the creation of individualistic habits of mind, which, in turn, generated a readership for the new novel.

Problems and Issues

The diversity, both theoretical and substantive, of accounts of the relationship between individualism and capitalism suggests a range of problems that need to be resolved. There is first the difficulty of periodization. A familiar objection to Marx's account of the relationship between capitalism and the Protestant religion is that, since Protestantism preceded capitalism, Marx must be wrong about the causal priority of capitalism. Similarly, Weber's suggestions on the same subject were met with the argument that, since capitalist activity could be discovered in early Renaissance Italy well before Calvin preached in Geneva, Protestantism could not be one of the preconditions of capitalism. Any account of the historical relationship of large-scale social structures seems to meet with objections of this kind. This is particularly the case when causal associations between bodies of ideas and social systems are specified; it is claimed that they are not in phase, or in period with one another.

Such problems of periodization are prominent in the discussion of the association of capitalism with individualism. For example, one of the difficulties with Goldmann's account is that he is not at all precise about the causal or temporal priority between capitalism and individualism. In a few pages he offers three versions. First, he says that Enlightenment beliefs are the consequences of changes in the organization of economic production. Secondly, he says that these beliefs are the precondition of these changes and, thirdly, that the system of beliefs is 'analogous' to the structure of the capitalist economy. Macfarlane (1978) points to similar complications when he shows that certain individualistic beliefs and practices were to be found in parts of England as early as the thirteenth century, a finding which he believes undermines the claim that capitalism and individualism are uniquely associated from the seventeenth century onwards. In short, any account of the relationship between individualism and capitalism has to be reasonably precise about their causal and temporal priorities and has also to cope with claims about the discovery of early instances of either.

The issue of periodization is closely related to a second problem, namely the *necessity* of the connection between capitalism and individualism. The point here is whether individualism, which is both an ideology and a way of behaving, is necessary or intrinsic to capitalism, or whether the economic system can exist without such ideology and behaviour. Doubt about the intimacy of these connections might suggest, for example, that capitalism in its contemporary form could do without the support of individualism in a way that it could not in its earlier stages.

There is also a problem with the identification of capitalism with exchange relations and their institutionalization in markets. Since exchange relations, markets and long-distance trade have existed in a wide variety of societies and over long periods of history, it is difficult to see why, in Goldmann's account for example, individualism should have arisen in the Enlightenment and had not appeared, say, in seventh-century Mecca. The identification of capitalism with a market economy, which is found among writers of widely different theoretical persuasions, is not wrong, but it is incomplete as a definition of capitalism. Capitalism has also to be seen as a mode of production, comprising distinctive relations of production, if it is to stand as a form of economic organization that can clearly be delineated from others. The failure to define capitalism correctly has bedevilled a number of areas of analysis, in particular the attempt to establish when capitalism emerged.

There is the issue of the political and economic dimensions of individualism. Marx stressed the economic effects of individualism: for capitalism to function, he believed that it was necessary that the subject should be constructed as a bare individual, and ideology in the form of individualism played an important part in this process. However, we might reasonably argue against Marx that individualism really has a *political* function. Individualism may have more to do with dissent than capitalism. We mean by this that an individualistic doctrine, which stresses the rights of the individual vis-à-vis other entities, can encourage or legitimate opposition to established authority. Theories of political obligation, which stress the rights of the individual, have historically played a role in the legitimation of dissent from absolutism. Individualism, therefore, may be taken up by any group that opposes the status quo and requires ideological legitimation of its dissent, since it is not only the right of individuals to make their own moral and political decisions, but it is their positive duty. In any consideration of individualism, therefore, attention has to be paid to its potential political function. The 'political' function is clearly not incompatible with the 'economic', however, and it is quite possible that individualism will appear first in a political guise but later come to 'fit' the requirements of capitalist society.

A further problem is the relationship between doctrines and behaviour. Intellectuals may produce theories that are individualistic, but this does not guarantee that capitalists or workers necessarily behave in accordance with these theories. In Goldmann's account, for example, it is not clear whether he thinks that the Enlightenment categories refer to what people *do* or what people *think*. Exchange is said to be made easier by the holding of certain doctrines, especially those concerning the freedoms of the individual. However, such exchanges are actually not directly made easier by capitalists *believing* in individualism; they are made easier by capitalists *behaving* as if people were individuals. Presumably it is possible for capitalists to believe what they like as long as they behave in the appropriate way. This is a difficult issue to resolve empirically. It is further complicated by a debate about the theoretical status of the concepts of ideology and knowledge. The debate is whether 'knowledge' can be seen as 'mental', as equivalent to ideas in people's heads, or whether it is inseparable from behaviour. Part of the solution is to separate the issue into several more limited questions about the relationship between intellectuals, on the one hand, and capitalists and workers, on the other, and about the social mechanisms that connect knowledge with social practice. In *The Dominant Ideology Thesis*, we referred to these mechanisms as the machinery of ideological transmission (Abercrombie, Hill and Turner, 1980).

This leads in turn to a consideration of another contentious issue: the importance of social classes. In the traditional sociology of knowledge, social classes have importance as intervening mechanisms that mediate between modes of production and bodies of knowledge. In his essay, 'Conservative thought', Mannheim relates rationalism to the rising bourgeoisie and conservatism to the nobility (Mannheim, 1953). Goldmann, similarly, writes as though individualism belonged to the bourgeoisie. These illustrate a familiar claim, which is usually justified by an appeal to the notion of class interest, that classes adopt beliefs that further their interests. In any particular case, such as individualism, the role of social classes, however, is an open question. Classes are only one of the possible intervening mechanisms between society and knowledge. These points draw attention, moreover, to an important methodological feature. This is the requirement to specify the social processes that relate knowledge to society. Sociologists and historians too often stop at the identification of a correlation between a particular social institution and a particular knowledge-form, without explaining the correlation by reference to particular social processes.

Individualism has been treated in the past in a fairly undifferentiated way. However, there are several elements in the concept that have to be sorted out in a proper account. There is a mistaken conflation of individualism and individuality. Individualism refers to the external – to ways of behaving in the outside world and to the quality of the social relations that connect the individual to society. Individuality is concerned with the interior of the subject – the development of sensibility, taste, consciousness, will and personality. Both notions differ from individuation, the process by which individuals come to be identified as particular *persons*, by means of marks, numbers, names and symbols.

These are familiar theoretical problems. We hope to resolve them in the following chapters, at the same time as we illuminate the substantive relation between individualism and capitalism. This investigation continues our discussion of ideology, the relationship of ideology to modes of production and, particularly, the relationship of ideology to capitalist relations of production, which we have presented previously (Abercrombie, Hill and Turner, 1980, 1983). We argued that ideology has been thought by others to have one of two functions. It may act as a form of social cement, unifying a society under the hegemony of a dominant class. In this formulation, there is often little to differentiate between sociological notions of 'general culture' and Marxist views of 'the dominant ideology'. Alternatively, ideology may function to ensure that members of a society act out their economic roles or fit appropriately into the economic system. *The Dominant Ideology Thesis* was largely concerned with the first function of social integration. Against the conception of ideology as social cement, we argued that subordinate classes are not incorporated or subordinated by ideology; their incorporation depends more on economic and political constraint or compulsion. We suggested, however, that the dominant ideology does have an effect on the dominant class: for example, it regulates family life in societies where the conservation and accumulation of private property in families are important. So ideology may function in the second mode. In this book, we discuss in greater detail the second function of ideology, by considering how, if at all, individualism contributes to the workings of capitalism.

Excursus: the Individual

In this study we are concerned to analyse the sociological issue of individualism and capitalism within a comparative and historical framework. Of course, this issue is also connected with certain key philosophical debates, but we cannot enter deeply and fully into problems that are essential to analytical philosophy. Philosophy, at least in the West, has been particularly interested in the problem of what is an individual. Since we are attempting to understand the emergence of individuals historically, we cannot entirely side-step the debate about what actually constitutes an individual person.

Although it may appear either formal or circular, we would define an individual as any agent who is socially recognized as a separate and different individual. This definition has the merit of drawing attention to the socially constructed and tenuous nature of what it is to be a person. All individuals are, in Cooley's expression, 'looking-glass' individuals because their autonomy and selfhood cannot be divorced from their essentially social character.

What then are the criteria by which agents are interpellated as specific, recognizable individuals? It is now almost conventional for sociologists to reject the Cartesian mind/body distinction in favour of the notion that persons are embodied agents. Embodiment is a critical feature of recognition, especially in a society where the representational self is fundamental to everyday status. It was Erving Goffman (1956, 1961, 1967), in his account of the presentation of self and face-work, who first systematically provided a sociology of recognition and encounters. We can argue that individuals are embodied social agents whose separate identity hinges on their possession of a unique body. One illustration of this banal fact would be the importance of fingerprints for a unique identification of persons.

However, having a body is not enough. We can always be impersonated, and identity parades are never unambiguous as a procedure of interpellation. In addition, we need consciousness and memory. To make a claim to separate status as an individual, we need a plausible history of ourselves, which recounts our past in such a way as to confirm our identity. Furthermore, to be an individual is to have a commitment to our identity. This commitment is taken to be validating evidence of whom we are. Our memory of this intimate story is a form of authorization. We are the author and topic of this story, which makes us an authority on our past.

These two features of individual status – a unique embodiment and authority over the validity of our biographies – are conventional elements of philosophy's interest in mind and body as the bases of individuals. Within sociology, these notions of embodiment, memory and continuity may not go far enough in specifying the individual, since a social individual is always an agent who is held responsible for his or her actions. An individual is, when defined fully, a legal personality. It is on these grounds that children, women and lunatics at various times have not been regarded as autonomous, separate persons. In French law, a woman on marriage traditionally found that her identity was submerged in that of her husband. Similarly, although domesticated dogs may have bodies, memories and personal names, they are not autonomous individuals because they are not held responsible for their actions. If Fido bites the postman, it is the owner of the dog who may be liable for damages. This argument, of course, makes the status of *corporations* somewhat uncertain, since they too are long-lived institutions, with 'memory' and a legal personality, even if they lack bodies.

In summary, a person is socially constituted as an individual through processes of social recognition, where separate identity depends on embodiment, autobiography (memory) and the attribution of legal rights. The emergence of these criteria is also bound up with the development of individualism itself and, more generally, with the evolution of an emphasis on the individual as separate and significant.

2

The Discovery of the Individual

Whatever ties of love or loyalty may bind us to other people, we are aware that there is an inner being of our own; that we are individuals. To the Western reader it may come as a surprise that there is anything unusual in this experience. It is to us a matter of common sense that we stand apart from the natural order in which we are set, subjects over against its objectivity, that we have our own distinct personality, beliefs, and attitude to life ... Western culture, and the Western type of education, has developed this sense of individuality to an extent exceptional among the civilizations of the world.

(Morris, 1972, p. 1)

In the Middle Ages both sides of human consciousness – that which was turned within as that which was turned without – lay dreaming or half awake beneath a common veil. The veil was woven of faith, illusion, and childish prepossession, through which the world and history were seen clad in strange hues. Man was conscious of himself only as member of a race, people, party, family or corporation – only through some general category. In Italy this veil first melted into air; an objective treatment and consideration of the State and of all things of this world became possible. The *subjective* side at the same time asserted itself with corresponding emphasis; man became a spiritual *individual* and recognized himself as such.

(Burckhardt, 1958, p. 143; emphasis in original)

It is a commonplace observation that the history of the West has involved a greater and greater emphasis on the individual. In the modern world, indeed, we take the importance of the individual so much for granted that certain features, individual names for example, are treated as if they were almost part of human nature. To forget someone's name is a source of great social embarrassment, at least in part because it appears to deny their individuality. Over time, European societies have gradually developed a way of treating, and thinking about, the human condition, which stresses the importance of individuals in relation to collectivities such as the tribe, the nation, the state, church or family. Not only is this a long-drawn-out process, with its origins at least in the twelfth century, but it is also pervasive and covers all aspects of human existence, from attitudes to death to the appearance of the novel form as a distinctive literary genre, from representations of the individual in painting and sculpture to religious experience. In the rest of this chapter we set out to illustrate this long-run historical process, which we call, following the book by Colin Morris (1972), the Discovery of the Individual. Clearly there is far too much evidence to present in any systematic way and we have chosen instead to focus on a few cases. Our argument in brief is as follows. There is a process of discovery of the individual in which individual characteristics are given greater and greater importance. However, this process is pitched at a very general level, for it merely asserts individual importance. It does not necessarily identify those *particular* characteristics that are important. Nor does its outcome *necessarily* result in greater freedom for individuals. It is quite possible that an emphasis on individuals permits greater ease of identification, which in turn allows more efficient surveillance and control.

Forms of Argument

There is a well-known sociological argument that individualism as a theory and the notion of the person as a self-conscious individual have their origins in the genesis of capitalism, and that the genesis of capitalism has its location in seventeenth-century English society. There is the equally convincing case that the importance of the individual is a peculiar feature of Western history and of Western society. We see no contradiction between these arguments, partly because they refer to different things. The discovery of the individual is the recognition of separate personality in place of collective identity and of differences among personalities. Individualism is a doctrine with a specific conception of the self. The issue of long-run and short-run accounts is tackled in this chapter.

A second argument that concerns us here is the contrast between contingent and determinant explanations. There is the view, for example, that individualism stands in a determinant relationship to capitalism, and there are fixed relationships between sets of beliefs and modes of production. Against this there is the notion that individualism is the outcome of a whole series of idiosyncratic and accidental features of Western culture.

In addition to these arguments, there is the problem of the so-called uniqueness of the West. Much nineteenth-century sociology was premissed upon a notion that Western society was peculiar, if not unique. Western societies are thought to be democratic and individual. They are thought to promote individualism and private property, both of which are connected with the individual rights of the private citizen. Western societies are thought to be oppositional and dynamic. By contrast, Eastern societies are held to possess characteristics that are diametrically in opposition to these positive features of Western civilization. It is easy to ridicule the epistemological assumptions of this naive East/West contrast; nevertheless, the problem of the emergence of capitalism in the West prior to the modernization of the East remains a historical and empirical problem. The emergence of Western rational modern society with its emphasis on achievement in the individual can be regarded simply as contingent, or it can be regarded as the determinant consequence of a set of necessary features of Western institutions and civilization.

We have, therefore, to consider in relation and separately three rather distinctive types of argument, which have characterized the development of sociological thought during the last century. There is no simple pattern of relationships in the literature. Long-run accounts that emphasize Judaic-Christianity tend to be deterministic and to maintain the singularity of the Occident. Short-run accounts, however, may be contingent, as when the development of modern Western society in the eighteenth and nineteenth centuries is explained in terms of specific features, or deterministic, when individualism is accounted for by its postulated link with capitalism.

The work of Max Weber is an interesting contribution to the analysis of the long and short runs. It is well known that Weber sought to reject the conventional evolutionary explanations, which were dominant in European social thought in the nineteenth century. He rejected the traditional evolutionary schemes, which saw the history of humankind as a unified history broken into regular stages of development. It is also well known that Weber had a specific concern with peculiar and contingent causes of any given historical event. Yet he was also interested in long-run historical changes; in particular, he sought to construct a secular theory of the uniqueness of rationalism in the West as it had developed over many centuries (Roth and Schlucter, 1979). He was therefore particularly concerned with the set of causes that gave rise to rationalism and the peculiar combination of circumstances that emphasized rationalism in the West. In his introduction to *The Protestant Ethic and the Spirit of Capitalism*, Weber said that he was concerned to understand what concatenation of circumstances had brought about instrumental rationalism in the Occident, a rationalism that had a universal significance and value. His rationalization theme is not an illustration of evolutionary thought and it is not an illustration of teleological history. Weber was specifically concerned to understand the contingent circumstances of particular events, but nevertheless he wished to show how these specific developments were part of a more general development towards rationalism. Rationalism was the unintended outcome of a whole series of peculiar circumstances and developments (Turner, 1981).

The issue of long-run determination versus short-run conjunctures has been particularly important in existing studies of the individual. In the last chapter we cited accounts that have located the origins of the doctrine of individualism in seventeenth-century political thought, which in turn is seen to be an expression of changes in property relationships and the organization of the market (Macpherson, 1962; Goldmann, 1973). Other writers (Chenu, 1969; Devane, 1977) have located individualism in the fourteenth and fifteenth centuries. By contrast, Macfarlane (1978) treats English society as essentially individualistic throughout the whole period of feudalism. Yet again, it is argued that Western society is necessarily individualistic as a consequence of the dominance of the Christian tradition. It would certainly be possible to exploit this confusion among writers in order to suggest simply that there is no special relationship between capitalism and individualism. There is no special relationship because individualism has existed under a variety of different modes of production and under a variety of different forms of political and social relationships. However, there seems to be no particular reason for playing off long-run against short-run arguments, since it seems perfectly plausible to suggest that, although the foundations of individualism were laid over a very long period, with the emergence of the individual over some 2000 years of the Judaic-Christian tradition, in capitalism this existing ideological tradition was developed and given, as it were, a special spurt and character.

Christianity and the Emergence of the Individual

Talcott Parsons's essay 'Christianity and modern industrial society' (1963) is an interesting example of the combination of long-run and short-run explanations, with its assessment of Christianity's contribution to the emergence of modern society. Parsons is primarily concerned to show how the church and the sacred became institutionally differentiated from society and the profane, but in his exposition he also provides a clear statement of how the Judaic-Christian tradition contributed ultimately to the emergence both of democracy and individualism. His argument is that the significance of Christianity lies in its substitution of faith for kinship and blood as the basis of social solidarity. The Christian community emerged as a community of individuals bound together by the subjectivity of their faith, not a community bound together by their blood and their descent. He says, therefore, that the most distinctive feature of Christianity was its development of a religious emphasis on the individual that departed sharply from the Jewish notion of the community as God's chosen people. In Christianity, the salvation of the individual soul rather than salvation of communities was important, and individuals needed consciousness if they were to be saved, because they were accountable for the actions of their souls. Christian individuals were admittedly connected together by ritual and worship, but the social and institutional link was definitely between individuals related to each other by faith, and not by primordial ties of tribe or descent or by marriage.

Christianity emerged therefore as an evangelical and universalistic religion with a doctrine of egalitarian salvation. Parsons argues that this universalism was also stimulated by the contact with Roman secular law, with its notion of natural order justic and law. However, these are to be seen as additions to a doctrinal core rather than as independent developments on the part of legal thinking.

39

Parsons goes on to argue that, given this core notion of the individual, we can see Christianity developing through various stages whereby the individual conscious is emphasized and liberated. The Reformation was a most significant stage in that liberation of individual conscious from the control of the church, which prepared the way to the emergence of what Parsons calls 'political democracy'. Protestantism provided a framework within which the responsible individual could function effectively; this religious framework provided some protection for individual rights while also demanding individual responsibilities. Parsons does not therefore see the secular activism and individualism of modern American industrial society as a departure from the Christian tradition; on the contrary, he sees American individualism as the final outcome and expression of a basic underlying Christian emphasis on the religious individual. In this sense Parsons denies the secularization thesis, because he sees modern democratic pluralism as the ultimate embodiment of the separation between God and Caesar. Parsons's contribution to the analysis of secularism and individualism is thus rather distinctive and separates him from other theorists of secularization and religion (Robertson, 1982).

In other respects, Parsons's argument is merely an application of Weber's views on the historical significance of Christianity. For example, it was Weber in *The City* who argued that

> The city church, city saint, participation of the burghers in the Lord's supper and official church celebrations by the city were all typical of the occidental cities. Within them Christianity deprived the clan of its last ritualistic importance, for by its very nature the Christian community was a confessional association of believing individuals rather than a ritualistic association of clans.
>
> (Weber, 1958, pp. 102–3)

The city in the West was therefore an association of co-religionists with equal rights under a universalistic system of law and religion. Weber, like Marx, thought that the occidental city was relatively autonomous from political interference by patrimonial states and therefore it was in the city that the independent urban burgher class could develop. The urban artisan and the urban burgher were vehicles for both rationalistic thought and individual aptitude. Moreover, Weber suggested that the city was an island of individual freedom for all social classes. The city was a radicalizing force in history, but at least part of its radicalness came from Christianity itself. For Weber, however, the paradox is that Christianity produces results which it does not expect and which stand in a negative relationship to Christianity as such. Unlike Parsons, Weber saw forms of secular individuality, especially economic individualism, as largely corrosive of Christianity's hold over the population. The price for Weber was antinomianism, but in other respects Parsons's argument converges substantially with that of Weber. Both saw Christianity as a force that brought about the de-tribalization of Europe and as a force that contributed to the emergence of autonomous cities as areas with a culture of individual freedom. The city was, so to speak, a social space within which the individual could be cultivated and protected. The church as a collection of equal and believing individuals provided a social model for the Western polity, that is, a political system based upon egalitarianism and the rights of individuals. The believer in the church paved the way for the citizen in the state.

Weber, of course, was characteristically ambiguous about such social developments. On the one hand, we can treat Weber's historical sociology as the study of the emergence of the person and the embodiment of reason and consciousness. Weber was concerned to analyse those historical processes that made the individual possible, that is, to understand how the individual emerged out of institutions and became, as it were, an institution. On the other hand, Weber tended to see the individual as an entity which was subject to a variety of external constraints and controls in a rational capitalist society. The individual emerges in history as the product of a whole series of changes (in particular, those brought about by legal theory and the Protestant Reformation). Weber saw the rationalizing potential of modern society as threatening the demise of the autonomous individual with the development of the iron cage of bureaucracy. In this respect, Weber's view is very different from the emancipatory perspective of Parsons.

It is interesting, therefore, to combine Parsons's position with that taken by other American sociologists of religion, for example, that of Robert N. Bellah in his celebrated article, 'Religious evolution' (1964). Bellah, like Parsons, treats American individualism both as an expression of a traditional Christian view and as a part of a new form of religiosity. Bellah quotes with approval Thomas Paine's aphorism, 'My mind is my church', and Thomas Jefferson's remark,

'I am a sect myself', as expressions of modern American religiosity. The new religiosity suggests that the individual must work out his or her own ultimate solutions for life, and the most the church can do is to provide a sympathetic environment for the development of such individuality. If religion historically discovered and elaborated the self, then modern religion is increasingly emphasizing human responsibility for the self. Although Bellah's position is interesting and innovative, it does of course bear a resemblance to the work of Tillich (1952), Lenski (1961), Luckmann (1967) and Berger (1969). However, we must remind ourselves that *all* of these positions go back to the work of Ernst Troeltsch in his study *The Social Teaching of the Christian Churches*, which appeared in 1908–11 (Troeltsch, 1912). He argued that the traditional opposition between the church type and the sect type would give way ultimately to an entirely new form of religiosity, which he called mysticism. Mysticism would be primarily the private religion of the isolated individual who was without extensive social contacts with other believers; religion would become increasingly privatized as the consciousness of separated individuals.

The thrust of these somewhat rather diverse accounts, however, is similar. First, they argue for the importance of the long-term contribution of Christianity to a history of the rise of the individual and individualism. Secondly, they emphasize the peculiar and special importance of the Protestant Reformation in the development of an individualistic consciousness and conscience. In short, these points of agreement combine both the long-run and short-run accounts of individuality and individualism, and there is no inherently problematic issue of periodization. In these accounts, Western culture is inherently one that elevates the individual, although it is also the case that the Protestant Reformation, and with it the emergence of competitive capitalism in the seventeenth century, made a special and unique contribution to the emergence of the conscience. The authors tend to differ over the question of pessimism and optimism rather than over the question of time-spans. American progressivists are optimistic in their appraisal: they do not see the importance of the individual as being threatened by modern society, but as enhanced and institutionalized by the rights of citizenship and the emergence of democratic politics. By contrast, Troeltsch and Weber had a highly pessimistic view of the future of the individual in a society where bureaucracy and control were dominant.

42

We can approach classical sociology, therefore, as a debate about the origins and characteristics of the individual and in particular of the modern self. The emergence of the modern self is the index of the decline of traditional, *gemeinschaft*-like community associations, estates, prescriptive and particularistic norms, and the division of societies into citizens and strangers. The emergence of the self is the index of secularization and the index of the impact of Christianity on Western culture and institutions. To say that classical sociology is concerned with the history of the self is to show the parallel with the later work of Michel Foucault (1976; 1979a). Despite varying secondary interpretations of his work, we can reasonably claim that he writes the history of subjectivity, the history of mentalities and the history of the soul. What has not yet been adequately recognized is the close parallel between Weber's interest in the rationalization process and Foucault's interest in the emergence of discipline, regulation and panopticism. Nor has the parallel between his notion of the disciplined society and Adorno's concept of the administered society been properly considered (Jay, 1984). We wish to suggest that both Foucault and the critical theorists were working within a legacy that goes back to Weber and Troeltsch; namely, a legacy that explores the relationship between the self, bureaucracy and capitalism. Weber and Foucault were concerned to understand both the institutional discourses that produced the individual over long historical time-spans and the social forces that were likely to bring about the termination of the self-conscious, practical, individual actor. The conditions that gave rise to the individual can be explored via a brief analysis of the history of the confessional in Western culture.

The Confessional Self

The relationship between the Christian confessional, the development of casuistry and the emergence of conscience is of importance in a sociological history of individuality. Moreover, the confessional rather neatly illustrates the problems arising out of the different forms of argument, a recurrent theme of this chapter. First, the confessional has a very long history in Christianity, but there were also specific times (such as the thirteenth and seventeenth centuries) when massive changes took place in confessional practice and the theology surrounding the sacrament of penance. The long and the short runs are both significant. Second, there is the difficulty of determining whether the notions of the confessional and the confessing self are peculiar to the Western Christian culture or are universal to all human communities. There is the issue of the uniqueness of the West. Third, we need to establish whether confession belonged to a particular type of moral system, which was itself specific to particular modes of production or to particular societies. Did the confession emerge as a result of a peculiar concatenation of circumstances or does it stand in a determinate relationship to given modes of production?

In *The Dominant Ideology Thesis*, we asked whether the confession could function as an apparatus of social control which regulated the life of the peasant or other subordinate groups, and approached this issue via the debate about the dominance of Catholicism in the medieval period. There we argued that the confessional may have played an important part in the ideological outlook and moral atmosphere of the dominant class, but the evidence did not support an argument that the confessional had an important role in incorporating the peasant – the peasantry were characteristically absent from the confessional box. While that analysis remains valid, it was a restricted and restrictive approach to the confessional as a topic of analysis. We now want to locate confession within a much broader sweep of history and in relationship to a more complex set of theoretical questions and problems. The confessional, like Christianity as a whole, preceded the emergence of feudalism, survived the onslaught of competitive capitalism and, according to some, flourishes in a capitalist system. In short, it would be difficult to show that confession was peculiar, say, to a feudal mode of production. But we can show that the confessional played an important role in the historic emergence of the individual, self-conscious person equipped with subjectivity and moral standards. The confessional is ultimately highly ambiguous, seeming to offer itself as a form of social control but also playing a crucial role in the articulation of the self and the emergence of the person. We shall now turn to the question of the uniqueness of the confessional to the Christian tradition, the relationship of the confessional to particular historical circumstances, and finally the problem of the periodization of confessional practices in Western civilizations.

The nature of the confessional and its special relationship to Western culture are complicated issues that raise intriguing theoretical questions. In approaching these issues we should at first reject any notion of a psychologically uniform nature of personality across cultures and over time, against many psychological treatments of confession and the confessional that suggest there is, as it were, a compulsion to confess which is indigenous to human personality. The notion here is that wherever there exists a moral norm (that is, in all societies) and wherever there is deviation from such norms, then we would expect the operation of guilt to drive a person to self-criticism. This view of the universality of the need to confess guilt is simplistic and unconvincing, and so, following the anthropological perspective, we would wish to distinguish between what are called guilt and shame cultures. In guilt cultures, social control is exercised as it were internally in the conscience of the individual, and behaviour is monitored by these forms of guilt reaction. By contrast, in shame cultures, social control is exercised through mechanisms such as public confrontation of the sinner, gossip and more public and overt forms of moral restraint. We also need to distinguish between spontaneous everyday confessions of guilt, as when people 'confess' to have forgotten to pay their bus fare, and institutionalized forms of confession, which are highly ritualized, publicly controlled and organized in very formal ways. In other words, we need to distinguish between everyday speech acts, which involve a form of self-criticism, and institutionalized arrangements, whereby individuals are organized into confessing activities. Thus, the question of the universality of confession will obviously depend on what definition we give to it. In Western cultures, the confession that emerged out of the Christian tradition was part of a sacramental system, that is, part of the sacrament of penance whereby sinners were regularly brought before the authority of the church to confess their misdemeanours. The question therefore comes to hinge on the existence of institutionalized practices of self-criticism, self-doubt and absolution. We may define confession, therefore, as an institution which establishes expectations that persons who have infringed norms will confess fully their misdemeanours to a person in authority, who has the power to absolve them of their guilt. The institution of confession presupposes the existence of a doctrine of personal guilt, a moral order against which the individual can sin, a system of pastoral authority which can receive and remove misdemeanour and, finally, a variety of techniques for speaking about and hearing such confessional statements. The emergence of such a system, namely a system in which conscience is a public form of social control, is particularly important for understanding the long-term historical emergence of a moral personality and of the self-conscious individual.

There are strong reasons for believing that a system of control by the inner cause of conscience was a very peculiar development in Western society; although certain analogous institutions are present in other societies, they did not develop to the extent that the sacrament of penance developed in the West (Hepworth and Turner, 1982). In the historical evidence, there are grounds for assuming a certain uniqueness in the development of the modern personality in Western society.

Anthropologists might wish to question these assertions on the basis that, as witchcraft, magic and sorcery have existed in a number of human cultures, confessional practices will be a regular feature of many societies. Anthropological studies of confessional activities inside witchcraft crazes and institutions of magic and sorcery are common (Rasmussen, 1931; Douglas, 1970; Lewis, 1971). These confessional activities certainly share some common features with the confessional system that developed in the West, but we can identify at least two distinguishing characteristics that differentiate these systems of confession. First, confession outside the Western tradition normally assumes a collective, group nature, that is, the confession is a reflection not of the state of the mind of the individual but a reflection of the character of the social structure. We would suggest that such confessionals are in fact very Durkheimian: they are statements about collective properties and forms of public thought, reaffirmations of public values and communal practices, rather than reflections of an interior mentality. Indeed, if we accept Durkheim's view that such societies are based upon 'mechanical solidarity', then we would argue that the individual in fact does not exist in such societies and so confessions are part of a public and exterior dynamic rather than features of an interior social meaning. Secondly, within such societies there can be relatively little differentiation between the notion of health and the notion of morality. Confessions of sin are part of a therapeutic technique for curing illness. In addition, such illnesses are often seen to be public and physical rather than private and interior. In short, the confession brings out a sickness that is not so much peculiar to the individual as a feature of the whole society.

These points can be illustrated in Knud Rasmussen's Eskimo studies (1931). Confessions were part of a larger system of shamanistic culture. Typically women would confess to having broken a tribal custom, such as entering an igloo during menstruation, and that this transgression explained the men's failure during fishing and hunting expeditions. Their sins were physical, namely the flow of blood in public places during menstruation, and the confession was performed in public before the tribe and involved an expurgation of such physical manifestations of group deviance. Such confessions involved no inquisition into the interior consciousness and subjectivity of the women but involved instead an acclamation of group practices and tradition. Rasmussen's analysis therefore supports a view that the confession in Western Christianity assumed an interior, private and subjective direction and can thus be contrasted with the public and conventional forms of confession in non-Western society.

To argue that the confessional tradition in Europe laid the foundation for the emergence of the modern personality as a self-reflective consciousness obliges us to inquire about the origin of this Western confessional tradition. There is clear evidence inside the Judaic tradition of a confessional practice. Jewish rituals that focused on the new year and renewal typically involved some statement of personal guilt and a request for forgiveness from sins. These confessional rituals in Judaism clearly laid the foundation for subsequent Christian developments, but they tended to assume a highly ritualistic and group nature. During the formation of early Christianity other influences from the Jewish environment came to bear. In particular, the Essene sects contributed significantly to the idea of confession of sins (Allegro, 1964, 1968; Dupont-Sommer, 1961). Other cultural traditions possibly bore upon Christianity and pushed it in the direction of regarding individual consciousness as the manifestation of some conflict between good and evil; there may well have been Zoroastrian influences (Hinnells, 1975, 1981). There is also the question of the later relationship between Islam and Christianity. There is evidence of a confessional tradition inside Islam (Gilsenan, 1973). In the case of Islam, however, it would be difficult to distinguish indigenous pure Islamic influences from a Christian overlay; where the confessional developed in Islam it appears to have had its origin in Christian missionary activity. The outcome of these comparative studies would be that Christianity

47

acquired a confessional tradition as a result of a rather mixed, traditional Jewish background, but that it was only in Christianity that the emphasis on private confession and the confession of the interior soul had a complete development.

In early Christianity confessions were irregular and could be made for a limited number of sins. Such confessions could also be made in public before the whole congregation. It was thus only over a very long period that there emerged the idea of the private confession before the priest, who had the authority to absolve sins in the name of the church. The notion grew that the church was a treasury of merit, a storehouse of the charismatic powers of Christ, which could be released through the hands of bishops: the notion of the keys of the confessional. The confessional as we know it has its modern origins in the thirteenth century when, as a result of the Lateran canon of 1216, confession became obligatory on all lay persons. Early in the thirteenth century there were moves to improve the educational standard of the priest and to incorporate the lay person within the orbit of the church via improvements in the nature of the ritualistic apparatus. This in particular involved the use of the confession to sound out heresy and discover sedition. The growth of the confessional, therefore, has to be seen in the context of a conflict between the church and secular society, where the church was seeking to influence lay opinion and lay practice by improving the quality of the priesthood and simultaneously educating the lay person. We might say that the goal of these changes in the confessional was actually an increase in the force of social control. Confession in many respects represents the ideal instrument of social control, because it encourages individuals to monitor themselves via a conscience of guilt under the view and control of the priest as the representative of churchly authority. Recent French history has brought to the surface many interesting aspects of this period, when confession was used as a way of monitoring society (Ladurie, 1980). However, we cannot simply dismiss the confessional as an instrument of social control from above, because these changes in the confessional were also part of a much wider movement in the emergence of conscience.

The confession was part of a new logic of personhood, organized around the key concepts of conscience, consciousness, feeling and sentiment (Huff, 1981). The re-deployment of the confessional in the thirteenth century has also to be connected with the new emergence of a culture of conscience through the development of casuistical morality, the norms of contrition and new sentiments relating to love and emotion. It has been suggested that the courtly love poetry and the tradition of the troubadours were important stages in the emergence of human sentiment (Lewis, 1936; Chenu 1969; Trinkaus and Oberman, 1974; Robertson, 1980). There is evidence that interior conscience, personal emotion, subjectivity and feeling were becoming more significant in the culture and everyday life of the upper classes.

These changes were also bound up with new attitudes towards women, at least in the upper circles of society. Controversially, it has been suggested that Christianity had always regarded women as persons. Jack Goody (1983) argues that the need of the early Church both to gain converts and to benefit from bequests of property reinforced the religious doctrine that all persons are equal in the sight of God, leading it to treat women as individuals endowed with reason, will and independence. Although women could still be part of the property settlement of families, some women were able to assert a role of cultural leadership within the upper class. Women came to play an important part in the refined cultural existence of the court (Heller, 1978). The argument is that, while the confessional was part of a fairly brutal apparatus of social control, it also played an important role in the civilization of society by encouraging the emergence of a new set of norms and practices which emphasized the emotional and personal life of the subject. Human beings became differentiated and their differentiation was signalled by the emergence of new forms of sentiment and emotion. These changes were reflected in new attitudes towards the spiritual life, and also in new attitudes towards sexuality, family and women. At least in the courts, women began to emerge as no longer merely sex objects or aspects of family property but as human beings with particular and unique personalities. The uniqueness of the confessional in the West is thus bound up with a more general problem concerning the nature of subjectivity and the person in Western society. These arguments therefore tend to run together, into questions about the uniqueness of Western subjectivity and emotional feeling.

This history of the confessional has been recently elaborated and developed by Foucault, who has treated the Christian confessional as an institution that gave rise ultimately to a confessing culture (1976). For him, Western culture does not dismiss or subjugate sexuality but, on the contrary, through the confessional discourse, Western culture elaborates, amplifies and distributes sexuality throughout a community. The confessional is a form of power whose effects are to be seen in a new knowledge of the self and the interior life. According to Foucault, we now live in a peculiar society where we are all compelled to confess and to explore our interior lives. Our culture has become essentially autobiographical. We might admit that these developments have a peculiar ambience in Western civilization and are the marks of Western subjectivity. We need to enquire, however, into the particular circumstances that gave rise to these developments. Are these long-run circumstances or were there peculiar and specific contingent causes that gave rise to the confessional in Western society? We need to enquire into the particular social circumstances that seem to encourage and develop confessional practices, and in particular we need to examine the relationship between cataclysm and confessionals.

Social Change and Confession

This study of confession and conscience provides a good example of how long-run and short-run arguments need not conflict. At the same time, it provides an argument about the problems of contingent versus deterministic explanations. We might argue that an emphasis on the subjective individual emerged in Western cultures because of the accidental presence of Christian beliefs about the soul. As a result of the destruction of the original Jewish-Christian church under Roman Imperial conditions, the Christian community emerged as a de-tribalized group of individuals bound together by faith and members of a community called the church. Because Christianity was originally a Jewish movement, which emerged and developed inside a Greek culture, there was less space for the influence of particularistic tribal allegiances. Christianity began to develop as a complex community with diverse ethnic origins. These circumstances favoured the development of an emphasis on the individual soul. The Christian emphasis on personal belief and loyalty to a universalistic god was further developed inside a Roman context, where Roman legal notions of the *persona* began to merge with Christian emphases on the soul. In other words, there was a fortuitous combination of a particular aspect of Roman legal theory and Christian theology to produce the notion of a subjective personality with rights and obligations. We have seen that, with the institutional development of the Christian church as a universalistic institution in feudal Europe, the confessional came to be used as an instrument for the control of heresy and political protest. The notion of conscience began to be used for largely political reasons, that is, to achieve control over the Christian hinterland, particularly in remote and mountainous regions. However, the confession in the society of the court also contributed to the flowering of a court culture, which to some extent was quite individualistic or at least favoured the individual development of personality. We have seen that this had a particularly important consequence for the emergence of women as private and unique individuals. Thus Christianity provided many of the ingredients that were necessary for the development of con-science and personality, and these ingredients were combined with a variety of other cultural circumstances in Europe.

It is difficult, however, to see any really precise or necessary connections between the individualizing culture of the confessional and the basic economic and political structures of either slavery or feudalism. In *The Dominant Ideology Thesis*, we argued that a confessional culture might aid the political dominance of the upper class, but the main role for confession would be in the surveillance and control of women and in the establishment of patriarchal authority in the household. Confession was quite well suited to the control of women via the priesthood in the interests of family stability and the transference of property. We might suggest that, while many accidental features went towards the manufacturing of a confessional conscience, there were certain necessary requirements within society for a system of beliefs and practices that would bring about the incorporation of women, the control of children and the maintenance of household authority. If a confessional or something like it is a necessary requirement of a society based upon private property, household structures and patriarchal power, then we would not expect a major disruption of confessional practice and belief in the transition from feudalism to capitalism. Feudalism was a society based upon forms of feudal land-ownership in which a peasantry could be coerced into providing labour for the manage-ment of large estates. A feudal society also required some form of household structure whereby this land could be distributed in a stable fashion from one generation to the next via a system of primogeniture. Although early capitalism has characteristics that are rather different from those of feudalism, it nevertheless also requires property distribution, forms of law that establish private property, and a household structure for controlling property from father to son. Feudalism and early capitalism are both patriarchal and both require forms of political control for the subordination of peasants and workers. We have also indicated in our previous work that the so-called transition from feudalism to capitalism is not historically significant, or at least not as historically significant as the transition from early to late capitalism. In other words, we have suggested the continuity between feudalism and capitalism. If we turn to the question of confession, we can see how this continuity is manifest in the continuity of confessional attitudes and practices.

The Protestant Reformation is conventionally thought to play an important part in both the emergence of the individual and the creation of circumstances that contributed, at least culturally, to the emergence of capitalism. In most classical accounts of modern society there is thought to be a very special relationship between the Protestant emphasis on the individual, the capitalist emphasis on economic man and the emergence of utilitarian ideologies stressing the autonomy of the individual. Even theories that seek to deny any validity to the Weber thesis normally suggest that there is a special connection between Protestantism, individualism and capitalism. That is, even Marxist critics of Weber often argue that Protestant individualism was associated with the emergence of individualism as a dominant ideology of early capitalist societies. Within our longer perspective, however, we have seen that Catholic culture even as early as the thirteenth century had begun to develop beliefs about persons within the confessional. It is therefore interesting that one common view is that confession actually disappears with the emergence of Protestantism, and so plays no role in the emergence of economic individualism inside capitalism. This conventional view of the history of confession is inadequate. The Protestant reformers did not so much object to confession as to commercialized absolution. They objected to the free market in the forgiveness of souls and they objected to a laissez-faire principle of indulgence. Lutheranism and Calvinism did not so much destroy the traditional Catholic confessional system as redeploy the confessional in new forms of belief and practice. Protestantism encouraged the individual to plead with God for the forgiveness of sins. In addition, Protestantism tended to encourage the development of the confessional diary, personal reminiscences and other forms of literary confession.

In Protestantism, therefore, the confessional became less a ritualized practice between priest and lay person and more a practice direct between God and the believer. In Protestantism, the confession of sin tended to become more diffuse and personalized. This involved a new conception of the nature of sin. In Catholicism, sins tended to be individualized so that they could be confessed in a statistical manner; the individual committed acts that were judged good or bad and these acts did not necessarily reflect on the essential character of the believer. In Protestantism, it was the total personality that was either saved or not saved, good or bad, evil or saintly. Because Protestantism emphasized the notion of man fallen from grace, sin was totalized and generalized. The personality became unified around principles of total evil and total holiness. Yet, even in Protestantism, regularized practices of confession tended to be quite common. For example, in the early Methodist sects it was common for the laity to meet regularly in class meetings, where individual members confessed their sins and the work of the Lord in their lives before their fellow lay people. The class meeting in Methodism was therefore a genuine form of confessional activity, involving public confession of interior guilt and sin. We might say, following the view of Weber, that the Protestant Reformation had the consequence of taking confession out of the confessional box and putting it in the family around the hearth. Confession became, as it were, democratized as a universal and regular practice of the believer, but it also became spontaneous and less organized around regular institutional assumptions. Protestantism placed much greater weight on conversion, and conversion was normally accompanied by confession. Emotional conversion inside the Protestant sect consequently came to replace the traditional institutionalized confession, and conversion involved the total personality in a reformation of life.

We can see in this illustration how long-run and short-run arguments can be combined and also how arguments about contingent developments and long secular deterministic trends can be joined. There were many accidental and contingent features, which made the confessional a central practice in Christianity, but there were also functional relationships between confession and the political and economic characteristics of both feudalism and early capitalism. It was Christianity which laid the general framework for the subsequent emergence of a special emphasis on the person, their rights and their needs. Bunyan's *Pilgrim's Progress* came to offer a general model of modern man equipped with guilt, subjectivity, consciousness, morality and sentiment. The confessional also provides a model of social control based not on overt brutality and constraint but on interior subjectivity, consent and feeling. The confessional provides an important link between the exterior institutions of the state and the interior practices of the mind, and the notion that one can only confess to a person in authority was an important feature of confession as an instrument of social control. It is clear, however, that these confessional practices had more importance and salience in the dominant class than in the subordinate classes. The confessing personality is also characteristic of late capitalism. Indeed, if we were to follow the arguments of Foucault, the guilt-ridden, confessing, self-critical personality would appear to be more dominant in the twentieth century than in the thirteenth, and more certainly dominant now than in the sixteenth and seventeenth centuries.

This is a good illustration of what we can now identify as a powerful paradox: namely, that on the one hand the individual in late capitalism appears to be highly regulated and standardized by social practices, but on the other is also highly emotional, narcissistic and guilt-ridden. In short, Confessing Man is simultaneously regularized and spontaneous, controlled and liberated, incorporated and opposed.

Conscience and Social Transformation

Both sociology and Marxism assume a great transformation of society with industrialization. In Marxism, the notion of a great transformation takes the form of a debate about the relationship between feudalism and capitalism. In sociology, the notion of transition is normally worked out in a series of contrasts between traditional and modern society, between rural and urban. In both versions of the great transformation argument there is an idea that modern society is secular. The history of capitalist society is the history of secularization. Marx and Engels thought that the growth of working-class socialism would gradually undermine the ideological dominance of the Christian churches. Durkheim argued that the growing complexity of modern society would result in the emergence of a whole series of new symbols and rituals, which would not be based upon traditional Catholic or Christian belief and principle. Durkheim's ideas, moreover, were in many respects an application of the ideas of Saint-Simon and Comte. There was the idea that a theological age would be replaced by a secular one. In Weber's classical notion of rationalization, it was assumed that the traditional dominance of religious beliefs, especially in the form of charisma, would be replaced by a society in which routine scientific belief and practice organized and dominated everyday life.

These ideas share a common theme or narrative. Protestantism helps to lay the foundation of capitalism by creating a culture which is individualistic and anti-traditional, but at the same time Protestantism liberates forces in society which come eventually to undermine Protestantism itself. These are the forces of rational inquiry, scepticism and hostility to tradition. These forces work in conjunction with urbanization and growing literacy to destroy the foundations of religious certitude. These developments have their impact on the confessional by undermining the authority of the priest to enter the family to hear confessions. Instead, the family and the household become separate and isolated from ecclesiastical influences, and the members confess to each other without the privileged ear of the confessor. All of this represents a decline in the authority of the institutionalized church in controlling and regulating the lives of its members. Instead, private individuals emerge equipped with conscience and consciousness, capable of adjudicating their own morality and lifestyles. Secular man is equipped with his own principles and beliefs, capable of judging his own lifestyle and deciding upon his own fate. Secular man is dominated by the needs for consumption, forced to choose between a multitude of commodities where these commodities are both material and immaterial. Modern man lives in a cultural world dominated by laissez-faire, where belief, morality, lifestyle and culture can all be chosen and selected as if he were selecting commodities. This history of secularization is of course faulty.

The strength of Foucault's position is that it draws into question this simplistic periodization of human history into ages of faith and ages of secularity. Like Weber, he does not see the past as a history of progress towards enlightenment, secularism, individualism and the private rational conscience of the person. The traditional Catholic confessional has not so much declined with the coming of modern society but has been redistributed into new practices which express power and knowledge.

> We have since become a singularly confessing society. The confession has spread its effects far and wide. It plays a part in justice, medicine, education, family relationships, and love relations, in the most ordinary affairs of everyday life, and in most solemn rites; one confesses one's crimes, one's sins, one's thoughts and desires, one's illnesses and troubles; one goes about telling, with the greatest precision, whatever is most difficult to tell.
>
> (Foucault, 1976, p. 59)

The Christian confessional has therefore been reconstituted and redeployed in medical, legal and scientific discourses on private life. The traditional rituals of the confessional box are now required to operate under new principles of scientific regularity. The confession is now a discourse that is part of the formal examination, the census, the questionnaire, the interrogation. It is no longer about what people consciously hide from themselves but is concerned with what is disguised from them in the unconscious.

The implication of this argument is that the traditional Catholic confessional was appropriated by the Protestant biography, then redeployed in the modern Freudian psychoanalytic confessional and finally re-instituted in bureaucratic forms of inquiry. There is, therefore, no great transformation of the confessional between the feudal and the capitalist mode of production. On the contrary, Christian institutions simply assume slightly different functions and moderations of form, while the confessional is still very much present in the clinical interview, the Freudian analysis and modern literary forms. The confessional mode becomes part of the bureaucratic apparatus of the state, designed to illicit the inner thoughts, attitudes and assumptions of the private citizen. The bureaucratic questionnaire provides the linkage between the individual citizen and the public world of politics and administration. Just as in the thirteenth century, when the confessional inquisition provided the apparatus which linked the church to the rural interior, so today's bureaucratic systems of investigation provide the link between the regulating state and the regulated individual. The confessional for Foucault is thus part of a massive system of surveillance, but a surveillance that is based upon micro-politics, that is a self-imposed, localized politics within the household. Of course this viewpoint is based upon a paradox, that in the democratic state the citizen is formally free and operates according to free market principles, but is at the same time the subject of innumerable bureaucratic details, surveillance, interviewing and measurement. The paradox is that we are simultaneously spontaneous and also controlled and normalized by social processes.

The result is that it becomes difficult to talk about definite periods in the history of confession, because the content and function of confession appear to merge from one period to another. There is no necessarily sharp break in the history of the conscience of the individual via the confessional, since the practices of the fifteenth century appear to blur with those of the sixteenth and there is no specifically sharp contrast between feudal Catholic confessional and Protestant capitalist ones. Similarly, the religious inquiry into the soul seems to overlap with the secular inquiry into the citizen. Rather than conceiving the subjective individual in terms of historical breaks, it often appears that the individual emerges through an evolutionary development of these detailed inquiries. There are no sharp breaks but slightly new directions and more elaborate forms of inquiry and expression.

Christianity and Individualism

We have considered various ways in which Christianity relates to individualism. Our argument is that Christianity is not individualistic in a strict or specific sense, and it certainly has not embraced individualism as a dominant doctrine. We have shown, however, that, over a very long period of its development, the church, through a range of institutions, emphasized the importance of the individual. Christianity developed, especially through the confessional and the sacraments, the notion that the individual was important in the spiritual organization of the world and history. We might argue that the church gave a special emphasis to the separate individual in the geography of grace.

This emphasis on the role of Christianity as a whole in the development of the individual appears to diverge from the usual position in the sociology of religion, namely that Christianity is, unlike other world religions, individualistic in both doctrine and practice. Our argument also appears controversial because we do not so sharply distinguish between Catholic and Protestant versions of Christianity. Within the tradition of Weberian sociology, we discover a very common argument that, while Catholicism did not support the development of individualism, Protestantism was crucial for the development of contemporary ideologies of individualism in both the political and economic realms. Clearly, the Reformation was a watershed in the historical development of individualism and it is the case that Protestant doctrine proved more congenial to the development of Western individualism. There are parallel relations between religious man in Protestantism and economic man in economic theory. Nevertheless, we wish to argue that Christianity, in both its Catholic and Protestant versions, was not itself individualistic and did not embrace individualism as an orthodox doctrinal stance.

Christianity, from its foundations, placed an important emphasis on communal obligations, an emphasis which derived to some extent from the Jewish emphasis on the people as a group chosen by God. As Christianity developed, it acquired ecclesiastical institutions which were derived from Roman social structures and it developed a range of social forms which were meant to help in the adaptation to a new European cultural and social environment. Although Christianity evolved in institutional terms towards a congregational religion, Christianity retained the notion of the church as the body of Christ in which the individual autonomy of its members was subordinated to the organizational harmony of the church as a whole. The church was an institution with a universal appeal, in which the whole was clearly greater than the parts. In order to maintain this unity, the church, as an organization, developed a number of processes and procedures, which were meant to guarantee orthodoxy and thus the unity of the people. This apparatus for establishing the harmony and continuity of the church over the individual included the confessional and the range of sacramental rituals, which guaranteed and enhanced the unity of the religious community. The Eucharist was an institution which stood at the centre of these unifying rituals and which emphasized the regulation of the person in the interests of communal goals. The Eucharist is a spiritual meal which, in anthropological terms, binds the individuals at the meal into a coherent social group.

Although the Reformation broke with many of the traditions of medieval Catholicism, we should not see the emergence of Protestantism as a total and complete rejection of its medieval Christian roots. The Reformation was a critique of the corruption of various ecclesiastical institutions, but the Reformation typically claimed to be returning to the values and practices of the primitive church as opposed to the corruption of medieval Catholic society. Although Protestants criticized the commercialization of the means of grace, they did not entirely reject the sacramental apparatus of traditional Christian institutions. We might consider Methodism in this respect, since Methodism is typically regarded as the individualistic religious movement *par excellence*. Although Weber thought that Methodism had incorporated an emotional element into the Protestant tradition, he also thought that Methodism was highly individualistic and contributed to the emergence of individualism, especially in the American context. Methodism, however, like many other Protestant sects, saw itself as modelled on the primitive church tradition. In particular, John Wesley criticized what he regarded as the corruption of Protestant religious idealism into the secular and materialistic individualism of the Anglican Church, which he compared to a rope of sand. Wesley's reform of Anglicanism involved a new emphasis on communal social relations within the Church, borrowing from what he understood to be the primitive Church tradition, as an antidote to the individualism of the society around him. As Methodism developed in the late eighteenth and early nineteenth centuries, various communal practices were evolved in order to bind the Methodist groups together. These new communal rituals involved the love-feast, covenant service, hymn singing and the class system. Finally, we might note that the Methodist Church referred to itself as a society and, like many Protestant groups, gave a strong emphasis to the importance of fellowship in the spiritual life of the individual. This communal emphasis in Methodism has, of course, been noted by a variety of historians (Hill, 1969; Devane, 1977; Huff, 1981), but these historical accounts fail to identify the importance of the contradictory relationship between communal norms, on the one hand, and the emphasis on the individual as the focus of spiritual development within the religious tradition, on the other. This tension between the value of the individual and the importance of communal regulations and norms was also characteristic of the Quakers, Baptists and some aspects of Presbyterianism. However, the emphasis on the individual in the Protestant sects must not be taken as equivalent to a doctrine of individualism. Furthermore, it is not accurate to argue that Protestantism was individualistic in a significant sense, since this is to confuse the notion of the importance of the individual with an articulated position, which we might characterize as individualistic. Like medieval Catholicism, the Protestant sects continued to regard the community of believers as the context for spirituality, continued to regard the church as essentially a form of fellowship and did not accept the notion of complete individualism, which would have undermined adherence to religious doctrines on matters, for example, relating to the authority of the Bible and the importance of a rational interpretation of spiritual history. The emphasis on the authoritative character of biblical truth is the clearest evidence of the fact that the Protestant Reformation did not, in practice, take the conscience of the individual as the only guarantor of truth and virtue. The Protestants, like their medieval Catholic forebears, knew that the notion of the complete autonomy of the individual was the first step to antinomian chaos. The sinful individual needed to be regulated by the church and, if necessary, by the state.

We cannot say that the history of the self is merely a history of Christianity and the religious self, since developments in the relationship between religious belief and social institutions are simply one feature of many changes going on in Western society, in terms of law and politics, economics and culture. We need to see other dimensions of the individual emerging and being developed by these institutional changes over both the long run and the short run. We need to consider the religious self and the religious history of conscience alongside a whole series of other histories relating to biography and autobiography, law and morality, economics and politics. The history of the self has many diverse and curious lines of development. The religious history of the individual, however, provides a rather useful framework and paradigm for the analysis of more secular and alternative histories. The dimensions of these various histories are infinite, so here it will be useful merely to select some features that help to reinforce part of the argument we have already established. We need to take other illustrations in order to re-examine some of these problems between long- and short-run arguments, between contingent and determinant features of historical development, and between arguments which assert the uniqueness of the West and which argue for the universality of the notion of conscience and personality.

Representations of the Face

Portraiture in the contemporarily accepted sense of conveying the individuality of the sitter is a relatively recent phenomenon. In medieval pictures of people, particularly in representations of the face, the artist's purpose was not necessarily to convey a likeness but to achieve other goals. Thus, in an introduction to an exhibition of early tomb sculpture at the National Portrait Gallery, A. Tomlinson argues:

> Portraiture, in the accepted sense, did not form part of the repertoire of the majority of medieval artists. What we sometimes think of as the characteristic face of a period or century is fairly often the common reduction of human features to a type, or norm, which was acceptable to a particular generation – how it liked to see itself. In fact, of course, faces were no more medieval than they are, say, modern or eighteenth century.
>
> (Tomlinson, 1974, p. 1)

In general, although obviously there were exceptions, artists in the period AD 500–1000 aimed at the depiction of office, of religious symbolism, or even of pattern and colour rather than individual likeness. As Ernst Gombrich says of the human figures in illuminated manuscripts:

> They do not look quite like human figures but rather like strange patterns made of human forms . . . One can see that the artist used some example he found in an old Bible and transformed it to suit his taste. He changed the folds of the dress to something like interlacing ribbons, the locks of hair and even the ears into scrolls, and turned the whole face into a rigid mask. These figures of evangelists and saints look almost as stiff and quaint as primitive idols.
>
> (Gombrich, 1982, p. 118)

A monk illuminating a manuscript sponsored by King Otto (973–1002) drew a portrait of the king, who then died before the completion of the manuscript. The artist simply changed the name beneath the portrait to that of Otto's successor, graphically illustrating that his intention was not to depict Otto's individual features but to display kingship.

Morris concludes, that 'About the year 1000, therefore, it is safe to say that artists were little, if at all, concerned with the recording of individual likenesses' (Morris, 1972, p. 89). It is important to stress that this is not a failure of technique on the part of the artists, any more than the non-representational quality of Chinese art of roughly the same period demonstrated technical deficiency. Quite the reverse. Medieval artists in western Europe were well acquainted with the methods needed to show drapery clinging to the human body, to represent shadow, and to foreshorten figures. If, to modern eyes, their pictures have a certain simple and 'unreal' quality in which individual likenesses do not appear, it is because their priorities were such that the person as an individual was not especially important. They wanted, among other things, to tell a story as clearly and simply as possible or to show the glory and splendour of kings and religious figures.

This medieval lack of interest in representing individuals has often been contrasted with the way in which the Renaissance is said to have discovered not only the importance of individuals but also the significance of representing nature. In the quotation at the head of this chapter, Jacob Burckhardt contrasts the Middle Ages with Renaissance Italy. He goes on to say that 'at the close of the thirteenth century Italy began to swarm with individuality; the charm laid upon human personality was dissolved, and a thousand figures meet us each in its own special shape and dress' (Burckhardt, 1958, p. 123). The individual became supremely important, an importance that Burckhardt sees as closely connected to the Renaissance quest for glory and many-sidedness of personality. As J. H. Plumb says of the Renaissance, 'the originality of its greatest artists lies not in the virtuosity of their technical experiments, or in the boldness with which they explored landscape and the naked body, but in their concentration on the uniqueness of the human temperament and the significance of individual experience' (Plumb, 1982, p. 10). There was a unique quality of personal destiny, and man could be what he chose. Artists owed little to the past or traditional models, but were able to follow their own genius in the choice of subject or technique. The result was that the faces that artists painted had individualized qualities.

Michelangelo is often supposed to epitomize the Renaissance 'independence of all rule and the individualism that accompanied it' (Blunt, 1962, p. 76). It is Leonardo da Vinci, however, who implicitly connects the need to work from nature, to paint what is there, with the consequent rendering of individual qualities. 'The painter will produce pictures of little merit if he takes the works of others as his standard; but if he will apply himself to learn from the objects of nature he will produce good results' (Leonardo, quoted in Bronowski, 1982, p. 177). If artists are to represent nature, then it follows that they will represent the individual qualities of the face, and that is nowhere more clearly seen than in Leonardo's famous self-portrait in Turin. The need to paint individual likenesses does not, of course, derive only from the injunction to work from nature. Leonardo further emphasized the individual qualities of his portraits by espousing the belief that the painter had to convey the emotions and ideas of the sitter in the portrait.

If there is a very general movement, from the early Middle Ages through the Renaissance, of an increasing emphasis on the importance of the individual, this process is not only reflected in the representation of the face but also in the social position of the artist.

Giotto's personal fame initiated a tendency to consider artists as individual creators. It was significant that *he* painted his pictures. He was not a simple craftsman who made things which he did not sign and whose personal contribution did not therefore outlast his lifetime. As Gombrich says, 'From his day onwards the history of art, first in Italy and then in other countries also, is the history of the great artists' (1982, p. 154). Later, Renaissance artists developed the spirit of independence, eccentricity, personal fame and egotism to new heights. A century before Cellini wrote his autobiography celebrating his own heroic virtues, Ghiberti was boasting that he had entirely transformed Florence single-handed. Michelangelo was the perfect example of the personal fame of an artist who was so sure of his social position that he could be rude to the Pope. At the same time he was the first example of the modern, lonely, demoniacally impelled artist – 'the first to be completely possessed by his idea and for whom nothing exists but his idea – who feels a deep sense of responsibility towards his gifts and sees a higher and superhuman power in his own artistic genius' (Hauser, 1962, p. 60). The importance of the artist as an individual creative personality was thus clearly recognized in the Renaissance. Not only was the notion of artistic genius developed, but work was now signed and biographies and even autobiographies of artists were written. There was considerable interest in fragments of sculpture and sketches which became just as important as the expression of the artist at work as the finished piece.

As both artists and their subjects became individuals, so the economic position of painters changed. In the early fourteenth century, artists, that is, painters and sculptors, were essentially craftsmen and were treated as such: they would not only create paintings or sculptures, they would also design and make tiles, produce patterns for carpets or tapestries, and draw up building plans. Artists were also members of a craft guild, which controlled techniques and conditions of work and also provided a supervised apprenticeship system. Artists' earnings were relatively low and the relationship between artist and patron might well be unfamiliar to twentieth-century sensibilities. For example, when giving a commission to an artist, the collector or patron would not only specify the exact subject in the greatest possible detail but also the colours to be used and their prices.

From the middle of the fourteenth century onwards, a number of factors began to change the artist's position. Manual crafts gradually became separated from 'fine arts' and works of art became thought of not as objects of practical utility but as intrinsically beautiful. Gradually artists won emancipation from guild control, their earnings increased rapidly and, what is more, they were able to charge greatly varying fees according to their popularity. Artists might still work to commission, but their relationship to the people and institutions that paid them was changing. As Blunt says: 'In his new freedom the artist was no longer a purveyor of goods which every one needed and which could be ordered like any other material goods, but an individual facing a public' (1962, p. 56).

So far, we have simply argued that representations of the face became more individual and less stylized in the period from 1000–1500. The increasing importance paid to individual differences that this signalizes is also reflected in the social position of the artist and the way that he becomes an individual creator rather than an anonymous craftsman. We have presented this Discovery of the Individual in terms of a conventional contrast between the art of the Renaissance and that of the Middle Ages. In fact, of course, such a dramatic contrast misleads; the Renaissance did not invent the individual, and such a notion of discovery misrepresents the slow and gradual processes of artistic change just as much as the parallel notion of abrupt scientific discovery misrepresents the course of scientific work. For example, *some* tomb sculpture acquires a certain individuality in the thirteenth century, particularly in France: 'before 1300 we have royal tomb figures which are unquestionably personal portraits, and sculptors had begun to work from death

masks, thus attempting personal portraiture of a very exact kind'
(Morris, 1972, p. 89). At the same time, stock figures appear often,
perhaps produced in a form of mass-production. The effigy of the
Black Prince in Canterbury Cathedral, for example, is a stereotype,
and widows would order stock figures for their husbands' tombs
without respecting their particular features (Tomlinson, 1974). In
sum, a conception of portraiture, of representing faces by a likeness
of an individual, arose gradually in the period 1000–1500 even if it
reached an early peak in Renaissance Italy. Such a conception stayed
with Western European art for a long time and probably still
informs the public notion of what a portrait should be. However, it
scarcely needs pointing out that a great number of painters in more
modern times have rejected this way of representing faces. Their
work is dominated by other aims than the depiction of the individuality of a sitter. We return to this point in later chapters.

Changes in Literary Form

The history of literary forms provides a valuable index of the
emergence of the individual and then the growth of individuality and
individualism. The idea that the novel is inextricably bound up with
the discovery of the individual is well established in literary criticism
(Watt, 1957). In addition, we find Karl Marx constantly referring to
Daniel Defoe's *Robinson Crusoe* in order to illustrate the characteristics of economic man in a competitive capitalist society. Crusoe's
adventures and his commercial ethic provided useful examples of
predatory utilitarianism and of the heartless nature of the new
economic order of English society. For Georg Lukács, in *The Theory
of the Novel* (1971), the emergence of a new prose form signalled
the decline of community and the emergence of a society composed
of competing, isolated and alienated individuals. Lucien Goldmann,
in *Towards a Sociology of the Novel* (1975), also emphasizes the
role of the novel in bourgeois society and culture. In his account, the
novel had been initially an expression of triumphant bourgeois
values, but during the crisis of capitalist society it came to play a
more paradoxical role. Individualism was under significant attack in
the 1920s and 1930s, yet it was during this time that the ideology of
individualism was most seriously asserted in the novel. The relationship between individualism and literature will be addressed by us in

subsequent chapters. At this stage we may simply note that in contemporary literature, especially in the literature of high culture, the individual appears to be under attack – the modern novel tends to portray anti-heroes and to emphasize the ineffectual character of the individual. It is paradoxical that the classical individual, whose will can be imposed upon society and nature, appears to survive mainly in pulp fiction, especially in thrillers and westerns.

The analysis of the novel as the literary form of bourgeois consciousness raises in a critical way the issue of long-run versus short-run arguments. It might be supposed that any literary description of human society would have to present some form of story involving human action and human activity, and that such activities would be the outcome of individual interventions. Literary characters would have to represent individuals in some form or other. Greek epic poetry and drama are full of powerful and forceful characters who leave their imprint on history and society. However, such heroic characters are typically pure social roles that embody some absolute virtue such as goodness or wisdom. They are ideal types of general forces, rather than particular persons with unique subjectivities and biographies. The nature of traditional characters in classical literature leads to a more specific debate about the nature and origins of autobiography.

Morris (1972) sees the religious confessional and the public confessions of St Augustine as early evidence of the discovery of the individual. He suggests that from the late eleventh century there was a great increase in the autobiographical content of published works, and he refers to Suger, Abbot of Saint-Denis, and Aelred of Rievaulx as particular illustrations of this new development. He draws attention to the autobiographical works of Otloh of Saint Emmeram, Guibert of Nogent and Peter Abelard as representatives of the new era of individuality. He also notes the growing popularity of letter collections and other literary forms, which gave expression to a new interest in the individual. Other developments in this period strengthen his argument, namely the new interest in the portrait as opposed to merely the picture of kingship. There was a new emphasis on representation in the memorial and tomb sculpture of the period, and Morris suggests that such direct representation of individual character was virtually unknown before 1080. These direct representations of the individual raise important issues in the analysis of the development of the person in literature and in the arts, and in our view they also bring out a striking difference between Western and Eastern art. The symbolic representation of spirituality in Islam and Buddhism, for example, seems to strike a sharp contrast with the Western tradition of more direct representation, although even these assertions may be open to some qualification (Gungwu, 1975).

In his *The Value of the Individual* (1978), Karl Weintraub disputes this periodization. He agrees that in classical literature the biographical details of the hero and his interior subjectivity are relatively unimportant to the unfolding of the narrative. But he asserts that genuine autobiography is relatively rare before 1800 and that forms of confession, for example St Augustine's confession, cannot be classified as autobiography because they do not significantly explore the interior development of consciousness on the part of a specific, differentiated individual. At best, the confessional literature of St Augustine and Abelard and the autobiographies of Petrarch and Cellini were anticipations of later development. The modern autobiography, he suggests, does not really start until the publication of Montaigne's *Essais*, which were composed between 1572 and 1580. The autobiographical form was subsequently developed by writers such as Bunyan, Baxter and Franklin in the Puritan tradition, but was only fully developed by Rousseau and Goethe. The rise and maturation of the autobiographical form, therefore, correspond to the development of a commercial bourgeois world, the freeing of the individual from traditional ties and the emergence of extensive trade and exchange relationships. The autobiographical literary form consequently fits neatly into the world of the bourgeoisie, and the autobiography could not fully develop until this bourgeois audience existed. The autobiography, according to Weintraub, did not fully exist before the beginning of the nineteenth century, yet since then nearly all forms of modern literature have become essentially autobiographical, or at least biographical.

We are by now of course perfectly familiar with such problems of periodization. These contrasting histories of the individual in cultural forms underline the importance of the difference between long-run and short-run arguments. Morris's evidence is indeed convincing, that there was an early discovery of the individual in Western culture. We suggest that this was initially simply a recognition of difference between persons, but with time and notably from the sixteenth century individuals were given a subjective individuality, and later still fully fledged individualism developed.

Perhaps the historical emergence of the subject may be conceptualized as a spiral, in which in various centuries a renewed and heightened emphasis is given to the individual person. Clearly, we cannot show that the emergence of the individual is a product of the emergence of capitalism and the market economy. We can claim, however, that the seventeenth and eighteenth centuries were significant for giving an overwhelming emphasis on the individual in a variety of spheres, namely the political, the economic and the cultural. This emphasis on the individual in literature was not peculiar to England but was widespread in European society. For example, Robert Finch (1966) notes a new emphasis on the importance of the individual in the French literary culture of the later seventeenth and the eighteenth centuries. He suggests that this individualist poetry 'puts feelings before rules, qualities before forms, pleasure before profit, and individuality before hierarchy' (Finch, 1966, p. 4). There appears to have been a fairly general transformation of European society, with the growth of the court civilization and the ultimate emergence of bourgeois culture. The main theorist of this historical transformation is of course Norbert Elias in his great work on the civilizing process (Elias, 1978, 1982, 1983).

The Individual and the Growth of Table Manners

In the history of Western societies there has long been a struggle between the centralizing forces of the court and the de-centralizing forces of the countryside. Feudalism saw this struggle between the court society, which surrounded the king, and the rural nobility, living in their castles or fortified houses with their own retinues. Periodically, the centre was strong and the rural hinterland was weak; on other occasions, the position was reversed. The general trend of most feudal societies in Europe was, however, towards a greater centralization and the emergence of absolutist royalty (Anderson, 1974). The strength of these absolutist states varied considerably. It was in France that the centralized court achieved its most complete development, whereas in England the king never fully achieved political and cultural dominance. Despite these variations, we can argue that over a long period of European history (between the twelfth and seventeenth centuries) there was a decisive move towards a centralized court, a codified form of law, the demilitarization of the knights, and the development of a national system of taxation. Outside England, we can also find the creation of standing armies and permanent bureaucracies. These changes provide the backcloth to Elias's argument about the growth of Western civilization.

We may note that to civilize and to cultivate represent analogies to the tending of gardens and the cultivation of nature. To civilize persons is to cultivate their mind and their manners. As Raymond Williams reminds us in *Key Words* (1976), the noun 'culture' has a complicated history that begins with the notion of cultivation, tending and inhabiting. To develop and to civilize thus grew out of the notion of developing crops or animals. However, to be cultured is ultimately to be cultivated: to have one's mind and sensitivity elaborated and developed through the emergence of civilization, that is, through the emergence of etiquette, everyday morality and interpersonal norms.

The gradual civilization of feudal society thus corresponds on the one hand to the formation of the state, and on the other to the cultivation of minds through the elaboration of manners. We can express this graphically, by suggesting that civilization is represented by the transformation from the man-at-arms on horseback to the courtier at the table. To civilize is to bring the violent man on horseback into the civilized atmosphere of the dining room, replacing the saddle by the tablecloth. It is for this reason that Elias sees civilization in the development of eating utensils and the formulation of appropriate manners for living round the table. Spitting on the floor or wiping one's nose on the tablecloth or pointing one's knife at one's neighbour are no longer gentlemanly or courtly forms of conduct. The gradual emergence of specialized utensils for eating, especially the fork, the spoon and the napkin, are symbolic both of a transformation of social structure and of a transformation of sentiment and mentality. The violent symbolism of the sword is replaced by the companionable symbolism of the eating knife. The more civilized we become, the more dense and elaborate are the norms governing eating and conduct in public places. At the same time there is an increasing individualization of eating manners. For example, originally the food would have been

69

communal, served at the centre of the table in large pots and containers, but over time each person acquired their own place, their own plate and their own utensils. Their food was served directly to them and there was little or no sharing of food at the centre of the table.

These apparently elementary transformations of practice represent very deep transformations of emotion and sentiment. Whereas militarized feudal societies were regulated by systems of violence and inter-communal conflict, the new society of the court depends much more significantly on personal control, on interior regulation of passions and feeling. Passion becomes much more detailed, organized and excluded from public exhibition. Our manners become individualized, but this means essentially the development of systems of self-control and the proscription of violent displays of untutored sentiment in the public arena. There is the paradox that the more individuals became self-controlled through their own regulation, the more society also depends upon a centralized absolutist state with a bureaucracy and monopoly over force. In these circumstances,

> the peculiar stability of the apparatus of mental self restraint which emerges as a decisive trait built into the habits of every civilised human being, stands in the closest relationship to the monopolisation of physical force and the growing stability of the central organs of society. Only with the formation of this kind of relatively stable monopolies do societies acquire those characteristics as a result of which the individuals forming them get attuned from infancy to a highly regulated and differentiated pattern of self restraint.
>
> (Elias, 1982, p. 235)

The whole development of courtly manners in the notion of courtesy represents, therefore, a major shift in the form of feeling and behaviour on the part of individuals. Collective forms of violence and control are substituted by individualized self-constraint. The transformation of the social structure is perfectly illustrated in the norm that when you pass a knife at the table you offer the handle to your neighbour. All suggestion of violence is thus expunged by the growth of such formal systems of etiquette and behaviour.

The Uniqueness of the West

We have tended to side with the view that the special emphasis on the individual is the outcome of the peculiar development of

Western civilization. The starting point was the original combination of the Greek philosophic tradition, Judaic-Christian spirituality and the emphasis in Roman law on the *persona*. The subsequent discovery of the individual in medieval and early modern Europe was dependent upon a variety of contingent features, including the growth of free urban spaces and the struggle for rights and civility. The emergence of the specific doctrine of individualism was due to a particular concatenation of circumstances, which we shall discuss in Chapter 4 in our analysis of the intensification and transformation of discourses of the individual in the seventeenth century. Our account, therefore, gives due weight to contingent circumstances and avoids teleology and evolutionism. All societies formulate views of the individual, however primitive and elementary these views might be. The Western emphasis on the individual is enhanced and elaborated by market and commercial pressures, by the nature of the city and urban life in continental Europe and certain special features of Protestant theology. Such an emphasis has always been uneven, because women were for so long denied a status as individuals fully equal to men or as citizens within the public domain. Nevertheless, it is difficult to avoid a position about the uniqueness of the West, since many of the central concepts of social discourse (such as religion, the individual and law) appear to be rather specific to the Western tradition. In drawing attention to the Discovery of the Individual in the West we are not necessarily advocating a special moral position that gives a privileged status to Western culture. Furthermore, our argument is not psychologistic, since we do not argue that the features of this discovery are inherent in personal psyche or that Western persons are essentially more individualistic in an ontological sense than Oriental persons. We are more concerned with cultural emphases on individuation and individuality, where the cultural emphases are the outcomes of political and economic developments, such as the particular features of feudal states and the special characteristics of European urban spaces.

Our argument is compatible with Max Weber's on the special significance of Western ascetic religious traditions for the growth of urban rationalism and liberal individualism. Weber saw a continuum of religions: on the one hand were religions that largely accepted the world and accommodated to it, and on the other were religions that rejected the world and any accommodation with secular powers. At one end of the continuum are the Calvinistic sects with their world-rejecting asceticism, and at the other end are those Asiatic religions that largely accommodated the world via individual mysticism or an ethic of secular success. Thus we might contrast the excessive emphasis on the individual in the Calvinist Protestant sects with the gentlemanly ethic of Confucianism and its stress on accommodation to courtly ethics.

The ethical system which we in the West have come to call Confucianism emphasizes the value of gentle humaneness rather than individuality and separate development for the person. It gives exceptional emphasis to the notion of filial piety and loyalty to the family. It is wholly different from the inner dynamic and logic of Protestantism, which isolates and separates the individual, liquidating any institutional support for the separate consciousness of the person.

CHAPTER

3

Discourses of the Individual

In the last chapter we formulated an argument about the way in which, in western European societies, the individual has gradually acquired an importance. Over a long period, individual differences become worthy of notice, collectivities become more circumscribed in their powers over individuals and notions such as the Dignity of Man acquire some real meaning. We referred to this long-run process as the Discovery of the Individual. However, this recognition of the individual remains a vague, specific and undifferentiated process. Individuals can, after all, be important in a number of different ways. Different social theories will find different qualities of the individual to be important, and societies and social groups will vary widely in the way that they esteem individual differences. In sum, besides the very general idea and process of finding individuals important, there are also much more *specific* theories of the proper relationship between individuals and collectivities.

What then is the relationship between the Discovery of the Individual and the specific theories? Clearly the relationship is both analytic and historical. In this chapter we are largely concerned to show the analytical differences between different specific conceptions of the individual and their relationship to the more general process of the Discovery of the Individual. One of the aims of the rest of the book is to show what the historical relationship of these discourses is. Discourses of the individual are not hermetically sealed universes, without *social* connections. Our argument will be that the specific discourses develop out of the general Discovery of the Individual, which is therefore a sort of primitive discourse that provides the historical ground for the development. Specific discourses are, in turn, appropriated by social groups, engaged not only in social struggle but also in ideological struggle, one of whose components is a debate over the proper role of individuals. One of the paradoxes of ideological struggle is that the parties to that struggle have to have some common ground in order to debate. There has to be a common set of moral, social and political categories in the same way that there has to be a common language. In our view, it is the Discovery of the Individual that provides the basic categories of the general importance of the individual, and the ideological debates between proponents of specific discourses are attempts to use those categories for different ends. We shall return to a more abstract discussion of the notion of ideological struggle in Chapter 6; in the rest of this chapter, we attempt to delineate four different specific discourses of the individual. We do this by presenting four, rather abstracted, ideal types, which are then used substantively in Chapters 4 and 5.

Anarchism and Socialism

The social and political theories of anarchism are popularly thought to celebrate the untrammelled rights of the individual above all else. This is an image that is, perhaps, derived from the alleged prominence of anarchist terrorism in the earlier part of this century. In this view, anarchy is a synonym for individuals creating disorder in society by doing what they like. There is, indeed, a streak of egoism in some anarchist doctrine, which can make the primacy of individual desires the foundation of a political philosophy. Max Stirner (1907), particularly, exalted the idea of the unique individual. For him, social rules and moral principles are only valuable to the extent that they do not repress the individual, which leaves them very little scope. Each person is the only rightful judge of his or her behaviour. 'You have the right to be whatever you have the strength to be.' Stirner is not, however, typical of anarchist theory and practice. Indeed, many leading anarchist theorists went out of their way to repudiate the ultra-individualist view. For example, Kropotkin held that views such as Stirner's could easily degenerate into a 'Nietzschean' individualism in which the belief in the right of the individual to act freely would entail the oppression of others. For Kropotkin, individuals could not be egoists, for there must necessarily be connections between them. 'It is impossible to conceive a society in which the affairs of any one of its members would not concern many other members . . . (it is) *impossible* to act without thinking of the effects which our actions may have on others' (Kropotkin, quoted in Miller, 1976, p. 238; original emphasis).

The general drift of Kropotkin's work, and of anarchist thought generally, is not individualist but collective. The prevailing source of inspiration is not individual but social. In as much as anarchists stress freedom, it is not freedom for individuals, but freedom for the community. Michael Bakunin, for instance, opposed what he regarded as the bourgeois ideology of individualism: 'I think that liberty must establish itself in the world by the spontaneous organisation of labour and of collective ownership by productive associations freely organised and federalised in districts' (Bakunin, 1950, p. 18). Kropotkin held that anarchist communities would function collectively, partly by the spontaneous recognition by individuals of each other's needs and wants, and partly by a system of mutual aid. The commune would be self-regulating, self-sufficient and responsible for the organization of work and for any discipline that would be necessary. Proudhon, Bakunin and Kropotkin all believed that the masses were spontaneously able to take action unless the impulse was powerfully repressed; political change is through revolutionary action and revolutionary action is spontaneously generated.

There is a strong sense, therefore, that the basic unit in an anarchist theory of society is not the egoistic individual but the commune. 'Freedom' is, of course, an anarchist slogan, but this is a freedom for the *people* from oppression by the *state*. The enemy is not social organization as such, but the imposition of political authority. The early anarchists saw the state as increasing in its power with increasing budgets, great armies, and a formidable bureaucracy, as Bakunin put it. The state destroyed the natural energies of the people. Both Kropotkin and Proudhon expressed the problem in terms of a conflict between state and society, a position which further illustrates the communitarian convictions of most anarchist thought. Kropotkin's view has been described thus: 'Society is the repository of all the good aspects of social life and organization – cooperation, sympathy, affection, initiative and spontaneity. While the State incorporates all the bad aspects of social interaction – coercion, force and domination; and politics

75

tend to be seen as the arena of force, fraud, and trickery' (Carter, 1971, p. 25). Proudhon complained that, with the growth of centralization, things reached the point where society and government could no longer exist.

The anarchist view of freedom is not, it should be said, entirely one of the freedom of the people, with their common interests, from the state. It also involves an interest in individual freedom, although, as we have already argued, this is subordinated to the self-regulation of the community. Individual freedom and the requirements of the community may clearly conflict, a point recognized at least by Kropotkin. That neither he nor other anarchist theorists could provide a coherent answer to this difficulty is not surprising; it remains a problem in a wider range of political theory.

Clearly, anarchism has a good deal in common with socialism. Both doctrines take the liberation and improved condition of the working classes as their point of departure. Their great difference lies in the view of the state, since most anarchists see socialist theory and practice as actually advancing the power of the state and increasing its capacity for oppression of the people and of individuals. It certainly is true that, of all the discourses of the individual considered in this chapter, socialism is the least concerned to provide a place for the individual vis-à-vis other entities. This lack of concern is both practical – the assertion of individual rights may be antithetical to the socialist society – and theoretical – there is no need to provide a theory of the place of the individual within socialist society.

Naturally, socialism's main target is capitalist society, one of whose prominent vices is egoism and the anarchy that the relentless pursuit of self-interest brings. Individuals treat each other instrumentally, creating disorder. Socialism, by contrast, restores unity and order, substituting collective action and an ideal of service to the community for individualized anarchy and desire for personal gain. H. G. Wells, in discussing the fundamental ideas of socialism, suggests that socialism is 'the denial that chance impulse and individual will and happening constitute the only possible methods by which things may be done in the world' (Wells, 1914, p. 22). Socialism 'has grown out of men's courageous confidence in the superiority of order to muddle' and is united with science in the demand for 'men to become less egotistical and isolated' (Wells,

1914, p. 23). 'In place of disorderly individual effort, each man doing what he pleases, the Socialist wants organized effort and a plan' (Wells, 1914, p. 26).

For socialists, the individualism of capitalist society is fundamentally damaging to liberty, equality and fraternity. It is also theoretically illusory. In no human society can individuals have the qualities that bourgeois social theory attaches to them. The notion of the unfettered individual free to act is mythical, because no individual can be free of social ties. Marx was himself particularly critical of those political economists who tried to derive the characteristics of society from those of individuals. The notion of a Robinson Crusoe – free and almost asocial – as the model of the individual in capitalist society struck Marx as absurd. Individuals are not free to construct their lives. To the contrary, individuals appear in society as *personifications* of social relations: a capitalist is not to be treated as a self-motivating human actor but as a representative of capital. This view of Marx has provided the basis for the even stronger doctrines of some recent Marxists. Louis Althusser (1970) holds that not only are human beings the effects of social structures but also that there is no such thing as human nature.

Socialism represents an emphasis on collective virtues and has, moreover, been implemented by means of a strong state apparatus. Within socialist theory, however, there has been some room for accounts of the appropriate place of individuals within society, not the least because socialism not only permits greater equality and fraternity but also encourages the active and real liberty of the subject. Socialists have seen capitalism as an unjust society and as repressive of freedom, especially that of the working class. Labourers are oppressed because they are forced by capitalist social relations to labour in order to live, and they may also be denied the freedoms of the liberal state because of the grip that capital has over the machinery of the state. In another and perhaps more fundamental sense, capitalist societies deny freedom. In this sense, capitalism prevents individuals from using and realizing their full powers as human beings. In reducing everything to commodities, people cannot exploit their particular gifts and talents. In this concern with the way in which particular societies may make life one-dimensional, socialists propose a view of the individual that has affinities with the discourse that we call individuality.

Individuality

Socialism and anarchism are clearly doctrines that are often espoused by political movements. This is not so obviously true of the next discourse of the individual – individuality – although this is definitely not to say that it is without social effects. The central point in doctrines of individuality is the need for the expression of each person's uniqueness. Individuality is concerned with the interior qualities of the person, with expressivity, and subjective conscience, and the development of sensibility, consciousness, personality and will. The cultivation of these qualities marks one person off from the next. For doctrines of this kind, society should be arranged so that individual qualities and differences can be recognized and individual talents developed. Self-development is a prime virtue. Further, the development of one's own talents, one's own unique qualities, is not necessarily rational or moral. On the contrary, cultivation of uniqueness might well lead to eccentricity or even socially destructive behaviour; the best way to stand out from the crowd might well be to be decidedly irrational. The importance of self-development and the cultivation of special and unique qualities of personality are well illustrated by the Romantic movement of the late eighteenth and early nineteenth centuries.

Many people associate European Romanticism with an absorption with oneself and the significance of individuality. As R. Furst says: 'It is a fundamental trait of the Romantic that he invariably apprehends the outer world through the mirror of his ego as against the objective approach of the Realist. What matters to the Romantic is not what *is* but how it *seems* to him' (1969, p. 58). Such a view of the creative powers of the individual produces a new attitude to art.

> Whereas previously art had been regarded as a skill, a proficiency in the manipulation of certain exacting rules . . . it now became an experience surrounded by a kind of mystique because it sprang from a very special sensitivity, the artist's inspiration. This change obviously stems from the new vision of the artist, no longer a propagator of knowledge, one who *does*, but a poetic soul, one who *is*. What matters, in other words, is the artist's individuality, of which the work of art is a direct expression, without the intervention of any conventions whatsoever.
>
> (Furst, 1969, p. 78)

This concern with the significance of individual experience and inspiration can lead to an interest in the idea of genius and the creation of Romantic heroes, like Byron's Childe Harold or Goethe's Werther, for example, or even Byron himself. It also leads to a belief that individuals are incomparable. Each person has unique qualities and talents given by Nature, and it is supremely important not to impose any measure of uniformity. Such a conception appears in a number of fields. Education, for example, should be tailored to the individual needs and requirements of each child. Rousseau in *Émile* argued that each stage in a child's development was unique and hence demanded its own appropriate educational technique. The Romantic interest in singularity, applied most obviously to individuals, can also be applied to nations as H. G. Schenk (1966) points out. Nations were also seen as having their own unique inner essences and this variety was a source of pleasure rather than of fear. Romanticism coincided with an upsurge in European nationalism, particularly Slav nationalism, and the use of partly forgotten regional languages for literary purposes. In sum, European Romanticism, whatever differences there were between its English, French and German varieties, had individuality, the celebration of individual uniqueness, as its centrepiece. Other conceptions of importance to the Romantics flow from this: for example, imagination and feeling only make sense as the legitimate expressions of the inner states of individuals.

The capacity to sustain and develop each individual's unique qualities implies a certain conception of freedom, one that is roughly described by Isaiah Berlin's notion of positive liberty (1969). To be able to cultivate one's personality means being left alone, in control of one's own destiny. Liberty in the positive sense is involved in the answer to the question, 'What, or who, controls what I do?' Negative liberty, by contrast, is expressed in the answer to the question, 'What is the area within which people can do what they like?' Positive liberty, then, is concerned not with the area of freedom or control but with its source. The source, in turn, is the individual:

> I wish my life and decisions to depend on myself, not on external forces of whatever kind. I wish to be the instrument of my own, not of other men's, acts of will. I wish to be a subject, not an object; to be moved by reasons, by conscious purposes, which are my own, not by causes which affect me, as it were, from outside . . . I wish, above all, to be conscious of myself as a thinking, willing, active being, bearing responsibility for my choices and able to explain them by references to my own ideas and purposes.
>
> (Berlin, 1969, p. 131)

The notion of individuality, and its associated concept of positive liberty are, as Steven Lukes (1973) points out, often thought of as characteristically German. For example, in Nietzsche's work, individuality is distinctive as a doctrine that emphasizes the development of sensibility, personality and will. It is concerned with interior perfectability and often regards the public sphere as incompatible with personal development. The authentic personality is realized despite, rather than through, the external public realm, which is regarded as false and valueless. By contrast, individualism is rejected as a conformist bourgeois theory of the legal subject, who adheres to utilitarian egoism without interior authenticity. One aspect of this difference can be seen in Neitzsche's rejection of utilitarianism. In Bentham's hedonistic psychology, people are motivated by the fear of social criticism and by the desire for social approval. This dependence on public opinion was part of the psychological basis of the panopticon scheme, which subordinated the individual to external observation. For Nietzsche, this dependence on external public observation was a denial of individuality; it signified moral cowardice and ethical slavery. Interior development could only be achieved by a radical separation of the individual from conventional society.

Even if the notion of individuality is associated with the work of certain German writers who may have carried it to extremes, it is not inevitably so. We have already noted the way in which the Romantic movement as a whole utilized this discourse of the individual. It is also represented in the aristocratic cultivation of taste and sensibility and disdain for those who are active in the world's work. In Chapter 5, we describe the way in which the discourse of individuality is invoked in contemporary societies.

In this account we have stressed individuality as essentially a discourse of the interior of the subject. A corollary of this is a certain passivity or inactivity. Individualism, the principal subject of this book, on the other hand takes little interest in questions of personality, taste or consciousness, and is much more concerned with the individual's active relations with the external world.

Individualism

Individualism is the discourse of the individual which has the widest currency and greatest importance in the history of capitalist societies in Europe and the United States. Like the other views of the individual, individualism is essentially a doctrine of human nature. It has four major features. First of all, individualism consists of a conception of human liberty. Individuals should be as free from interference in their activities as it is possible to be. Law, custom, and social pressure should be minimized. Individuals should, for example, be free to sell property or labour to anyone without legal or customary impediment. Such freedom is the natural state of mankind and is only not achieved because of pressures from repressive institutions, such as those of the state or church. Naturally, it is recognized that there have to be some limitations on this freedom, and theorists of individualism debate on where to draw the line. None the less, the essence of the position is that there should be a sphere of thought or action that is free from interference. Notably, J. S. Mill argued that the individual was *sovereign* in matters concerning his or her self. As a consequence, there is 'a sphere of action in which society, as distinguished from the individual, has, if any, only an indirect interest; comprehending all that portion of a person's life and conduct which affects only himself, or if it also affects others, only with their free, voluntary and undeceived consent and participation' (Mill, 1946, p. 9). This conception of freedom is roughly equivalent to Berlin's notion of negative liberty: 'By being free in this sense I mean not being interfered with by others. The wider the area of non-interference the wider my freedom' (Berlin, 1969, p. 123).

The second theme is that individuals have the capacity for *action* in the transformation of their environment, natural and social. There is in this rather a clear contrast with individuality, where the emphasis is on being and not doing. Robinson Crusoe is the archetype of the value of activity and the importance of being able to control nature. He is devastatingly single-minded in the improvement of his island, in the bending of his environment to his will and, incidentally, to his advantage. This impulse to activity is seen, indeed is accentuated, in the quality of restlessness and the pursuit of novelty that so many commentators have detected in the culture of capitalist societies. For example, the American historian Draper writes of the northern United States, that its 'population was in a state of unceasing activity; there was a corporeal and mental restlessness . . . This wonderful spectacle of social development was the result of INDIVIDUALISM; operating in an unbounded theatre of action. Everyone was seeking to do all that he could for himself' (Draper, 1871, pp. 207–8; quoted in Lukes, 1973, p. 29). A similar point, in an entirely different context, is made by the art critic John Berger. Writing about a portrait by Frans Hals that gives the impression of great energy in its sitter, not random movement but confident and purposeful action, Berger says: 'What distinguishes this portrait from all earlier portraits of wealthy or powerful men is its instability. Nothing is secure in its place. You have the feeling of looking at a man in a ship's cabin during a gale . . . At the same time, the portrait in no way suggests decay or disintegration. There may be a gale but the ship is sailing fast and confidently' (Berger, 1980, p. 164). This quality of individualism is neatly summed up in the title of Marshall Berman's book, *All That Is Solid Melts into Air* (1983). For Berman the characteristic of modernism is a restless, ceaseless and relentless activity *in the world*, which results in a transformation of the environment. This tendency is symbolized individually in Goethe's Faust. Faust's bargain with the devil does not bring him wealth, power, immortality or sex. Instead, it gives him speed and the capacity to transform the world through his own activity. It is as if the *process* of development was what moved Faust, not the result. As Faust says: 'It's restless activity that proves a man.'

The activity, even restlessness of individualism, it should be stressed, is not random or irrational in the way of some of the Romantic proponents of individuality. Quite the reverse, individualism advocates *rationality* in activity in the world. Free activity is not irrational but is planned and calculating and is the more effective for being so. An obvious illustration of this point is Weber's contention (1930) that Calvinism created isolated individuals whose conduct was highly rational, because rationality ensured worldly success, which was in turn a sign of election to a state of grace.

We have defined individualism as incorporating a concept of freedom, an emphasis on the capacity to act and to transform the natural world, and a stress on planned and calculating action. The last element concerns responsibility and motivation. The notion is that, if individuals act freely and rationally, they do so by virtue of some inner drive and they take responsibility for their actions. Individuals are self-actualizing. The energy that there is in society, on this view, comes from individuals, and society or the state perpetually threaten to block this energy by controlling individuals. Motivational energy belongs to individuals, who can transform nature through work. As one advocate of an individualistic way of life argues:

> The Americans have never accepted the 'hair-shirt' theory of work. Work for them, rather, is essential to self-development and personal achievement ... Work, for the American, means striving for excellence in performance, which requires putting one's self into it. Only by freely assenting to his work can a man claim the performance as his, and it can improve the self only because it belongs to the self.
>
> (Miller, 1967, p. 189)

One way of representing this aspect of individualism is to use D. C. McClelland's phrasing and to talk of achievement motivation (1961). In the discourse of individualism, high levels of achievement motivation are positively valued. The impulse to achieve, it should be stressed, is therefore a motivational issue: it is an inner drive. It should not be confused with blindly taking risks, for high achievers calculate the possibilities and will take only those risks that are necessary to achieve the goals. Neither should the inner drive for achievement be confused with ambition. In many ways, the outcome, or reward, is not the important thing; it is the successful fulfilment of the task that pushes individuals onwards. As D. C. McClelland says: 'achievement satisfaction arises from having initiated the action that is successful, rather than from public recognition for an individual accomplishment' (McClelland, 1961, p. 230). Such a conception of achievement also implies that individuals take responsibility for their actions. If an inner drive rather than external constraint compels individuals to carry out tasks successfully, they also bear responsibility for these.

From these four connected aspects of individualism – freedom, activity, rationality, and self-motivation – a number of corollaries flow. Individuals have the capacity and the freedom to rise out of their social status at birth, for example. More significantly, these motivated and restless individuals, free to act energetically on the world, are likely to *compete* with one another. This signifies a major difficulty inherent in the notion of negative liberty: one person's freedom impinges on another's.

Struggle and Alliance between Discourses

We have emphasized the differences between discourses of the individual. For example, we contrast individualism with individuality, largely because the former emphasizes the external relations of the individual with the environment, while the latter stresses the interior qualities of the subject. Again, the socialist view of the individual differs from individualism with regard to the area in which the individual can be free vis-à-vis the community. We have constructed the four discourses as ideal types and have drawn on sources over a wide range of societies and historical periods. The result is almost an ahistorical set of constructions. We have chosen to do this in order to present the analytical differences between the types as clearly and as polemically as possible. However, in the study of real societies, one cannot sharply preserve the analytical boundaries between the four discourses. Clearly they overlap to some extent and there are various points of contact. For example, the objection to the state in anarchism and the concept of negative liberty in individualism are obviously related. One point of contact here is the work of Robert Nozick (1974), which offers a bridge between anarchist doctrine and theories of laissez-faire derived from individualism. Similarly, individuality and anarchism may share a belief in the unique qualities of the individual and both may look to the work of Stirner for inspiration. Again, individualism and individuality can easily overlap, as in their common invocation of concepts of privacy and autonomy, and their joint, if sometimes contradictory, presence in Mill's writings (Lukes, 1973).

In sum, for our purposes in this book, we show how these four discourses of the individual differ from one another and are all differentiated out of the primal Discovery of the Individual described in Chapter 2. However, these *analytical* separations are achieved at some cost. Not only do discourses have significant conceptual overlaps but also an advocate of any one of the discourses will find it difficult to describe this position without contrasting it with others. Different discourses, as part of social life, typically refer to each other. They elaborate their views of the individual by contrast with others. For example, conservative theorists, advocating a doctrine of individuality, may do so by contrasting its virtues with the vices of individualism; the latter discourse, by concentrating on the individual's activity in the world, is seen to neglect the development of the authentic inner self. Discourses contest common ground and they make reference not only to each other but also to other features of society that excite praise or blame. This makes it possible for the analyst to describe discourses as dominant or oppositional. For example, in Chapter 5 we try to show the way in which individualism in the late twentieth century has become an *oppositional* doctrine that is critical of prevailing social arrangements. The same is true for dominant discourses, whose principles of organization and methods of argument show that they have no serious rivals.

Discourses, then, are involved in struggles with one another. Such struggles require some sort of common ground; there has to be something for them to argue about. In this case, we believe that the common ground is provided by the Discovery of the Individual. As we have seen, this provides a rough-and-ready set of categories about the importance of the individual, which can be manipulated by the rival specific discourses. This permits engagement with one another, while allowing each discourse to advocate a particular view of the individual and, by implication, different theories of human nature and of the desirable ends of human life.

The corollary of our position – that discourses of the individual are engaged in struggles with one another – is that they can equally well form alliances. The very fact that discourses are not closed universes leaves room for partial agreement over the proper role of individuals, particularly against a common enemy. For example, early nineteenth-century conservatives and socialists agreed that individualism was destroying the unity and harmony of society by stressing the egoism and selfishness of individuals, even though they disagreed about the proper solution.

These considerations of the interrelationships of discourses of the individual, and the way in which they convey their subordinate or superordinate position in a hierarchy of discourses, inescapably suggest the significance of considering discourses as *socially* organized entities. They are not simply sets of disembodied ideas, to be analysed merely as doctrines; they are competing social theories used in real social struggles. Discourses are socially organized and relate socially to one another; discursive struggle and social struggle are intertwined, but neither can be reduced to the other. These statements leave open the question of *how* discursive and social struggles relate to one another, how discourses of the individual have social effects and are appropriated or rejected by particular social groups. This is the question that informs the next three chapters, empirically in Chapters 4 and 5 and more analytically in Chapter 6.

4

The Bare Individual of Pioneer Capitalism

Capitalism

In order to study the relationship of individualism and capitalism, we require definitions of both concepts. Whilst individualism is a term that has been widely used but defined loosely and inconsistently, capitalism has been defined more tightly. Nevertheless, definitions still vary. J. R. Holton (1985), for example, identifies three types of definition. The first is capitalism as a system of exchange relations, which has the market at the core of its definition and is associated with a tradition that stretches from the classical political economists to modern economists such as W. W. Rostow, on the one hand, and Paul Sweezy, on the other. A second defines capitalism as a mode of production and emphasizes the centrality of the social relations of production associated with private property and commodified, free wage labour, the major tradition within Marxist analysis. The third is Weber's fusion of market and production relations, and his distinctive emphasis on capitalism as being in addition a mentality that exalts the diligent and rational seeking of profit as an end in itself.

We see no particular problem in reconciling elements of these definitions, because they refer to aspects of capitalism that are mutually compatible. Capitalism is a distinctive economic form with particular social relations of production, that operates via markets and is geared to profit, as both Marx and Weber have indicated and as a number of modern commentators accept (for example, J. R. Holton, 1985). The real difficulty is to define capitalism in such a way that it is separate from individualism, which most accounts do not. We have to avoid building individualism into the definition of capitalism, for the obvious logical reason that the analysis of their relationship would otherwise be circular. There is, in addition, a more substantive issue, that capitalism has various forms (for example, early and late, competitive and monopoly, Occidental and Oriental), some of which may have little to do with individualism. If there are indeed non-individual forms of capitalism, an individualistic definition would simply rule these out of consideration.

Capitalist economic organization involves the production and exchange of commodities with the aim of accumulating a surplus value, that is, profit, with some part of this profit being re-invested in order to maintain the conditions of future accumulation. Capitalism has a number of distinctive features as a mode of production. First, it uses commodified labour which, like other commodities, may be traded on the market. While commodified labour in the particular form of free wage labour is regarded as constitutive of capitalism in Marxist and Weberian traditions, we suggest that labour as a commodity may have varying degrees of freedom. At one end there is free labour, a system in which workers have rights as individuals to choose employment; at the other end are labour markets where individual rights are denied. Secondly, labour is separated from the means of production and subsistence, which makes it dependent on others for its own survival. Thirdly, capitalism functions with exclusive property rights in the means of production and the products of the labour process. The characteristic feature of property rights is that they serve to exclude others and thus monopolize effective possession. In choosing to emphasize exclusion and possession, we disagree with those who see absolute ownership as constitutive of capitalism. We believe that exclusionary possession is 'private' property. But 'private' in our definition does not refer solely to individual or personal property, since exclusionary property rights may also be attached to collective and corporate bodies. These rights, moreover, are created and protected by the state.

The market is the mechanism whereby profits are realized from commodity production. It also compels capitalists to act in systematic, rational and profit-seeking ways. If one wishes to talk of the 'spirit' of capitalism, then this can be seen as a systemic constraint of the market system, which need not be an orientation to action among individual capitalists, since survival in the market place

87

demands a certain course of action irrespective of beliefs and attitudes of individuals. This was recognized by Weber who argued that, once established, capitalism no longer required the Protestant Ethic.

The Doctrine of Individualism

Individualistic doctrine as an elaborated and coherent theoretical discourse, whose core is the individual, is associated with the philosophical and normative revolutions that occurred in seventeenth-century England. At this time, the notion of individual rights was developed as a systematic alternative to political obligations founded in scriptural prescriptions and the natural law of hierarchy and to social obligations deriving from an organic and collectivist Christian tradition. Charles Taylor describes the essence of this new discourse thus: 'The central doctrine of this tradition is an affirmation of what we would call the primacy of rights' (1979, p. 37), which ascribes rights to individuals and denies the centrality of the principle of belonging. Social and political obligations, indeed the very existence of social and political communities, are secondary and derivative, because they are conditional on an individual's consent or because they promote individual interest. Individualistic social theory as it developed at this time is seen as laying the intellectual foundations of later British and American liberalism, indeed of the whole genus of modern atomistic conceptions of society (see, for example, Macpherson, 1962; Taylor, 1979; Stone, 1980).

The English transformation, associated with changes in political theory between Hobbes and Locke and the protest theology of radical Protestantism, formed an important break with the medieval world view. It accelerated and changed the direction of the long-run discovery of the individual. Medievalism embodied 'the thesis of the corporational structure of society' (Ullman, 1967, p. 36), which regarded the individual as subordinate in hierarchical relationships of political and religious authority, and as inferior to and dependent upon an organic social community (Ullman, 1961, 1967; Pocock, 1975). Individuals were reduced simply to subjects, without the right or even the capability for independent action. The Christian confessional tradition did embody the idea of individual conscience, but in their public behaviour people were subordinated to collective organization. Walter Ullman (1967) notes that the synthesis of canon law and elements of Roman law, which produced this corporate vision of human organization in which all authority descended from above, was countered in England after the middle of the thirteenth century by feudal law ('common' law) that embodied principles of consent, reciprocity and rights, the 'ascending' image of society and authority. In Italy, the first signs of civic humanism also challenged descending principles in the later medieval period. However, the assertion of the rights of subjects in England occurred within a collectivist ethos, which informed the values and activities of all levels of society (Reynolds, 1984), so we should be chary of attributing too much individualism to feudal principles. Nevertheless, embryonic common law did contain the seeds of a later individualistic interpretation of rights.

The transformation of theoretical discourse can be interpreted as the novel synthesis of several strands of thought, some deriving from medievalism, some from older traditions, while others were new. The revival of Aristotle's republican ideal in Florence during the first quarter of the sixteenth century has been described by J. G. A. Pocock (1975) as the 'Machiavellian moment'. The Florentine linkage of a man's moral worth as an individual with citizenship (in the sense of his active and effective participation in the political community) and with independence (that is, being beholden to no one and bearing arms to defend his autonomy) coloured individualism in seventeenth-century England and later in America. The influence of Machiavellianism on James Harrington (1656) in the middle seventeenth century – though it may also have had some influence on earlier generations of English political thinkers – was twofold: his identification of moral worth in individuals as the ownership of private property (notably freehold land), which provided material independence of others, and the right to bear arms to defend oneself; and his conception of balanced government as one in which individuals of sturdy independence, owing favours to no one, had a major voice.

Puritan theology, resurrecting the primitive Christian tradition that believers stand in a direct and individual relation to God, which had been submerged in medieval Catholicism, emphasized the loneliness of the individual before God and the significance of individual conscience. While this emphasis on the individual contributed to the emergence of individualism, Protestantism was not itself individualistic. The Protestant sects believed that individuals would only develop their spirituality within the community of believers, and so there was also an emphasis on fellowship and communality.

Puritanism also placed weight on what Lawrence Stone (1979) had termed 'affective individualism', the right of individuals to choose their marriage partners on the basis of love and for the church to join them in holy matrimony, irrespective of the wishes of parents or the wider family. Jack Goody (1983) has emphasized that such individual choice was central to the theory and perhaps the practice of the very early Christian church; thus Puritanism once again reaffirmed a much older position. It can be argued, however, against the view that affective individualism was truly individualistic, that this aspect of the Christian tradition might conflict with the Christian conception of marriage as a permanent, lifelong union, because it could imply terminating a marriage if affection waned. John Milton provided a powerful argument for divorce in his view that marriage should be based upon mutuality and compatibility. Between 1643 and 1645, Milton published a number of pamphlets on divorce, in which he attempted to offer a moral argument in favour of the dissolubility of marriage within the Christian tradition. The main point of Milton's defence of divorce was that marriage is not primarily or only about sexual reproduction but also about companionship; where this mutuality collapses, divorce is a reasonable solution to marriages that have become empty and painful. However, Milton's was a lone voice and his views were abhorred by his contemporaries. It is notable that Milton proposed that husbands alone or husbands and wives jointly should be able to initiate a divorce, but the right should not be allowed to wives acting independently. Wives were individuals, but they were not equal to men.

Another strand was the tension within the later medieval inheritance, which, in the case of property rights, saw common law develop the rights of the individual as against those of wider groupings (Pocock, 1975). The evocation of such rights in the parliamentary debates of the early and middle seventeenth century, however, should be seen partly as special pleading and not as strictly accurate accounts of the historic rights of the English. Finally, economic individualism, the right of individuals to pursue their own material interests without political or legal hindrance or consideration of wider social obligations, and a new conception of the individual as the sole proprietor of his or her own person (which we discuss below) appears to have been a novel element developed in the seventeenth century itself. We should note, however, that it was not until the late eighteenth century that the classic liberal justification of economic individualism, as individuals promoting the collective good when they freely pursue their own economic interests, was propounded in Adam Smith's *The Wealth of Nations* (1776), nearly a century after John Locke (1690) wrote his seminal work on political individualism.

Seventeenth-century individualism also provided the basis for a critique of patriarchy and the monarchical principle. In the first half of the seventeenth century, writers like Sir Robert Filmer in *Patriarcha* had attempted to draw a powerful connection between the authority of God, the power of kings and the rule of husbands over their households. Written around 1640 and published post-humously in 1680, *Patriarcha* was a defence of monarchy against the contractualist theories of writers such as Hobbes in *Leviathan*. Filmer's argument arose in the context of changing attitudes towards the family and the role of the father in the wake of Puritanism. Celibacy ceased to be the norm of a religious vocation and there was greater theological emphasis on the duties of family life. Filmer argued that family authority is natural and that political power is identical to the power of fathers (Schochet, 1975; Turner, 1984). Although they are better known for their contractual theory of government and their treatment of individual rights, John Locke's *Two Treatises of Government* also represented a powerful political argument against Filmerism, which used individualistic assumptions to challenge the hierarchical conception of the family that was an essential element of the patriarchal theory. Locke's view of family organization was that fathers and mothers were jointly responsible for their children, and their authority was that of trusteeship, rather than the father alone having responsibility on the basis of absolute power.

Individualism has long been recognized as laying the basis of political opposition to traditional monarchical government and the development of liberal conceptions of parliamentary government, and more clearly so with Harrington, Locke and the Puritan theorists of the Putney Debates than with Hobbes, who did not break completely with the collectivist tradition and also justified absolute sovereignty, legitimizing the political dissent of the two revolutions. C. B. Macpherson (1962) has suggested that a politically oriented doctrine of individualism also embodied a coherent vision of economy and society. According to his account, individualism was 'possessive' because people were seen as the sole proprietors of their own capacities:

> The individual, it was thought, is free inasmuch as he is proprietor of his person and capacities. The human essence is freedom from dependence on the wills of others, and freedom is a function of possession. Society becomes a lot of free equal individuals related to each other as proprietors of their own capacities and of what they have acquired by their exercise. Society consists of relations of exchange between proprietors. Political society becomes a calculated device for the protection of this property and for the maintenance of an orderly relation of exchange.
>
> (Macpherson, 1962, p. 3)

Moreover, possessive individualism, the term now commonly used to describe the theoretical discourse of the period, embodies three sets of assumptions that are peculiarly appropriate in a capitalist society according to Macpherson (1962, 1975). The social world is pictured as a market, and human society is essentially a series of market relations. As individuals are free agents and have property in their own labour, they can choose to contract their labour power in the market place. Absolute private property in oneself leads to absolute private property in things, since what one mixes one's labour with becomes one's own, which justifies the private ownership of capital. Thus possessive individualism is to be found not only in the individualistic political doctrines common to England and America, but also in their conceptions of property and social relations.

Individualism and Capitalism Connected

The emergence of individualism in the early modern period has frequently been linked with the development of capitalism. Analysis mainly takes place at two levels: changes in articulated, theoretical doctrine and changes in the actual practices that constitute social and economic organization. The congruence of changes in these two levels is often taken as evidence of their linkage. An intervening level, of beliefs in peoples' heads and the effects of these on their activities, has been more rarely tackled, because of the great difficulty in finding adequate evidence. Weber's attempt in the Protestant Ethic thesis, to prove the direct linkage between doctrines and practices mediated via individual attitudes and motives, foundered in part because of his lack of information about individual economic agents apart from Benjamin Franklin (Marshall, 1982). Nevertheless, linkages between doctrine and practice are made, and are variously interpreted as doctrines causing structural change, being caused by such change, or simply as functional relationships with little specification of causality. Whatever the view, individualism and modern capitalism are thought to be closely related.

The growth of the individualistic practices thought to be essential to the development of capitalist social and economic organization is conventionally charted by a comparison with traditional society conceived as a 'natural economy'. This is found in the writings of Marx and Weber and among modern historians (Macfarlane, 1978). Characteristically, the natural economy is seen as a domestic mode of production, or a socioeconomic system based on the peasant household, with the following features: subsistence agriculture dominates; product, labour and capital markets are largely absent; the household both produces and consumes, thus fusing social and economic functions in one unit; land has few, if any, of the modern attributes of alienable private property and is typically familial property in which, if an individual has any rights, these are simply temporary rights of management; co-residence of kin is the norm; individualistic practices are restrained by the collective restraints of the corporate structure of traditionalism, and by a culture based on a collective orientation and expressed in the organic world-view of traditionalism. The structural and value changes associated with capitalism, however, amount to the decollectivization of traditional society and the end of ascriptive ties, since capitalism embodies individualism. Three crucial elements of individualism as practice and doctrine associated specifically with capitalism, and not just with the rise of a market economy, stand out. These are: the nature of capital as private property, labour, and business behaviour.

Individualistic practices are manifest in the rise of individual property rights in place of collective or feudal property, neither of which had given the individual owner an absolute right to alienate or otherwise use land as he wished. Marx regarded the growth of absolute private property between the fifteenth and eighteen centuries in England as a mirror of the growth of the capitalist mode of production, denoting the development of a new conception of land based on absolute individual ownership rights and with a purely economic interest, divorced from 'all its former political and social embellishments' (Marx, 1974, p. 618). This transformed land into a capital asset that could be bought and sold in the market. Weber (1961) also emphasized the rise of modern individual property, associated with the development of the market, as one of the factors that helped destroy the peasant economy and promoted the decline of collectivist traditionalism. Macpherson links the transformation of rights in land with the growth of possessive individualism as a doctrine and the emerging capitalist mode of production: a new kind of absolute property right was 'required by the capitalist market society, that is property as an exclusive, alienable right to all kinds of material things including land and capital' (Macpherson, 1975, p. 112). Property which gave only temporary rights of use or was common property, or, in those rare cases where private property did exist, was legitimized on ethical and theological grounds which encumbered it with social obligations, had to become a saleable commodity with no limitations over its use, 'to let the capitalist market economy operate' (1975, p. 109). Tenurial and legal changes marked a factual shift in the nature of property towards what capitalism required. The seventeenth-century ideological changes associated with possessive individualism, which culminated in the modern conception of property, marked the intellectual rationalization of this shift into a coherent philosophy of absolute private property. A similar view of the origins and importance of individual ownership is to be found in the work of other modern historians such as H. J. Perkin (1968) and J. G. A. Pocock (1975).

A second individualistic practice associated with capitalism is the rise of free labour. Following Marx and Weber, the creation of a class of landless wage labourers has been seen widely as a defining characteristic of modern capitalism, capitalist development being thought impossible without the historical spread of property-less labour from the sixteenth century onwards. The expropriation of the peasant from the means of production meant that labour was no longer tied to the land and the peasant household, but was now 'free' (in reality, obliged) to sell itself on the market, and thus came to assume the status of a commodity. In Marxist and Weberian accounts, free, commodified labour promoted individualism, by separating the labourer from the nexus of obligations and communal relationships of precapitalist society, and by elevating certain market principles over older principles of community. These principles are that individuals are free to choose which contracts they enter, and marketable commodities, including labour, have a purely economic and impersonal quality without ethical or social obligations. Furthermore, Marx suggested that an essential condition of free labour was the development of a particular conception of the self:

> labour power can appear upon the market as a commodity, only if, and so far as, its possessor, the individual whose labour power it is, offers it for sale, or sells it, as a commodity. In order that he may be able to do this, he must have it at his disposal, must be the untrammelled owner of his capacity for labour, i.e., of his person.
>
> (Marx, 1970, p. 165)

Free labour markets recognize the principle of possessive individualism, that labourers are the absolute owners of their own capacities and labour as a commodity is thus unique because it embodies an individuality that cannot be possessed by others: employers in effect rent rather than own labour power, and employees are free to choose which employment contracts they will enter. Labour markets are also free in the sense that they are places of economic exchange between bare individuals, employers and employees who are free of all non-contractual and non-economic obligations towards each other. In Marxist and Weberian analyses, this characteristic promotes the rational utilization of labour within capitalist enterprises, allowing employers to hire at the best price, and quickly and exactly to match the amount and quality of the labour they use to the demands of their business. This compares with inefficient use of labour in other modes of production where labour markets do not provide employers with the same flexibility. Consequently, capitalism both commodifies something that cannot be owned in the same way as other objects, and creates a continually operative market for this commodity.

Individual private property in the capital market and individual ownership of labour power in the labour market are both essential to the rise of capitalism in these accounts, while the Marxist canon also stresses that their ideological legitimation, as in the possessive individualism that informed British and American liberalism, is intrinsic to capitalism.

There is a third component of individualism, associated initially with Weber and with a continuing tradition among social scientists, that modern capitalism requires a new type of mentality and behaviour among businessmen. As is well known, Weber at times linked economic practices and ethical doctrines tightly together: for example, when he spoke in *General Economic History* of the 'ethics and the economic relations which result'. Weber's analysis of business behaviour immediately prior to the rise of modern capitalism takes for granted that merchants and other entrepreneurs displayed an acquisitive attitude, the 'economic impulse', but that this was constrained in its practical application by an ethos of traditionalism that stood in the way of rational, long-run, economic resource-maximizing behaviour. Gordon Marshall (1982) has distinguished two traditionalistic orientations to business activity in Weber's accounts. One is the pursuit of a customary level of earnings with the least exertion and the most comfort, and in conformity to communal norms; the other is a combination of avarice, conspicuous consumption and unscrupulous, opportunistic speculation. This latter orientation Marshall describes as 'rampant individualism' (1982, p. 104). For Weber, the rational pursuit of profit characteristic of modern capitalism is an individualistic ethic. Weber's thesis, that Calvinist Protestantism was a necessary, though not sufficient, condition of the rise of modern capitalism, suggests that Protestantism gave individualism a special character. Protestantism emphasized autonomous and self-motivated activity, diligence in pursuit of a calling, and calculative rationality as an orientation to action. Individuals socialized into this value system acquired a mentality that matched the requirements of modern capitalism. Calvinism fostered in individuals a sense of separation and isolation from other people, and a sense of responsibility for their own salvation, the 'unprecedented inner loneliness of the single individual' (Weber, 1930, p. 104).

This individualistic stance had various economic consequences. Entrepreneurs no longer had solidary social relations with employees and business associates in the manner of traditionalism, and economic relationships became purely instrumental, allowing the exigencies of the market to determine the nature of social relations in the economy. The individual's single-minded pursuit of a calling, combined with asceticism and a steward-like attitude to resources, fostered among businessmen both the profit-maximizing attitude and a propensity to accumulate capital. The emphasis on individual choice and individual responsibility for actions fostered rationality in the choice of the means that entrepreneurs employed to realize ends. The net effect of these was a form of individualism peculiarly suited to the 'formal rationality of economising' embodied in modern capitalism (Poggi, 1983). Weber also suggested that the Protestant Ethic had an effect on labourers, Puritanism promoting diligence and effort at work.

Weber's thesis can be located within a wider perspective of the European development of conscience as a necessary component of modern individualism. The research of Benjamin Nelson has shown that the Protestant emphasis on personal consciousness was not the invention of Luther and Calvin but a re-emphasis of a series of debates in the Middle Ages (Huff, 1981). If we regard Nelson's work as an exploration of the roads to modernity, then Nelson showed that the debate about rationales of action in medieval society prepared the way for a Protestant attack on traditionalism in action and opinion. Nelson's study of the medieval *summa*, casuistry and the cure of souls demonstrated that we should perceive Protestant-ism or special cases, such as the English tradition, as parts of a much larger landscape of culture where conscience and an emphasis on the individual formed a continuity rather than a transition away from a more basic religious tradition.

The view that economic growth depends on a particular form of individualism within the business stratum can also be found among more recent commentators. D. C. McClelland developed Weber's hypothesis, that the Protestant Ethic fostered individual personality traits which partly accounted for economic growth in the early modern period, suggesting that the Weber thesis was a specific case of a more general phenomenon, namely that parental encourage-ment of self-reliance and mastery in early childhood was responsible for an achievement motivation in adults. The innovation, risk-taking and inner-driven activity characteristic of entrepreneurs were expressions of a strong achievement motive, and 'achievement motivation is in part responsible for economic growth' (McClelland, 1961, p. 36). In the English case, motivational changes (measured by means of a content analysis of literary sources) could be seen to precede economic changes by between thirty and fifty years in the period 1550–1880 (McClelland, 1961). Child-rearing patterns were identified as being crucial to the formation of individual personality and external influences, such as religion, worked via this mechanism. E. E. Hagen (1962) put forward a somewhat similar view, that innovative individuals were necessary for rapid economic development, that such people displayed personality traits of high needs for achievement and autonomy, and that these were developed in particular forms of home life and social environment. Traditional society normally created authoritarian personalities but, under certain conditions, social change would throw up new, innovative individuals. Neither theorist equated economic growth necessarily with capitalism. However, the emphasis on the entrepreneurial function and its performance by individuals appears to have been rooted in the historical experience of the capitalist industrialism of Britain and America.

The conviction that capitalism and individualism are inextricably fused can be seen in a variety of contemporary analyses. Individualism is, of course, almost endemic to economic theory which largely accepts the *homo economicus* of traditional utilitarianism. Economic debate about want-satisfaction and utility is still grounded in the classical notions of rational action whereby the market is explained through the struggles of individuals to satisfy their needs. This individualism in economic theory has been significantly challenged by writers such as Talcott Parsons and Neil Smelser in *Economy and Society* (1956) and the critique of economic individualism was fundamental to Parson's theory of social action. While there has been criticism of economic individualism at this level of action theory, the whole tradition of economic theory survives in the sociology of entrepreneurship, where the individualism of the economic actor is associated with initiative, change and radical reorganization of economies through the entrepreneurial spirit. There is a well-established debate on the connections between achievement motivation, entrepreneurial activity and rapid social change. The classic works in this tradition would include Daniel Lerner, *The Passing of Traditional Society* (1958) and Alex Inkeles and David Smith, *Becoming Modern* (1974), in addition to those of D. C. McClelland and E. E. Hagen already mentioned. These works insisted on the centrality of indi-

vidualism and individual entrepreneurial activity to the whole
economic process. This association between individualism and
capitalist economies has also found a classic expression in the work
of Daniel Bell who, echoing Weber's thesis, states:

> Capitalism is a socioeconomic system geared to the production of
> commodities by a rational calculation of cost and price, and to the
> consistent accumulation of capital for the purposes of reinvestment. But
> this singular new mode of operation was fused with a distinctive culture
> and character structure. In culture, this was the idea of self-realization,
> the release of the individual from traditional restraints and ascriptive ties
> (family and birth) so that he could 'make' of himself what he willed. In
> character structure, this was the norm of self-control and delayed
> gratification, of purposeful behaviour in pursuit of well-defined goals.
>
> (Bell, 1979, p. xvi)

Two modern historians who align themselves with the Marxist
tradition have succinctly summarized the linkage between capitalism and the broader components of individualism, in the following
manner:

> The extension of capitalist development ... depended upon a free
> market in labor-power and upon absolute property – in short, upon the
> maximum mobility of capital, land, and labor. In addition, full capitalist
> development depended upon, even as it encouraged, an appropriate
> ideology of work, saving, and individual autonomy.
>
> (Fox-Genovese and Genovese, 1983, p. 32)

This statement seems to us to encapsulate the perspective of commentators who, regardless of their theoretical persuasion, also see
the rise of modern capitalism in terms of these socioeconomic and
value changes.

Medievalism

Some historians have recently questioned the view that the sixteenth
and seventeenth centuries marked the rise of new individualistic
practices, and that these were associated with the rise of capitalism,
since their research into medieval and early modern English society
has failed to confirm the absence of individualism in the earlier
period. Alan Macfarlane (1978) attacks the conception that medieval England was a peasant-household socioeconomic system, with

tightly knit organic communities, household units, non-individual property, a non-market and non-cash economy, and low rates of geographical mobility. He suggests that medieval social organization was individualistic, since individual action was constrained neither by collective, communal restraints nor, indeed, by those of the immediate family. In his discussion of Weber, he refers to the 'defamilization of society', a state that he, unlike Weber, identifies as existing as early as the thirteenth century in England. His evidence from Earls Colne in Essex and Kirkby Lonsdale in Cumbria points to the following: a 'modern' nuclear family structure, in which households contained no extended kin and adult children left to establish their own households; a distinction between the family and the farm, which indicated the separation of social and economic realms; considerable geographical mobility. Moreover, individualism was also manifest in the growth of capitalist economic institutions, including: a market for labour; land treated as a commodity and with effective private ownership, which allowed it to be traded on the market; the declining importance of inheritance as the mechanism of transmission of land; farming for a profit and with rational accounting methods. Macfarlane suggests that such evidence discredits conventional notions about traditional values and collectivism: 'it is not possible to find a time when an Englishman did not stand alone. Symbolized and shaped by his ego-centred kinship system, he stood in the centre of his world' (1978, p. 196). Moreover, this individualistic society was also capitalistic: 'a capitalist–market economy without factories' (p. 196).

The extent of local variation even within a single county in medieval England makes generalization about the whole society difficult to substantiate, and so Macfarlane's wide-ranging assertions have met with some scepticism among medievalists. Nevertheless, his own and other studies suggest that individualistic practices were indeed more widespread than hitherto has been recognized, at least in the South-east and parts of the Midlands after the fourteenth-century plagues (see the evidence Macfarlane, 1978, cites on pp. 95–100 and 147–54). Modern historians of the family agree that there is no evidence for

> the supposition, formerly very widespread amongst scholars of the organization of work, that the original state of Europe, and of the rest of mankind, has to be called a 'natural' economy, in which every family

group itself produced everything it needed to satisfy its wants . . . .
(Laslett, 1983, p. 539)

Even medievalists who disagree with his interpretation of the
thirteenth century and see pre-plague society as conforming to the
peasant-household model recognize that the massive depopulation
resulting from the plagues profoundly changed traditional society,
leading to greater geographical mobility, smaller households with a
changed composition as adult children left home to enter the labour
market or to establish their own farms, the rapid turnover of
tenants, the growth of larger farms that produced a marketable
surplus and employed non-familial wage labour:

> the very high mortality of the late fourteenth century did more than
> temporarily reduce the population and improve the prospects of wage-
> labourers. By extinguishing ancient peasant families with their long-
> established grip upon customary land, and by triggering off a period of
> intense geographical mobility which threw into confusion notions of
> servile and non-servile peasant status, the plagues swept away the
> established tenurial and tenemental structure . . . With so much land
> available and tenures irrelevant, new and larger holdings emerged . . .
> Many of these new tenements . . . required extra-familial help to run
> them, while the small, twelve-acre holding characteristic of the pre-
> plague period virtually disappeared. The nature of the tenemental
> structure at Kibworth had thus been profoundly altered and with it the
> size and composition of the household.
>
> (Howell, 1983, p. 236)

We feel that parts of Macfarlane's argument should be treated
cautiously, notably the suggestion that capitalist institutions were
highly developed and that individualism was untrammelled by
family or community considerations. A land market did clearly exist
in medieval England and examples can be found even in the
thirteenth century (King, 1973; Postan, 1973; Jones, 1979; Howell,
1983). However, this evidence is fragmentary and not sufficient to
support the view that the market was the dominant or even a major
mechanism of transmission. It is quite compatible with an interpretation that markets were used at the margin, to acquire or dispose of
small parcels of land – to consolidate holdings into more efficient
farming units or to lease out acreage surplus to immediate requirements. Macfarlane establishes that land *could* be alienated, but there
is insufficient information available to decide the extent of such

101

alienation, or whether land was more often sold than leased (if leased, it would ultimately return to the family). The suggestion that land was routinely and permanently alienated via a market depends heavily on evidence for the extensive and continuing turnover of surnames in the land records of the fourteenth century. Given the pandemic recurrence of plague that may have reduced the population by half between the late 1330s and 1400, it seems reasonable to suggest that evidence of tenurial instability reflects a demographic context, in which tenants and all their kin are wiped out, as well as individualistic practices of alienation. Some historians have noted the reassertion of hereditary practices in specific areas once the population stabilized after the pandemics (Hilton, 1975; Howell, 1983). On a more theoretical level, we would question that defamilialization was carried to extremes, since we believe that familialism coexists with individualism and is not only compatible with, but is central to, capitalism prior to the twentieth century. This is a theme that we develop later in this chapter.

In an analysis of local communities throughout Western medieval Europe, Susan Reynolds (1984) suggests that the collective values and activities of lay society were considerably more important in England than Macfarlane's picture suggests, while England did not differ from the rest of Europe. She acknowledges that there was a tendency towards individualistic activity in various forms, including farming for the market and geographical mobility, but believes that this was counterbalanced by a trend to collectivity. Medieval society 'was a network of communities in the sense that it contained a mass of local groups, often overlapping with each other, which acted collectively in running their agriculture, their parish churches and fraternities, their local government, and perhaps a good deal more besides' (Reynolds, 1984, p. 152). The implication of her argument is that, while Macfarlane's model of a local peasant community as sharply bounded, homogeneous, inward-looking and antagonistic to others was not to be found in England, or elsewhere in Europe for that matter, rejection of this extreme ideal type need not mean accepting that individualism had triumphed over other forms of communality, because rural people throughout Western Europe 'were all highly collective in their habits and attitudes but very flexible about the units in which they acted' (Reynolds, 1984, p. 139). It is pertinent to note that, where agricultural production was organized on a communally regulated strip basis, individual land ownership did not carry rights to effective control of the means of production.

A labour market for agricultural and industrial workers also flourished in the medieval period. But not all wage labour had the characteristics conventionally associated with capitalist 'free' labour. Agricultural wage labour included part-time by-employments for small farmers who were economically self-sufficient, and full-time employment for independent cottagers whose landholdings could supply many of the necessities of family subsistence. The balance between these groups changed in the fifteenth century as the number and size of small farms decreased (Howell, 1983), but in neither case was labour entirely separated from its own means of production. The agricultural labour force also included landless wage labourers, the huge numbers of servants found in contemporary documents, who approximate more closely to the characteristics of a capitalist labour force. Male and female children were routinely put into service in other peoples' homes, hired by the year and provided with board and lodging, while the 'exporting' family hired its own labour as required (Hilton, 1975). In Coventry, at the end of the fifteenth century, free wage labour could be found. This comprised labourers and journeymen, neither of whom had any means of subsistence apart from the sale of their own labour power and skills. They formed their own households but were employed by substantial masters, some of whom were large-scale absentee financial capitalists (Phythian-Adams, 1979). Contrary to Marx, who maintained that wage labour was exceptional prior to the sixteenth century and thus was not constitutive of the mode of production, modern evidence suggests that in its various forms it was widespread and central to medieval England.

The issue of economically rational action, a defining characteristic of the new individualism in Weber's account, is also raised by Macfarlane's analysis, as it has been by other recent commentators. There are some illuminating examples of economic rationality prior to Protestantism. Marshall has shown how difficult it is to prove an absence of rationality in medieval economic life, arguing that the choice of rational means for a given end depends on the context within which action takes place, and cannot be understood outside this context. Discussing the research of Eileen Power and Sylvia Thrupp on medieval guilds, he suggests that, where the market for guild products was local and relatively inelastic, this localism constrained business activities and businessmen responded in ways typical of Weber's first form of traditionalism. Where markets were wider and more elastic, and so presented greater opportunities, then businessmen adopted individualistic, resource-maximizing strategies. In each case, business activity may be seen as a fairly rational response to the structure of opportunities (Marshall, 1982). H. E. Hallam finds 'capitalist' attitudes in the thirteenth-century monasteries of eastern England, based on notions of regularity, order, subjection, hard work, a conception of time marked by the clock, enumeration and accounting (Hallam, 1975). These attitudes promoted economically rational farming on church lands – evidence that 'materialism was hard grained within the Christian tradition' (Hallam, 1975, p. 49) – and, in addition, appear to have spread beyond the monasteries, to the greater secular landlords. Weber was aware of these monastic practices and attitudes, but denied that they were significant precursors of the capitalist spirit (Poggi, 1983). Hallam's evidence suggests, moreover, both rational economic men and rational economic corporations in the medieval period, monasteries being one of the earliest collective economic agents. J. H. Hexter cites estate books from the fourteenth century which show 'a methodical interest in gain, in "driving the most to their profit"' among the English landed gentry, to demonstrate the long-established tradition of economically rational land-management prior to the sixteenth century (Hexter, 1961, p. 89). Obviously we do not know how extensively such economic rationality was spread among the commercial and landed interests, but the evidence is sufficient to counsel caution in endorsing the view that rationality was a novel attribute of modern capitalism, or indeed a trait possessed only by individual agents.

Early Capitalism

Various 'modern' individualistic practices are clearly recognizable in medieval family and economic organization, and in well-developed forms. It is also possible to discern embryonic 'capitalist' practices, notably the widespread use of wage labour, some sort of a market in land and a limited amount of market-oriented farming. However, systems of belief were predominantly collective, both at the level of the 'official' religious and political doctrine described by Ullman and the lay culture that Reynolds recreates from local records, although feudal notions of reciprocity, consent, mutual obligations and rights, potentially had individualistic as well as collective implications (Ullman, 1967). The early modern period did not witness the origins of individualism, rather its continued development from earlier beginnings in the practices described above. But possessive individualism as a coherent system of belief did not develop until the seventeenth century. The development of capitalism as an economic system can also be located more firmly in Tudor and Stuart England than earlier.

The conventional view of a transition from feudalism to capitalism in Marxist history has been challenged on a variety of grounds (Holton, 1985). Both within and outside Marxism there is some awareness that there is no such thing as *the* transition to capitalism but a variety of separate and distinctive transitions. To some extent this problem was recognized by Nicos Poulantzas (1973) who criticized the idea of a royal road to capitalism, by noting the significant differences in the British, French and German cases. There could be no single road to capitalism because the class structure and contingent circumstances of these cases were significantly different. As there is not one transition but many, the outcomes of these transitions also vary significantly. These debates were largely anticipated by the work of Barrington Moore in *Social Origins of Dictatorship and Democracy* (1968), who, demonstrating that the special relations between peasant and landlord in different societies created entirely different political systems, showed also that there is no necessary or fixed relationship between political forms and capitalist conditions. These wide-ranging historical differences indicate why it has proved theoretically so difficult to specify a particular causal link between individualism and capitalism.

The late sixteenth- and early seventeenth-century English economy contained three dynamic sectors, which may be described as capitalist since they produced goods and services for private profit, realized via the market, and depended to a growing extent on the employment of commodified labour. Agrarian capitalism was the leading sector. Commercialized food production in the period of continuously rising food prices and developing produce markets (which had begun in the second quarter of the sixteenth century and lasted until population growth eased in the 1660s), plus a demand for wool from the clothing industry, created the conditions for the expansion of agrarian capitalism. Cultivation became more extensive, as the margins of cultivated land were extended and more intensive with enclosing (Coleman, 1977). There also appears to have been an extensive land market. Early industrial capitalism depended on the growth in the extractive industries throughout the sixteenth century, though slowing after the first quarter of the seventeenth, and the expansion of clothing and other manufactures. Industrialism was primarily a rural phenomenon, with a small urban element. Wage labour, though extensive, was frequently combined with subsistence production on cottage smallholdings, even small farms. The agricultural and industrial labour forces were interconnected, since the putting-out system prevalent in textiles and metalworking meant that landless agricultural wage labourers and small farmers, and their families, could be involved in both agricultural and industrial occupations according to the season (Coleman, 1977). We may characterize as merchant capitalism the commercial and financial activities of urban merchants, who dominated overseas trade via the monopoly trading companies, much of the clothing industry, some urban handicraft manufacturing (where the social relations of production in guild-regulated trades became more capitalist with a polarization into large masters and dependent artisans and labourers) and the distribution of agrarian produce.

Unlike some of its continental successors, English capitalism of the early modern period was not a bourgeois growth, since it was dominated by landed interests in the agrarian sector. Moreover, the various sectors became interconnected: the larger landowners provided financial capital, invested in merchant companies, and participated in rural industrialism via the extractive and sometimes the clothing industries, while merchants purchased land. By the end of the seventeenth century, as the more substantial landowners and farmers took advantage of the commercial opportunities that the less substantial could not hope for, English rural society had moved towards a tripartite structure: large landowners; substantial tenant farmers with some security of tenure; a mass of landless wage labourers (Stone, 1980). Urban society was also in the process of becoming three-tiered: substantial merchants and financiers in London and other major cities; smaller merchants, tradesmen and independent artisans, shopkeepers, employers of labour in manufacturing; wage labourers (Hill, 1980; Stone, 1980).

Links between the development of English capitalism at this time and individualism have been hypothesized in various ways. The growth of Puritanism as an individualistic religious ideology has of course been linked both directly and indirectly with capitalism. The direct link is the suggestion that Puritanism provided an ideological rationalization of the new individualistic practices of capitalism: as a justification of economic individualism it followed the growth of capitalism, but in some accounts it in turn reacted back on the economy by encouraging the further development of an individualistic mentality among capitalists (Marshall, 1982). These are essentially restatements of the notion of an 'elective affinity' between a Protestant Ethic and the spirit of modern capitalism. The indirect link is that Puritanism became part of the ideological challenge of the new social forces associated with capitalism in their struggle to change the traditional social and political order, and that the bourgeois revolutions of the seventeenth century established a new political framework which promoted capitalism. The old 'rise of the gentry' thesis associated with R. H. Tawney (1941) and then Christopher Hill (1969) was that a capitalist gentry, in alliance with urban merchants and employers, constituted new social forces, which displaced the aristocracy and assumed social and political power, thus influencing government in the interests of capital, and that Puritanism was the religion of these new groups.

Both links have of course been disputed. The direct link depends on Puritanism being widely spread among capitalists. The evidence suggests that it *was* the dominant form of religious belief among urban merchant capitalists and small businessmen, but that the rural-capitalist squirearchy, which was equally committed to the pursuit of individual material interests, was overwhelmingly Laudian (Manning, 1976; Stone, 1980). The direct linkage of Puritanism and capitalism receives some support, but it is of restricted applicability. The idea of a close and direct relationship between capitalism and individualistic beliefs remains in recent historiography, though the nature of the link – causal, functional, correlative – is not clearly specified. But individualism is now more broadly conceived, as the philosophy of possessive individualism which bears no necessary relation to Puritanism.

> Possessive individualism is also peculiarly associated with an urban middle class and with a squirearchy living off commercialized agriculture.
>
> (Stone, 1980, p. 44)

Among 'the social forces accompanying the rise of capitalism' we must include not only the individualism of those who wished to make money by doing what they would with their own but also the individualism of those who wished to follow their own consciences in worshipping God . . . .

(Hill, 1980, p. 112)

Possessive individualism as it developed after Hobbes was a politically focused doctrine, formulated as part of a challenge to traditional conceptions of government and culminating in Locke's second *Treatise on Government* and the premise that individuals, particularly men of property, had certain rights which the sovereign could not violate even in the name of the public good. This doctrine was developed in the course of political struggle and was not simply the product of detached intellectuals – in 1646, for example, the Leveller Richard Overton both anticipated Locke's conception of individuals as sovereign over themselves and their possessions and formulated this in language that bears a remarkable similarity to that of Locke (Macpherson, 1962). The theoretical development of individualism did run ahead of the practical political consequences, however. The egalitarianism found in the Putney Debates and in some Leveller writings, the logical conclusion of the notion of individual rights, was not to reach fruition in universal adult suffrage for more than two centuries in Britain, though its influence was felt earlier in America. Similarly, the right of individuals to full religious toleration and freedom of speech took time to be realized. But after the two revolutions of the seventeenth century, individualism was embodied in concrete constitutional and legal changes, which allowed individuals – or rather men of property – freedom to pursue their interests with much reduced state interference: the counterweight of Parliament to the Crown; contractual monarchy and constitutional checks on the executive; the legal rights of the person and property in place of rights discretionary on the sovereign's will. In the political sphere, this marked the triumph of the conception of the individual as *citizen*, defined by Walter Ullman as 'autonomous, independent, and with indigenous rights . . . entitled to take part in public government itself' (1967, p. 6).

The indirect link between individualism and capitalism has been reformulated. The idea of a bourgeois, Puritan revolution has given way in modern historiography to an interpretation of the seventeenth century as the 'transition from a Tudor aristocratic order, breaking down in the first half of the seventeenth century, to a Whig aristocratic order first brought into being during the second half of that era' (Pocock, 1980, p. 10). But this aristocratic order differed from the old. The ascendancy of possessive individualism (rather than Puritanism *per se*) in constitutional and legal spheres meant that the interests of men of property, landed and commercial, now had greater protection; indeed, the political influence of the House of Commons ensured that these interests could not be ignored. Moreover, the aristocracy itself was by now more heavily involved in commercialized agriculture and financial capitalism: 'the peerage was sociologically a very different class from the hangers-on of James I's Court' (Hill, 1980, p. 121). This new political configuration arising out of the two revolutions facilitated the expansion of capitalism (Hill, 1980; Stone, 1980). It did so negatively, by preventing the re-emergence of royal absolutism, which may have impeded economic development, and by more positive acts.

Various positive changes have been cited. The first was the partial dismantling of Tudor and Stuart economic controls, which had been designed 'to restrain human greed and to protect the economically weak against the strong' (Stone, 1980, p. 45), by the abolition of monopolies and the encouragement rather than restriction of enclosure. However, in the economic sphere, individualism continued to be restrained by customary notions that government should attempt to influence prices and interest rates and oblige local authorities to provide assistance to the poor. The second positive change was to turn 'lordship into absolute ownership' (Perkin, 1968, p. 135) and to create, for large landowners, absolute private property secure against the Crown, as the result of abolishing feudal tenures and the Court of Wards in 1646, 1656 and 1661. Smaller farmers were denied a similar tenurial revolution in the 1640s and 1650s, when moves to transform copyhold were defeated, and in 1677, when insecurity was extended to small freeholders unless they could provide a written title, thus consolidating landowners against the peasantry (Hill, 1980). Insecure tenures, the rapid extension of enclosure, and other economic forces speeded the decline of small farmers, while large landowners grew stronger. The third change was the creation of the colonial system after the Navigation Acts of 1650, 1651 and 1660, supported by successive governments in foreign policy and enforced by military means, which provided substantial and secure opportunities for merchants and financiers. The fourth change was the triumph of common law, with its characteristic orientation towards individual rights.

The effect of the two revolutions was to create an environment in which men of substance could advance their economic interests, were secure against governmental control of the economy without parliamentary assent, and were able to expand as large-scale capitalists at the cost of the small (Hill, 1980). There is agreement that political changes, inspired by and expressing possessive individualism, thus created the conditions of further capitalist expansion. Economic development depended on political conditions as well as on the logic of capitalism.

The ideal of citizenship permeates the seventeenth-century opposition to traditionalism. We can see, following the analysis of T. H. Marshall (1977), that citizenship has evolved through three stages. The civil element in citizenship is composed of the rights that are necessary for the development of individual freedom (that is, the liberty of the person and freedoms of thought and speech, the right to own property and to conclude economic contracts). Many of these civil rights developed in the seventeenth and eighteenth centuries in association with the theories of Locke and Hobbes. The second component of citizenship is the political, which embraces the rights to participate in political power as a member of a political body invested with authority and as an elector of members to such a political institution. This was extended to men of substantial property in the seventeenth century, and more widely in the nineteenth century after successive widenings of the franchise included the male working class into the electoral process. But it was not completed until the universal adult suffrage of the twentieth century. The third component of citizenship is social and this involves a basic right of economic welfare and security. This social dimension to citizenship was particularly important in the early twentieth century as subordinate groups gained access to welfare and economic rights within the social system. The institutions which correspond to this form of citizenship are educational systems and social services. While early notions of citizenship stressed the individual and the notion of individual rights, later forms of citizenship have given greater prominence to the idea of collective social rights and welfare institutions.

Modified Individualism

We have accepted a number of assumptions about capitalism in relation to individualism that have been made in the literature. This is the place to scrutinize these more closely against the historical evidence. We believe that the relationship between individualism and capitalism is neither intrinsic nor necessary. Such a relationship only appears to hold if, as it often is, capitalism is *defined* as a series of individualistic practices, so that the capitalism–individualism nexus becomes tautologous. We agree that English society can be characterized broadly as individualistic, but we feel that, at the level of economic practices, this individualism was perhaps not so complete as the development of the doctrine of individualism would suggest. We argue that early capitalism in England grew within a framework of practices that embodied individualism in varying degrees.

The assumption that capitalism requires individual and absolute private property rights may be questioned in the context of the English agrarian capitalism of the late-seventeenth and eighteenth century, which was still the dominant economic sector. Absolute private property depended on the abolition of feudal tenures and, from the early years of the sixteenth century, on the steady development by the courts of a common-law policy that was hostile to most restrictions on the ability of individuals to alienate land and which effectively prevented landowners binding their heirs in perpetuity (Bonfield, 1983). Yet, despite the freedom that landowners gained to dispose of their property in their own lifetimes, their dynastic impulses were such that they continued to seek ways of maintaining the integrity of their estates through succeeding generations. By the early seventeenth century, settlements designed to pass estates intact to children and grandchildren were easily broken by life tenants, who became tenants-in-tail and could do as they wished with their lands. However, the new device of the trust to preserve contingent remainders, developed in the mid-seventeenth century and subsequently refined, protected the interests of unborn children and prevented life tenants gaining absolute ownership. The practice of making *inter-vivos* settlements between fathers and sons at the time of sons' marriages restrained life tenants in possession from alienating land. Thus marriage settlements restricted alienability for one generation and, provided each tenant in possession entered a settlement with his heirs, in principle land could be entailed for generations. Paradoxically, the mid-seventeenth century saw the possibility of more effective restraints on alienation than had existed for the previous century, and formed a counterweight to the individualistic trend of the common law.

With further development in the early eighteenth century, and notably in their extension to provide portions for daughters and younger sons as charges against the estate (Bonfield, 1983), strict settlements became established as an important feature of landed inheritance. H. J. Habbakuk (1950) has estimated that about half the land in England was covered by strict settlements by the middle of that century. His celebrated thesis, that the trend in land-owner-ship from the later seventeenth century was towards the extension of large-scale landholdings in the hands of the magnates, the decline of the gentry and lesser peasant freeholders, and, by the mid-eighteenth century, a sharp contraction in a previously exten-sive market for land, rests on the development and spread of the strict settlement (Habbakuk, 1939–40, 1950). Strict marriage settlements, adopted more rapidly and widely by the largest land-owners, provided the means to conserve landed estates and slow the rate of sales. Legal developments relating to mortgages and the growth of long-term in place of short-term mortgages meant that settlements could now provide for daughters and younger sons by means of cash portions raised against the estates, rather than by transfers of land. The eldest sons, inheriting larger estates, were thus able to offer larger jointures to their brides, and so were likely to marry women of substantial wealth, and the practice of using the bride's portion to invest in more land added to the estate. At the same time, the less substantial gentry and smaller freeholders tended to sell rather than buy land in the market, because they, unlike the greater landowners who had financial remuneration from office-holding and investments, had insufficient resources to cope with the heavy land taxes after 1692. However, merchant capitalists, who did have the resources and were potential buyers on the land market, found more appealing investments in trade and finance. The Habbakuk thesis suggests that the strict settlement created greater family control over the disposal of property, if this became necessary to raise cash for any reason. Land sales could only be made at the time of resettlement, because life tenants could not alienate in fee, with the consequence that decisions to sell would involve both the father and his eldest son, and perhaps the bride's family.

Although this thesis for long informed accounts of land-ownership and inheritance, recent research has begun to question the linkage of marriage settlements and the rise of great estates. Summarized in J. V. Beckett (1977) and L. Bonfield (1983), this research indicates that Habbakuk's generalization from evidence pertaining to Bedfordshire and Northamptonshire to the whole of England may not be tenable. Evidence on the land market suggests that the concentration of property in fewer hands and the relative decline of lesser owners undoubtedly occurred in a number of counties, but in Lincolnshire there was no such trend. Moreover, the land market itself appears to have both contracted and expanded at different times, demand fluctuating in inverse proportion to the price of government securities. The incidence of land tax seems to have varied in different regions and does not necessarily seem to have affected lesser owners in the way suggested. Analysis of family records shows that settlements could leave part of the estate unsettled, for disposal by sons as they wished, and there may have been greater freedom to use the bride's portion in ways other than extending the estates. Demographic patterns are also significant, since failure to produce a male heir or death of the father prior to a son's marriage would break the pattern of intergenerational settlements. There is some evidence that such breaks would have been more common in the first quarter of the eighteenth century than later, when the supply of sons increased and thus reduced the amount of land available for the market. Recent research is suggestive rather than definitive, however, and touches on aspects of the land market and family practices that are relevant to H. J. Habbakuk's overall model as well as to the issue of strict settlements. What matters from our point of view is the strict settlement, which was widely used to restrict absolute property rights: settlements were found not only among the magnates but also among the large and small gentry alike (Bonfield, 1983). While this may dent Habbakuk's linkage of the rise of the great estates with the differential uptake of strict settlement, the evidence of a wider spread of settlements is germane to the frequent limitation in practice of individual rights in private property.

Capitalism in the rural sector developed, therefore, within a system of property rights which gave many landowners restricted rights of alienation. The 1774 edition of *Tenants Law* described how even land held in fee simple was so 'spotted and involved' with encumbrances that individuals were denied effective absolute titles and unimpeded rights of disposition, suggesting how problematic in practice the notion of absolute private property could be (quoted in Neale, 1975, pp. 98–9). Moreover, commercialized agriculture and mineral exploitation were also conducted on the basis of leaseholds as well as ownership, because landowners rarely worked all their own land and routinely leased out substantial amounts. Yet the role of tenant farmers, mineral and building leaseholders is ignored in accounts that link absolute private property with capitalism.

R. S. Neale (1975) has argued that the somewhat restricted property rights typical of seventeenth- and eighteenth-century English rural capitalism profoundly shaped the institutional and legal framework that fostered subsequent capitalist developments, and shaped even the notion of capital itself. He suggests that the development of trusts, mortgages, and leaseholds as financial instruments, and the corresponding legal elaboration of the equity of redemption and the law of trust, created an elaborate, flexible and functional financial base for capitalist development. Leaseholds, ground rents and building mortgages underpinned the urban and transportation infrastructure of industrial capitalism, while trusts provided a legal framework for a variety of eighteenth-century merchant and industrial ventures in the absence of a freely available joint-stock company form after the Bubble Act of 1720. Indeed, trusts could create organizations that functioned almost as corporations. Neale (1975) cites certain great estates in which the creation of tenancies distinguished ownership from management and use, the claims of mortgagees (in effect, investors) were given preference, the claims of all beneficiaries put pressure on salaried estate managers to maximize income, and major policy changes were discussed and approved by what was in effect a board of trustees. A. B. Dubois (1938) provides examples of equitable trusts in manufacturing and insurance that functioned in a manner analogous to joint-stock companies, with separation of management and ownership, limited liability, transfer of shares and a continuing existence via a board of trustees, though without the right to corporate ownership of assets. Both the landowning class and the urban bourgeoisie made use of these financial and institutional instruments (Neale, 1975). Despite what contemporary political theorists said about absolute private

114

property, the law came to embody notions that property was the legal title to income from land rather than ownership of the land as an object, that these titles were divisible, that present and future income was property, and that paper titles such as mortgages and bills of exchange (in other words, credit) were equally property (Neale, 1975).

Although Marxists have commonly drawn a close relationship between the emergence of legal individualism and capitalist society, connecting the emergence of the legal subject as an absolute entity and the growth of commodity markets (Poulantzas, 1973; Pashukanis, 1978), it is clear that this relationship is complex and variable. The relationship between legal individualism, juridical forms and capitalist production of commodities will depend greatly on whether we are talking about absolute or provisional legal rights of ownership. We have shown, following the work of modern historians, that capitalism may have developed without absolute rights of property ownership and that, on the contrary, restricted rights of alienation in the legal sense were quite common.

Strict settlements are indicative of another facet of English capitalism that is surprisingly ignored in accounts of individualism: namely, that prior to the late-nineteenth century familial principles restrained pure individualism, as the widely used phrase 'family capitalism' suggests. The assumption that capitalism denies the collective ties of the family and involves a process of defamilialization is untenable. Family capitalism was not the peculiar product of the inheritance practices of the eighteenth-century English landed aristocracy and gentry, but was the normal form of early capitalism, including industrial capitalism before and during the industrial revolution. Weber identified 'stewardship' as an important component of the Protestant Ethic and correctly pointed to the way this orientation promoted capital accumulation and investment in productive assets rather than consumption. But stewardship, while serving God, also served the family, particularly in Puritanism with its strong family ethos, and there is no suggestion in Weber's account that God's will might better be served by vesting the ownership of capital assets in religious and charitable corporations rather than in the family, which is not a fanciful scenario given the success of the early church in raising endowments and the practice of some modern businessmen who bequeath their assets to charitable trusts. One line of reasoning might perhaps have advised the

115

Sovereign Individuals of Capitalism

ideal-typical capitalist to avoid creating a family, because relatives
are potentially a conduit through which profits leak into consumption that inhibits accumulation and re-investment. This was something that Scrooge fully appreciated, and perhaps those eighteenth-
century landowners so burdened by the weight of the portions
charged to their estates would have concurred. Against this, it is
clear that familialism was often an indispensable ingredient of the
accumulation of capital and the creation of a successful commercial
enterprise.

Habbakuk's illustration of how careful marriage strategies
enlarged estates demonstrates the broad significance of families for
successful entrepreneurs in early capitalism. Modern surveys of
industrialists during the early industrial revolution show that the
older view of the individual entrepreneur rising from humble origins
by means of self-help, as popularized by Samuel Smiles, is wide of
the mark: industrialists typically were neither of humble origin nor
solely dependent on their own resources (Foster, 1974; Honeyman,
1982; Evans, 1983; Howe, 1984). Financial, managerial and
marketing assistance from kin, family contacts and, among
members of religious sects, co-religionists, could be drawn upon by
substantial numbers of the industrial bourgeoisie. By the time that
industrial capitalism in textiles matured in the second quarter of the
nineteenth century, the hereditary succession of industrialists within
family firms was clearly established (Foster, 1974; Howe, 1984).
John Foster has suggested, that the employer in Oldham

> saw himself as son and grandson to an estate and judged himself within
> this familial (still almost peasant) perspective. He was successful if he
> increased his inheritance. The pattern of industry itself made wealth more
> familial than personal. The capital requirements of high profit pro-
> duction meant that a firm's assets could not be divided up every
> generation.
>
> (Foster, 1974, p. 180)

Anthony Howe (1984) notes, among the cotton masters of the
mid-nineteenth century, a tendency towards partible inheritance
rather than the impartible, exclusive inheritance commonly found
among landowners. Partible inheritance created a number of individual ownership stakes within the enterprise that in principle could
be alienated freely, although some firms were structured as tenancies
in common, a legal device that made alienation more difficult

116

(Foster, 1974). The earliest manufacturers seem rarely to have used the strict settlement to perpetuate dynastic control (although family trusts became more common later). Yet partibility seems to have co-existed with strong family-firm links, and indeed created organizations that, in family terms, were *inclusive* rather than exclusive in the manner of landed estates (Howe, 1984). Kinship was significant in other ways, with nephews, brothers-in-law, and sons-in-law being recruited as partners or to managerial positions, often to perpetuate the family firm when sons were lacking (Howe, 1984).

Family capitalism was indeed normal during early industrialization in France and Germany as well as in Britain, and with similar functions (Kocka, 1978). It has been noted how the major German industrial pioneers formed 'old and complex bourgeois dynasties, often interrelated, and quite like aristocratic dynasties in their marriage policies, except that with them it was not so much a matter of increasing their territories as of increasing business, entrepreneurial skills, and capital' (Kocka, 1978, pp. 510–11).

We contend that there is potentially a tension in capitalism, between the emphasis on individual economic rights and individualism more generally and the importance of the family and family unity as a condition of the conservation and inheritance of economic wealth across generations. The importance of individual rights and conscience was not always reconcilable with the economic requirement of family unity as the condition for economic accumulation within the context of a kinship group. The potential tension between individualism and economic accumulation frequently appeared in the nineteenth-century novel, even if it was eventually resolved by the fortunate coincidence of love and inheritance, as in Trollope's *Dr Thorne*. In the French context, the novels which constituted the so-called human comedy of Balzac were also reflections upon the problem of the family's survival in the post-revolutionary era, where the egoistic interests of a rising commercial class had to be contained within the framework of the family's economic strategy. These points indicate that, although individualism was discursively dominant in early capitalism, it clearly conflicted with other discourses like familialism.

A third assumption also deserves some modification: namely, that capitalism requires formally free labour with individual choice and contracting. We would not question the assertion that labour becomes a commodity and is valued solely for its productive potential under capitalism, but we do query the necessary linkage of capitalism and free labour markets. Modern capitalism has operated with labour markets of varying degrees of freedom. These include the unfree conditions of South Africa, systems of bonded labour for immigrant workers in Western Europe in the 1970s, and a dual labour market structure in Japan in the 1950s and 1960s that effectively denied primary sector employees normal labour market freedoms and tied them to one company, because primary employers refused to hire the ex-employees of other companies. John Rex has argued, against the contention that free wage labour is the only form compatible in the long run with the logic of capitalism, 'that capitalism is compatible with a variety of forms of labour' (Rex, 1971, p. 404). This view has been endorsed in the debate about labour forms and capitalism (Wolpe, 1972; Corrigan, 1977).

From the early modern period onwards, English capitalism at home developed a free wage-labour system. Compared with modern labour markets, there were clearly some restrictions on freedom. These include the old Poor Laws, which in theory limited geographical mobility and the individual's choice of employment, the survival of serfdom in Scottish mines until 1799 and the continuation of the only marginally less unfree, bonded labour of English mines in the North-east (Pollard, 1978), and the linking of some agricultural wage labour to the land through tied cottages. But the system was still recognizable in essence as free wage labour. Alongside this there was the semi-independent labour force of urban artisans and rural cottagers and putting-out workers, owning some of their own means of production (tools, small plots of land, spinning wheels and looms) but dependent on paid employment for full subsistence. With time, this merged into the free wage-labour force (Snell, 1985). The relative abundance of labour, due, prior to the mid-seventeenth century and again after the mid-eighteenth century, to a rising population, and in the intervening period (when population growth slackened) to rising agricultural productivity and enclosures, ensured that fairly free labour markets operated much as Marxists and Weberians have claimed.

English capitalism abroad, however, did not use free labour. Whereas English merchants in the East merely 'made their way into the trading networks of existing economies', in the Americas they became producers as well as traders (Coleman, 1977, p. 66). The fruit of this form of English merchant capitalism was slavery, since

118

the development of sugar plantations in the Caribbean, and cotton and tobacco plantations on the American mainland in the seventeenth century, depended on imported slaves in the absence of an abundant, indigenous labour supply. Slavery, of course, does not simply limit the individual's freedom of choice, but transforms an individual into the possession of another. Slaves are not the absolute owners of their own capacities, nor do they have an individuality which cannot be possessed by others. Slavery is thus the *purest* form of commodified labour, devoid of that peculiar character of free labour as a commodity, namely that the purchaser only rents an individual's labour power. On the market, slaves are bought and sold, not hired and fired.

In volume III of *Capital*, Marx maintained that slavery was directly contradictory to the capitalist mode of production, because capitalism presupposed labour as free wage labour. But elsewhere he recognized that slave plantations were anomalous, because they were owned by capitalists and existed within a world market based on free labour. There has been considerable debate among contemporary American historians on whether slavery is compatible with capitalism, and, in a recent contribution to this debate, E. Fox-Genovese and E. D. Genovese (1983), following Marx, argue vigorously that slavery did prove incompatible, because in America it was replaced by a conventional capitalism, while merchant capitalism generically was parasitic on a variety of different modes of production rather than being central to the capitalist mode. Yet they concede that the English slaveholding class of the seventeenth and eighteenth centuries should for all practical purposes be regarded as capitalist. From our point of view, the significance of merchant capitalism abroad lies in the demonstration that a non-individualistic form of labour was central to the functioning of a major sector of the English economy.

The later use of convicts to develop the Australian economy indicates that unfree labour, far from being exceptional, was commonly used within pastoral capitalism when there were inadequate supplies of indigenous labour. Even where convicts were freed, they often became ticket-men, who were not entirely free workers. Slavery and convict settlements were thus essential to the development of colonial capitalism in peripheral regions (Connell and Irving, 1980).

119

CHAPTER

— 5 —

Cultural Contradictions of Modernity

Our argument in previous chapters can be summarized as follows. There is a long-run historical process, the Discovery of the Individual, which results in individuals being given, in a very general way, greater and greater importance. Out of this process develop more specific discourses of the individual, which identify particular qualities of individuals as important. Two historically significant discourses of this kind are individualism and individuality. Of the possible specific discourses of the individual, individualism achieves a certain discursive dominance. Because of this dominance, it enters into a functional relationship with capitalism, as this rises as a dominant economic form. It is because both these forms are dominant that there is a functional relationship between them; it is not because they have any elective affinity with one another. One side of the functional relationship is that individualism provides a particular form for capitalism, a form in which the individual is the economic subject. Capitalism can take other forms and, indeed, empirically it has done so, as we shall illustrate in the first section of this chapter. Our claim is definitely *not* that individualism has any causal priority in the genesis of capitalism. We do want to argue, however, that it helps to determine the *form* that capitalism will take. The other side of the functional relationship is that the dominance of capitalism in turn promotes the continued significance of individualism.

There is no necessity for the functional relationship between individualism and capitalism. As it was made, so it can be unmade; functional relationships can become unstuck. It is our view that this is precisely what is happening now: individualism and capitalism no longer serve each other. Capitalism has outgrown individualism and is now less shaped by it than it was before. Indeed, there are signs that individualism in the modern world may be dysfunctional for capitalism. At the same time, the changing position of the individual reduces the efficacy of individual action. Such developments result in individualism losing its position of discursive dominance in contemporary culture. This has three consequences. First, there tends to be a 'pluralization of life worlds' (Berger, Berger and Kellner, 1973), or a 'bewildering variety of cultural demesnes' (Bell, 1979), so that the cultural structure becomes more differentiated. Secondly, discourses of the individual become oppositional, losing their confident self-assertion. Thirdly, discursive alliances are formed, so that it becomes increasingly difficult to separate individualism from individuality. The rest of this chapter is devoted to illustration of these various arguments.

Non-Individualistic Capitalism: the Case of Japan

Japanese late capitalism differs considerably from the Occidental model found in Western Europe, the USA and among the former British colonies. Its essence has been described by Michio Morishima as 'nationalistic, paternalistic and anti-individualistic' (1983, p. 18). We shall show how contemporary Japanese practice reflects these principles, how Japanese industrialization followed a different path from the Occident, and how contemporary differences may be explained in part in terms of the autonomous influence of a distinct culture that preceded industrial capitalism and shaped its course. Our case is that Japanese capitalism differs because it embodies collectivism, which underpins the three characteristics cited by Morishima.

In Japan, the Meiji Restoration of 1868 prompted the deliberate destruction of feudalism and the creation of new institutions which would promote industrialization, the goal of the new government being to modernize in order to match the economic and military strength of the West – the famous policy of a 'rich country with a strong army' (Lehmann, 1982). The new institutions were consciously copied from Western practices. The abolition of feudal landholding, the destruction of territorial power and political centralization under a constitutional government have attracted the interest of political historians, but the economic institutions are of more concern here. These included the creation of absolute private property, free labour, a market economy, and the joint-stock company form with individual shareholding (Masao, 1968; Sumiya and Taira, 1979). In the economy, the Japanese created a formal institutional structure, which reflected the European principle of the supremacy of individual rights. The Meiji bureaucrats also followed the continental European pattern of a state-sponsored capitalism that expedited economic growth, relying less on the autonomous activity of self-interested, private profit-seeking, individual entrepreneurs found in the British transition to industrialism. Like the Prussian government, the Japanese state created and managed factories, some for military purposes and others as models for private entrepreneurs, founded banks (with the enforced participation of merchant capital), modernized the transport system and favoured private capitalists by means of subsidies and trading privileges (Yamamura, 1978). Capital formation was a mixture of state activity, funded by the taxation of peasant agriculture, and the private funds of individual entrepreneurs, their families and friends. In the 1880s, the state sold off its manufacturing plants at knock-down prices to favoured individuals, thus creating large-scale capitalists, though it continued to subsidize these individuals directly and indirectly (by means of trading privileges and military procurement policy). In the same period, private banking developed after legal changes allowed more profitable trading, and individual shareholding grew rapidly (Yamamura, 1978). After the early pump-priming, the state continued to invest in the educational and transport systems, but productive capital was in private hands. The labour market and employment relations showed only a few signs of the later paternalism, and approximated commodified labour traded on a free market. By the end of the nineteenth century, therefore, the Japanese seemed set to develop along the lines of Western capitalism.

The development of Japanese capitalism in the twentieth century, however, has clearly not followed Western practice, despite the early emulation of the Western model. Nationalism has had major implications for the Japanese system, affecting the character of entrepreneurship, the relationship between the state and private capital and the structure of the economy. It has been argued that the

Japanese capitalists of the Meiji era were motivated as much by nationalism as by private profit-seeking, with the 'rich country with a strong army' inspiration providing the drive to industrialize. In an early form, this argument suggested that the state officials who founded manufacturing plants and banks were ex-samurai socialized into the nationalistic community spirit of Japanese Confucianism, and many of the entrepreneurs in the private sector came from the same ex-samurai stratum, while the merchant class, which had not been socialized into elite culture, continued to seek private profit in traditional forms of trade. More recently, historians have shown that intermediate status groups, including the merchants, were more involved in state and private capitalism, and in the private sector were concerned with their own individual and family interests. Nevertheless, they continue to emphasize the importance of nationalism as a dominant motivation. In the first place, the non-samurai strata had been exposed to the same elite culture and internalized a similar nationalistic ideology (Yamamura, 1978). In the second, the links between private capitalism and the state, and the consequential dependence of industrialists on continuing state patronage, subordinated private capitalism to governmental policy that was nationalistic (Morishima, 1983).

State domination of the economy in the pursuit of nationalistic goals had certain consequences prior to 1945. Private capitalism lacked real autonomy and functioned as an instrument of government, for example in the development of a modern armaments industry and the industrialization of Manchuria. Yet the process was not unidirectional, since with time capitalists in turn came to influence government by means of political corruption, which enabled them to buy the support of leading politicians. It was for this reason that the military sponsored a new class of dependent industrialists in the 1930s, believing that government was no longer capable of promoting the national interest as the military saw it (Morishima, 1983). The effect of state sponsorship was to concentrate the Japanese economy into an oligopolistic structure after 1918, as government and then the military transformed a handful of firms into giant combines, the 'old' (formed in the early Meiji period) and 'new' (post-1930) *zaibatsu*. These were family-dominated conglomerates, each being partly owned and wholly controlled by a family holding company, with the family interests organized as a family trust covering both stem and branch lines.

They spanned industrial, commercial and financial sectors, and dominated the economy: what they did not own directly, the *zaibatsu* were able effectively to control via their banks and their manufacturing subsidiaries' control of product markets. This pattern of economic growth has led one Japanese economist to describe Japanese capitalism as being administratively guided from its inception:

> This economic growth was certainly not achieved through using the mechanism of free operation of the economy; it was the result of the government or the military, with their loyal following of capitalists, manipulating and influencing the economy in order to realise national aims. In the final stage this kind of state capitalism was eventually transformed into a controlled economy . . . .
>
> (Morishima, 1983, pp. 96–7)

The militarism of the Meiji period clearly no longer informs late capitalism in Japan, and the *zaibatsu* were broken up during the postwar reconstruction imposed by the Americans. Yet state direction and economic nationalism continue to distinguish Japanese capitalism. Government has consistently guided the economy, aiming to promote Japanese dominance in specific sectors. The planning of industrial policy has involved consultation and close working arrangements among bureaucrats, financiers and industrialists. The role of the governmental agency, MITI, in this process, as the forum in which businessmen and bureaucrats meet to agree national priorities and as the agency which then implements the agreed view, is well known (Johnson, 1982). Private and autonomous corporations, while influencing governmental strategy, in turn agree to formulate their own business policies in line with state guidelines. In part they are constrained, since the levers of economic control in the hands of government (which include soft loans, development funds, tariff and non-tariff protection) are significant mechanisms. Yet industrialists themselves appear to accept the necessity and desirability of an industrial policy that directs growth along centrally determined lines, so that both those selected for growth and those who are sacrificed support state policy. There is widespread acceptance that the national economic interest comes before private interests, that government should define the national interest, and that individual companies jointly form a 'national team', which competes with other nations as a united body (Morishima, 1983). The collectivism manifest in nationalism outweighs the individual pursuit of private interests.

A second feature that marks off Japanese from Western capitalism is paternalism. The paternalistic organization of employment relations, or welfare corporatism, has been extensively documented and is familiar to many outside Japan: it covers the offer to employees of lifetime employment with a single employer, seniority wage and career structures (the latter allowing manual workers to rise into staff or junior managerial grades), continual in-company training of employees, extensive non-wage benefits (including housing, medical and social facilities). The system embodies the principles that employers value the continuing employment of workers rather than their short-term contribution to production, that companies provide security while employees owe loyalty and obedience, that payment should reflect seniority rather than individual performance, and that employment relations are diffuse and embrace the whole man rather than being contractually specific exchanges of labour for wages. In addition, no-poaching conventions among large corporations reduce the possibility that individuals will use the formally free labour market to move between firms, while the tame, company-sponsored unions of the postwar era have upheld company power over labour. Some Japanese commentators view modern paternalism as the adaptation to an advanced industrial setting of traditional communal and collectivist values, that in the early nineteenth century had guided master–apprentice relations within crafts and the *ie*, a corporate residential group which, in agricultural enterprises and merchant houses, was also a managing body (Yamamura, 1978; Sethi *et al.*, 1984). In the large-scale corporate sector, lifetime employment may not be absolute, since there is some job mobility; nevertheless, the contrast with the West is considerable.

This Japanese system is in fact confined to a very narrow section of employees: the permanent male labour force of large companies. Women, temporary workers and workers in employment past the official retiring age in large companies, and the employees of smaller companies, are excluded. The system binds employees in various ways. On the one hand, it disseminates an ideology of trust and belongingness, with apparent success. On the other, it also contains a most powerful form of economic compulsion: since only the aristocracy of labour in primary sector companies benefits from the material rewards of welfare corporatism, and enterprise trade unions provide little protection against corporations, the individual has little realistic alternative but to comply.

Paternalism developed mainly after 1918, although some early roots can be found in the state-owned plants of the early Meiji period. Like their counterparts in Europe, early industrial employers in Japan found difficulty in recruiting and retaining labour, and the early factory labour force was notable for its high rates of absenteeism and turnover. Japanese employers tried various strategies to combat these difficulties. State textile firms employed the daughters of ex-samurai, in the hope that the samurai culture of nationalism and obedience would bind them to the firm (Morishima, 1983). Private textile employers adopted more coercive policies, demanding deposits as guarantees, housing their female employees in barracks guarded by security staff, even kidnapping employees (Saxonhouse, 1976; Lehmann, 1982). In the heavy industries employing men, the subcontracting of labour recruitment and organization to gang bosses, who exploited the particularistic ties of kinship and villages to build stable work-teams around themselves, was common. While in the state-sector engineering and shipbuilding firms a primitive form of welfare corporation has been noted (Dore, 1973). Paternalism subsequently developed in part as a response to employee instability, as an attempt to bind workers to a firm by means of self-interest and feelings of loyalty. Such instability had also produced paternalistic responses in the West on occasion, most notably among large-scale German employers (for example, Krupps) in the second half of the nineteenth century (Lee, 1978). Japanese paternalism was also a response to the exhortations of a government, affronted by contractual relations based on the cash nexus and unalloyed commodification, that employers should create a more humane and morally acceptable employment system, to the government's willingness to legislate employee rights, and to the fear among employers of the growing appeal of the radical labour movement to wage labourers (Taira, 1978).

Anti-individualistic and pro-collectivist principles distinguish capitalism in Japan. Within companies, group identity is a major principle of work organization at all hierarchical levels. Among male manual workers, this probably stretches back to the gang-boss system and, in the present period, can be found in the widespread use of quality circles and work teams in production (Cole, 1979; Bradley and Hill, 1983). The Western stereotype of Japanese workers, that they subordinate themselves to the group and to the wider collectivity of the firm, and so suppress their individuality, is confirmed by anthropologists and sociologists (Smith, 1983). At management level, group decision-making processes depend on consultation and consensus among peers and on collective responsibility, which ensure that no individual manager is associated with a particular decision (Ouchi, 1981). These processes are clearly alien to Western management practices that demand individual initiative and responsibility, and to a culture that sanctions the pursuit of policies that are unpopular elsewhere within the organization, provided that they can be presented as technically correct (for example, the endorsement of 'macho' managers who demonstrate their individual strength of will by taking 'tough' decisions against opposition). Decision-making is influenced by the *ringi* principle: groups of subordinates discuss a proposal among themselves and, when they are in agreement, forward their view to their superior for consideration; he in turn consults with his peers and, on the basis of their consensus, will forward the proposal to the next level of management, reject it, or send it back for further consideration. In theory, the process stretches from shopfloor groups to company presidents, though the practice may not always correspond to the aspiration. Decision-making that depends on group consensus and the participation of subordinates can legitimately be described as non-individualistic. The *ringi* procedure originated in feudal administration, was extended by Meiji bureaucrats, and was adopted by private firms at the onset of industrialization (Yamamura, 1978).

Relations between firms are also idiosyncratic when viewed from the West. Despite the destruction of the prewar *zaibatsu* and the enforced sale of family shareholdings, the Japanese economy remains concentrated into a number of industrial 'lineage' organizations (Clark, 1979). Vertical groupings of smaller firms around a parent company, with the parent company as the majority shareholder or in the position to change the top management of subsidiaries and subcontractors, are not uncommon in the West, though the degree of integration to be found among hierarchically organized Japanese groups does appear stronger than elsewhere. Horizontal groupings, however, are unique to Japan. The six main groups, heirs of the *zaibatsu*, have no obvious hierarchical structure. The component parts are autonomous companies, which are linked via a group bank (which acts as the lead bank for each company though rarely accounts for a majority of their loan finance) and by means of reciprocal minority shareholdings and some overlapping directorships. These groups are not conglomerates, since they are neither centrally owned nor directed, nor are they cartels, since their constituents operate in diverse fields, and the only visible and formal group activity is the monthly meeting of company presidents (Dore, 1983). Yet these independent companies form easily identifiable groups, using common names and trademarks, establishing reciprocal long-term trading relationships within the group in preference to dealing with outsiders, and with employees identifying themselves as group members and not just as members of a particular firm (Yamamura, 1978). The power of collective ties preserves industrial combines even forty years after they were legally disbanded.

Ronald Dore suggests that a general characteristic of inter-firm trading relations in Japan, most highly visible within lineage groups, is relational contracting: that is, the moderation of individual self-interest by goodwill or 'give-and-take' within a framework of long-term relations, where both parties value the relation as an end in itself as well as a means of promoting private ends (Dore, 1983). In contrast to the utilitarianism of English individualism, that people (natural and legal persons) in their dealings with others should follow the Smithian precept in the *Wealth of Nations* to 'address ourselves, not to their humanity, but to their self-love, and never talk to them of our necessities but of their advantages' (Adam Smith, 1776, quoted in Dore, 1983, p. 459), Dore argues that the Japanese ethic is to create 'moralized trading relations of mutual goodwill' (1983, p. 463). The principle of inter-firm relations is that losses and gains should be shared and both parties to a contract should try to ensure the survival of the other, even by forgoing an advantage that could be won at the other's expense. Relational contracting describes both intra-group corporate relations and employment relations within corporations, the system of welfare corporatism. Recognizing that individual interests will conflict, it is an attempt to reduce the disruptive potential of self-interest on communal relationships.

The peculiarities of Japanese advanced capitalism reflect the shaping of the economy by distinct cultural or ideological forces. 'Try as one might to avoid terms like "national character" . . . it is clearly national differences in value preferences, or dispositions to action, with which we are concerned' (Dore, 1983, p. 469). Japanese and Western scholars suggest that the Japanese form of Confucianism has produced a 'Confucian capitalist society', which is simply different from the sort of capitalism that emerged in the Christian West (Morishima, 1983). The crucial difference is that Confucianism as an ethical system is collectivist and anti-individualistic. In comparison with Christian doctrines, which do emphasize individuality, the lack of concern with the individual in Confucianism has been explained as a consequence of the absence of a transcendent God: there is no God in relation to which the individual has a special role, no notion of individual equality before God, and no conception of individual salvation in another world (Koschman, 1978; Smith, 1983). Stress on collectivity arises when the sacred is seen as group life and a moral individual as one who grows as a social person. Confucianism teaches 'that the meaning of social life lay not in seeking salvation in another world . . . but in cultivating relationships among members of society built on trust . . . and, above all, a commitment to loyal action on behalf of others' (Nishimura Shigeki, quoted in Smith, 1983, p. 16).

The ramifications of these values are extensive and have been identified in a variety of spheres. J. Victor Koschman (1978) characterizes political culture from the nineteenth century through to the American-inspired, democratic reforms of the postwar constitution as being the expression of two attitudes: the preservation of social harmony, if necessary by repressing conflict, and the lack of a universal conception of individual rights to counter power in hierarchical relations. An ideology that recognized neither conflicts of interest nor rights of individuals had no need, in turn, for a political theory of contract. Koschman argues that traditional attitudes toward authority and conflict, and the status of the individual in relation to political authority, persist today. Robert J. Smith (1983) similarly finds that an emphasis on social harmony rather than individual rights continues to permeate the practice of the legal system, where conciliation is more important than contract mentality, and informs more diffuse cultural values which emphasize obligations to others and the restraint of individual desires. He notes how the structure of language itself downplays individuality, because 'identification of self and other is always indeterminate in the sense that there is no fixed centre from which, in effect, the individual asserts a non-contingent existence' (Smith, 1983, p. 81). Smith suggests that the Japanese *do* have a sense of self, but this individuality is less well formed than in the West, as can be seen by the use of personal references: whereas Western children use 'I' and 'you',

> the Japanese male child . . . by the age of six must master . . . at least six terms of self-reference; girls of that age will employ five. (For persons addressed or referred to . . . both boys and girls regularly use a minimum of fourteen such terms.) Japanese children also use names, kin terms, and place names, but the really striking contrast with the American child's speech habits is that none of the possible options is clearly dominant among Japanese children. With overwhelming frequency they use no self-referent of any kind.
>
> (Smith, 1983, p. 79)

Within the collectivist thrust of Confucian ethics, specific aspects of Japanese Confucianism have proved highly congruent with capitalism. The virtues of benevolence and harmony underpin the groupness and consensus apparently characteristic of the modern economy. Benevolence covers various ideas: that human nature is naturally good; that the affection found among family members should be extended to all; that human nature becomes perfect when suffused with such affection. Harmony is necessary if benevolence is to flourish, and involves individuals being in accord and preserving collective mutuality. Both favour particularism over universalism in human interaction and primary over secondary association: inter-personal mutuality and 'dense' networks of relationships in place of the instrumentality and absolute criteria that characterize many non-familial relationships in Western capitalism. Morishima (1983) suggests that the Japanese emphasize four additional Confucian virtues, namely loyalty (to the state and other superordinate bodies), filial piety, faith toward friends, duty to seniors. Given this ideologi-cal context, it is scarcely surprising that a nationalist-capitalist economy should have arisen, and that it should do so on the basis of welfare corporatism, the subjugation of individualism, perhaps even individuality, to collectivity, and relational contracting within and among corporations. Moreover, Confucianism as a rational and intellectual doctrine that values wisdom and learning is compatible with scientific knowledge. 'Thus a capitalist economy which was managed in an entirely different spirit from English capitalism – an economy combining Japanese soul and Western technology – was set up in Japan' (Morishima, 1983, p. 87).

It is not sufficient merely to show that there is an ideology which has a functional fit with economic practices, however. Two issues remain: whether the ideology has become *dominant* in society and how it may be *effective* in shaping behaviour. We have already cited evidence that Confucianism was dominant among the state and private entrepreneurs who fostered capitalist industrialization in the Meiji period, and that Confucian values shaped their choice of action. Confucianism in the late nineteenth century was, however, an elite value system with little purchase on the mass of the population, proving effective among capitalists but not among labour – witness the problems of labour instability and lack of discipline. Outside the higher strata, Buddhism dominated and was widely regarded among Meiji bureaucrats as promoting moral corruption in the masses (Smith, 1983). The crucial development is widely seen as the creation of a universal system of primary schooling in the 1870s, which covered 98 per cent of the population by 1904, and the decision of state officials to use this for the dissemination of Confucian values among the population at large. The aim of education was to create loyal and obedient subjects – the 1890 imperial rescript on education was known as the *Way of the Subject* – and the paramount purpose of schooling was held to be the development of the correct moral character among children (Dore, 1964). In contrast to the British situation, which we have discussed in *The Dominant Ideology Thesis*, in Japan there has been an ideology at once coherent, dominant, and, so the consensus of scholarly opinion would suggest, effectively transmitted. Thus there is some reason to believe that Japanese values have helped shape its distinctive form of modern capitalism.

Individualism and Changes in Western Capitalism

Individual, exclusive private property places both the ownership of capital and control of its use in the hands of individuals. Individual property of this sort was clearly central to the industrial and financial capitalism found in Britain in the nineteenth and early twentieth centuries, initially with partnership and later with joint-stock capital structures. Family capitalism vested ownership either in the hands of individuals, subdividing the equity, or, through trust arrangements, in the hands of bodies representing families as entities. In either case, individuals were the beneficiaries of capital ownership and, because of the fusion of ownership with management, could determine the use of capital. Since firms were often founded by more than one individual or later received an infusion of capital from non-familial sources, several unrelated partners might share the ownership; thus family capitalism need not imply a simple identity of one familial group with the firm. Individual and family ownership and control were also normal in the USA and Japan during early industrial capitalism.

The tendency in many British and American companies after the First World War was for stock ownership to become more fragmented and dispersed among a wider circle of individuals, with a decline in the position of founding individuals and families from being sole owners, to majority owners, to minority owners and finally, perhaps, to insignificance as owners of a company's stock. The need to raise new capital through issues of equity as companies grew in size, inheritance taxation, and the disinclination of the old owners to have their personal fortunes dependent on the performance of a single company combined to promote this trend. Capital ownership remained individual but was no longer so concentrated. (The tendency in Japan between the wars was to greater family concentration.) The celebrated thesis of a 'managerial revolution' suggested that the fragmentation of ownership would be accompanied by a separation between the ownership and control of capital: as the relative size of single stock holdings in individual companies declined, the multiplicity of minority owners would individually have insufficient stock to control a company's activities and effective control would pass into the hands of management, salaried employees with little or no ownership stake (Berle and Means, 1932; Burnham, 1941). In the event, empirical research conducted in the 1960s and 1970s suggested that such managerial control might prove the exception rather than the rule, since substantial individual minority shareholdings and constellations of interests (a number of minority owners acting jointly) were sufficiently widespread for most large companies *potentially* to be controlled by a section of their stock holders (Scott, 1979; Francis, 1980; Hill, 1981).

Various developments in company ownership and structure have been significant for the relationship of individualism and capitalism. The first concerns the nature of the individual property rights that go with the ownership of a company's stock. Stocks themselves do constitute absolute property that can be freely acquired and alienated. But the property rights of stockholders in public companies in modern Britain are surprisingly limited, the major ones being the right to a revenue when the company's directors declare a dividend, to elect the board, to formulate policy by majority decision at the general meeting of shareholders, so long as a policy resolution does not usurp directors' powers of control, and to wind up or otherwise dispose of the company. Shareholders delegate managerial power to the board of directors and cannot override its discretion, thus they have no say in the appointment of managers or in the determination of how the business is run, except in so far as the need for directors to seek re-election makes them amenable to influence. The directors have fiduciary responsibilities, but they act as trustees for the company and not the individual shareholder. A shareholder has no ownership right in any of the company's assets, which belong to the company as an independent legal entity. Daniel Bell has claimed that, in the American context, 'ownership is a legal fiction', and 'one can treat stockholders not as "owners" but as legitimate claimants to some fixed share of the profits of a corporation – and to nothing more' (Bell, 1974, p. 295).

Not only are property rights restricted, but comparatively few stock owners can exercise even these effectively. For the majority of shareholders, ownership of stock effectively carries only the right to receive a revenue, since the size of investment required to influence board elections in a heavily capitalized company, even when acting in concert with other stockholders, is so great as to rule out all but a few large shareholders. Conversely, where a limited number of substantial shareholders can effectively determine the composition of the board, they may use this influence in ways that are not necessarily in the interests of other holders of stock. (The 1980 Companies Act in Britain has now somewhat improved the remedies available to individual shareholders whose interests are threatened.) Stockholders usually act as investors and *rentiers* of capital rather than as the owners of corporations. They transfer their capital between different shares, and between equities and other forms of investment, with little long-term commitment to any firm or interest in how it is run. An often-heard criticism of investors in Britain and the USA is that they do not exercise their right as owners to replace the board of unsuccessful companies, preferring to sell a company's stock rather than attempt to turn its performance around, and thus share responsibility for unsatisfactory performance.

The second development has been the growing depersonalization of capital ownership in capitalist economies. The tendency is for individuals and families to be superseded by corporate bodies as the major providers and owners of stock. Ownership of the equity of public companies is now highly concentrated in the hands of other companies and financial intermediary institutions such as pension funds, unit and investment trusts, insurance companies. In Britain, individuals owned only about 28 per cent of the shares in publicly quoted companies in 1981, the rest being owned by companies, financial institutions and the state, with the financial institutions alone owning about 55 per cent (Stock Exchange, n.d.). In Japan, individual ownership stood at 29 per cent in 1980, with corporate and financial ownership at 71 per cent (Steven, 1983). In the same period, approximately half of the shares in publicly quoted American companies were owned by individuals and half by institutions (New York Stock Exchange, 1985). At the same time, in all capitalist economies, companies finance the vast majority of their capital requirements without recourse to new equity, either by self-financing out of retained profits or through various forms of borrowing. The financing of borrowing is met overwhelmingly by institutions.

Paradoxically, depersonalization has increased the potential for control by the providers of equity and non-equity capital over the use to which their capital is put. Institutional shareownership has reversed any tendency towards fragmentation of shareholdings, and single institutions or a few acting jointly have substantial minority stakes in a large number of publicly quoted companies. To give one extreme example, the UK's largest insurance company, the Prudential, had holdings of more than 7 per cent in thirty-four of the fifty largest UK industrial companies in 1976–7 (Utton, 1982). The size of equity stake needed to create the potential for control varies with the fragmentation of stockholding and the ability of shareholders to combine. In highly fragmented companies and where shareholders do not act together, as small a holding as 5 per cent may suffice, but in practice a larger proportion is more likely to be required. Equally, the providers of loan capital may demand some say in company policy, even representation on the board.

The actual exercise of control is more difficult to identify. Institutions that hold shares in several thousand companies lack the resources, and probably the capability, routinely to intervene in these companies and prefer to protect their interests simply by selling the shares if they are dissatisfied with performance. However, there have been several publicized cases in Britain during the last twenty years of institutional shareholders replacing boards. It is generally held that such cases are exceptional and institutions prefer to act covertly – by means of informal contacts with company chairmen and through non-executive, external directors acceptable to the institutions, many of whom have multiple directorships – and that their influence is over broad strategy, not detailed application. We might expect the potential control of the institutions to be translated into effective control more often in the future, however, as the changed structure of the equity market now makes it more difficult for large investors simply to disinvest from companies that underperform. Given the magnitude of the institutional holdings, a decision to disinvest runs the risk of flooding the market with a stock and depressing its price. Moreover, when the market for shares is dominated by a limited number of institutions, with professional fund managers sharing similar information and similar investment criteria, it becomes increasingly difficult to find buyers of stock except at bargain prices.

The third development has been the rise of giant corporations and economic concentration in this century, particularly in Britain, the USA and Japan. A characteristic feature of late capitalism is the growth of so-called monopoly capitalism, a term that conveys the change from an economy based on many small units operating in a competitive market, to one where a small number of large firms dominate. The process of concentration in Britain and the USA has been based on companies owning other firms, acquired via merger, takeover or the creation of new subsidiaries, and on diversification into a number of related and unrelated industries (Zeitlin, 1974, 1978; Scott, 1979; Prais, 1981). The British economy, indeed, appears to be among the most highly concentrated of all. By 1976, the largest 100 manufacturing companies accounted for 42 per cent of net output, approximately double the proportion accounted for by the top 100 in 1949. The 200 largest employers accounted for 46 per cent of manufacturing employment in 1972 (Utton, 1979, 1982). The financial sector has become similarly concentrated, with four clearing banks dominating commercial banking, four or five insurance companies accounting for 30–40 per cent of business in that sector, and four unit trusts handling 43 per cent of managed funds in the 1970s (Utton, 1982). While the development of monopoly capitalism has caught the attention of many commentators, there still remains a large number of small and medium sized firms in advanced capitalism – although, by world standards, Britain is unusual in having so few smaller firms in manufacturing (Prais, 1981) – and so some form of dual structure is normal: a restricted number of large corporations, with a high degree of institutional financing, coexisting with a multitude of independent medium and small firms, many owned by individuals and families.

We believe that these developments have significant consequences for the relationship of individualism, specifically individual private property, and capitalism. The first is that modern capitalism functions with a significant amount of private property that is not owned individually or even by families. Indeed, the dominant form of ownership in large-scale capitalism is corporate. We are not claiming that private property no longer has relevance to capitalism, as have recent commentators such as Daniel Bell (1974). Instead, we suggest that capitalism now functions with corporate and not personal private property. Secondly, the rights associated with private property seem somewhat restricted in comparison with the absolute rights thought by many to be constitutive of capitalism, in particular ownership as the right to revenue and not to the physical assets that provide this revenue. Thirdly, there is effectively a separation at least of individual ownership from control: institutional owners may have sufficient ownership power to control a corporation's activities, through their capacity to determine the board, but the vast majority of individual shareholders are too small to have any effective control over the usage of their invested capital. Fourthly, substantial minority owners or organized constellations that can translate potential into effective control are in a position to pursue policies that the majority of owners may not favour.

This analysis of the modern corporation and the changing role of individual private property also informs the concern shown by F. A. Hayek, intellectual heir of the classical English liberal tradition, with the position of the individual in corporate capitalism. He is taxed by modern developments, because, following John Locke and Adam Smith, the core of his philosophy is that the institution of individual private property is the guarantor of personal liberty and individualism; thus he abhors anything that weakens this institution. He suggests various legal remedies to restore the full property rights of individuals (1967). The first is that the individual should have a legally enforceable claim to his or her share in the *whole* surplus of the corporation, instead of the existing situation where a majority of stockholders (acting on the advice of the management) decides for all what part of the net profits will be reinvested in the corporation and what part will be distributed. He implies, moreover, that it is bizarre to give a legal person (the corporation) the property rights of a natural person, because this 'turns the institution of property into something quite different from what it is normally supposed to be' (p. 309). A consequence is to give corporate institutions voting rights in other corporations in which they own shares, which is clearly

> contrary to . . . the conceptions on which the system of private property rests – an artificial separation of ownership and control which may place the individual owner in the position where his capital is used for purposes conflicting with his own and without his even being able to ascertain who, in fact, possesses the majority of votes. With the grant of voting rights to corporate stockholders the general presumption that the corporation will be run by persons whose interests are the same as those of the individual stockholder is no longer valid.
>
> (Hayek, 1967, p. 310)

His second remedy, therefore, is to deny voting rights to corporate holders of stock, while allowing corporate stockholding simply as investment.

The new gigantism of individual companies that have expanded and diversified and the retreat of owners from direct, day-to-day control of their property have, as is well known, produced a cadre of professional managers who perform many of the functions that were previously done by capitalists. While the 'managerial revolution' and its implications for control and private property have continued to absorb commentators, the joint effects of size and the decoupling of ownership from administration on the internal organization of enterprises have attracted less attention recently. The transformation of older organizational arrangements into corporate bureaucracies is the fourth important development in company ownership and structure. This was of great concern to earlier generations of sociologists, precisely because of its implications for the individual. We shall elaborate below what we see as the positive dysfunctionality of individualism for the effective bureaucratic organization of large capitalist enterprises. What we wish to note here is that changes in business organization have elevated conformity to rules, deference and obedience to superiors, custodianship of other people's property, and collective organization instead of individual autonomy, so creating bureaucratic organizations that are authoritarian and constrain individualism. The currently decentralized, multi-divisional (M-form) structure of major British and American companies fragments the solid uniformity of these giant monoliths and allows for a diversity of semi-autonomous subsidiary organizations. But the modification of unitary (U-form) companies into multi-divisional profit centres, although it may have partly de-bureaucratized the giant company, has not reversed bureaucratic organization within the divisions, many of which are still huge and complex organizations by historical standards and depend on formalized bureaucratic procedures. Whereas individual autonomy and entrepreneurial creativity may have fitted the smaller, less differentiated, proprietorially managed firms of early capitalism, such individualistic traits bear no obvious functional relationship to the organizational forms typical of more recent capitalism.

There has been a pervasive theme in analyses of the modern world, that suggests we have witnessed the growth of an administered society that constrains the individual. The bureaucratization of business enterprises is but one element in this broader development, which led Weber to his pessimism about the future of individual autonomy in a society where the state and bureaucracy became increasingly dominant. While capitalism ostensibly requires free markets in which untrammelled individuals act according to their own utilities, in practice it also seeks the stability of decision-making and reliability of procedure that modern bureaucracies make possible. The market context of capitalism requires state intervention to provide a secure environment. In particular, capitalism requires rational law and state administration. Weber's view that modern life would be dominated by bureaucratic processes and the growing reach of the state has been echoed by subsequent German sociologists, and the notion of the administered society is dominant among critical theorists (Jay, 1984). The roles of the modern state in the economy and local government in urban life point to the power of supra-individual agencies to override individual property rights in the interests of wider collective goods.

With the growth of highly organized and centralized enterprises in

138

societies where the state plays a crucial role in the development of the economy, it is increasingly obvious that the concept of the self-reliant economic individual in the tradition of Robinson Crusoe no longer relates to or reflects the underlying economic and political development of modern capitalism. Although there is much talk about the decline of the economic role of the state as Keynesian economics are superseded by the monetarism of economists such as Milton Friedman, in reality the state becomes the necessary feature of all modern economies and those societies with monetarist policies have in practice to rely extensively on state intervention (Samuelson, 1965). Economy and society are complex structures that simply cannot depend on the force of individual utilities for their integration and direction. Hence the recognition that individualistic practices do not constitute the dominant organizing principle of modern economy and society, even if ideologies of individualism claim that they do.

We have argued that the functional relationship between capitalism and individualism has become unstuck. Now we wish to go further, to show how the values and practices of individualism may actually hinder profitable accumulation and prove positively dysfunctional for the contemporary organization of large-scale corporate capitalism.

The rise of Japanese manufactures to pre-eminence, the inability of American industry to match Japanese levels of productivity growth and product quality, and the fact that every dollar invested in Japanese industry produces greater added value than a dollar invested in the USA have led to considerable reflection during the last fifteen years on why US capitalism proves less effective than Japanese (see the vast literature cited in Sethi *et al.*, 1984). Several factors are cited, which include the more effective role of the Japanese state and the higher level of investment. What is relevant here, however, is the realization that Americans have also been less efficient at organizing large-scale capitalist enterprises. This inefficiency results from the practices and values of management, and the root cause of the problem is individualism. The American inheritance of the English doctrine of individualism proved highly congruent with the proprietorially managed capitalism of small and medium-sized enterprises in the nineteenth century. American values emphasized self-determination, self-fulfilment, self-reliance

139

and self-discipline; the primacy of individual interests and rights rather than duties; the equality of individuals and the consequential right to participative government; a hard-nosed materialism that defined individual utility as private prosperity; the sanctity of individual property rights; the pursuit of self-interest in aggressive competition with others (Sethi *et al.*, 1984; Cochran, 1985). Sometimes it is said that it is the corruption of traditional values that causes contemporary problems; for example, that self-determination and fulfilment were compatible with capitalism so long as they were tempered by self-discipline, whereas now they have degenerated into pure hedonism. Significantly, however, even in the nineteenth century when the values were presumably pristine, observers of American business pointed to the unsuitability of Americans, imbued with individualism, for managing others' property and running large corporations. H. V. Poor in mid-century and Andrew Carnegie at the turn of the century described big business as in effect alien to American values (Cochran, 1985).

The large-scale and complex divisions of labour found in modern corporations require well-co-ordinated, co-operative social organizations that are geared to realize supra-individual, corporate objectives. Moreover, the future viability of any company requires long-term planning, even at the cost of immediate gains. The problem is that the orientations and practices of the individuals who staff these enterprises tend to be atomistic, competitive and self-serving with a short time-horizon.

One often-noted difference between American and Japanese companies is that US management have a perspective that concentrates on the next set of corporate results, whereas the Japanese have time-horizons stretching years into the future and will accept low profits now in anticipation of what will come later. The willingness to defer gratification and forgo immediate reward is, of course, supposed to be one of the key indicators of capitalist rationality and an essential ingredient of the Protestant Ethic. The apparent failure of American corporate management to give priority to the long-term interests of capital may be variously accounted for. Explanations include: pressure from shareholders who, because they are more *rentiers* than owners, expect good dividends every quarter or half year; payment-by-result schemes for individual managers that reward immediate results; a competitive, individual career system and high rates of job mobility among managers, which ensure that self-interested individuals have a vested interest in short-term 'success' irrespective of the long-term consequences of their actions; a disinterest in the future of the corporation among individuals whose personal career paths are likely to take them to other firms.

Bureaucratization does not fit easily with individualistic values, as we noted above, yet paradoxically it is intensified by individualism. The modern form of the bureaucratic vicious circle rests on two characteristics of individualism. First, employee mobility will be high when a free labour market works within a cultural environment that elevates the purposeful pursuit of individual utility in the form of material rewards, and treats employment as an instrumental and specific, not diffuse, contractual relationship that continues only until a better opportunity occurs elsewhere. It has been claimed that the average US manufacturing company in 1980 lost 4 per cent of its employees each month (Cochran, 1985). Large corporations may try to bind certain key lower-level workers in various ways (Edwards, 1979), but less effort is made to incorporate other employees. The second characteristic is the need to build a co-ordinated social organization, one in which the people assigned to different parts of the division of labour co-operate effectively and harmoniously with each other, out of human resources that have been trained to compete rather than to co-operate and to pursue private rather than corporate interests. Bureaucratic rules and regulations therefore become essential. This is so because detailed and formal role definitions are required when employee turnover is high, with the result that organization cannot be maintained on the basis of an internalized corporate culture and knowledge learnt on the job. Such roles are especially necessary, moreover, to promote co-operation among self-serving competitors.

It might be anticipated that various and considerable costs will follow from this mismatch of individualism and the requirements of a rational capitalism. Employee mobility and the lack of long-term corporate horizons stand in the way of systematic in-company training. Hence US corporations tend to buy skills on the external market and neglect the training of their existing employees (Sethi *et al.*, 1984). The administration of a large volume of recruitment and severance is clearly expensive, while companies incur additional but less visible costs as long as employees are not fully effective because they have not yet reached the tops of their learning curves. Companies are preoccupied with devising structures that will motivate

141

employees by rewarding individual performance. Hence the time and expense lavished on defining and evaluating jobs, evaluating performance, and then finding appropriate systems to match performance and payment. Control systems cannot rely on the force of internalized social and corporate values. Instead, they have to be designed to regulate and motivate managerial employees and others whose commitment to and involvement in the corporation are unreliable. The elaboration of formal procedures and the surveillance or monitoring of performance consume time and corporate resources. Decisions taken by individuals in an environment of competition with others, and where the decision-takers are individually rewarded or penalized according to the outcome, do not benefit from the wider pool of knowledge and judgement possessed by the corporation, and to that extent are less than optimal. Individualism, moreover, seems to produce a specialized labour force rather than employees with a general competence. This can be explained partly as the result of individual strategies to maximize utility and minimize dependence through the market, where specialist knowledge is more easily assessed than a general competence, and partly because individualism fosters the conception that people have property rights in particular jobs. The result is an excessive specialization and technicism among managers, which impedes a global view of a company's interests and a collective corporate culture (Sethi *et al.*, 1984). We might also add, in this regard, the resistance among workers to job flexibility.

Individual success in bureaucracies involves diligence, judgement, obedience to rules, acceptance of authority and subordination of the self to collective organization. The first two principles are compatible with individualism, but the others are incongruous with autonomy, equality and self-reliance. A combination of controls and material inducements has always managed to reconcile the discontinuity at a reasonable level of efficiency. It is only with the realization that the US economy now consistently under-performs the Japanese – indeed, it is now clear that since 1850 it has also performed less well than a number of other capitalist economies, when measured by annual rates of increase in *per capita* income (Cochran, 1985) – that the appropriateness of the structure of US business to efficient capitalism has widely been questioned. Some suggest the wholesale adoption of Japanese practices: W. G. Ouchi (1981), for example, advocates replacing the hierarchy and rigid rules of bureaucracy with a shared corporate culture that will create employee commitment and foster trust, co-operation and involvement, and new working relationships that prevent rivalry and competition. Others suggest redesigning the organizations to increase their fit with individualism rather than trying to eradicate individualism, arguing for further decentralization, the maintenance of performance-based individual rewards but a change in the criteria to promote the long-term value of capital, or the extension of arrangements such as franchising that retain scale economies while allowing individual initiative to flourish (Sethi *et al.*, 1984; Cochran, 1985).

Individualism: From Optimism to Pessimism

Our discussion of individualism prior to the twentieth century focused mainly on English society. We should also be aware of the development of individualism in the settler capitalism of the eighteenth and nineteenth centuries (Denoon, 1983). In the colonial, plantation and pastoralist societies of the then global periphery (Canada, America, South Australia, Southern Africa and New Zealand) there was relatively little restriction on political and social activity, and individuals could expand in a geographical space which was wholly uninhabited. It was in these societies that the frontier thesis of Frederick Jackson Turner had its greatest relevance. Turner's argument in *The Frontier in American History* (1920) was that the special circumstances of a frontier environment encouraged and required an individualism of self-reliance. This brand of individualism celebrated the autonomy and activism of the isolated individual who could not call upon social or political supports in an environment that was essentially threatening and dangerous. It was this self-reliant individualism that gave rise to a society based upon the six-shooter and barbed-wire. It may even be the case that individualism in these circumstances could acquire a distinctive set of characteristics, somewhat separate and distinct from the individualism of the established urban industrial capitalist societies. In the Australian context, it was this frontier mentality which gave rise to the peculiar male version of individualism, 'ockerism' and mateship, which celebrated simultaneously the virtues of male social support and rugged individualism that were essentially anti-authoritarian (Spearitt and Walker, 1979). In America, it has been suggested that this frontier individualism, which was based upon private land-ownership and self-reliance, has been gradually replaced by a different form of 'individualism', which emphasizes self-expression rather than political autonomy (Potter, 1965). These differences, between aggressive self-reliant individualism and non-conformist dissenting modifications, may be associated with David Riesman's distinction between other-directed and inner-directed individualism (1954), that is, individualism and individuality.

Whether we are talking about the wide open spaces of America and Australia or about the competitive rigour of early English capitalism, there is some agreement that the early, self-reliant forms of individualism are no longer relevant to modern society, and indeed may be incompatible with it. There are indications in the literature that the character of Western, specifically English-inspired, individualism may have changed, as individual and family capitalism declines, as the state intervenes significantly in social and economic life, as the market place is increasingly organized by large and multinational corporations, and as much of the old ideology of unrestrained capitalist expansion is brought into question by Keynesian economic principles. The result is a growing pessimism about the autonomy and authenticity of the individual in modern capitalism.

Within a variety of traditions, the nature and location of the individual in modern societies have been questioned. In the 1920s, writers such as John Dewey were beginning to ask whether the traditional individual of American society could survive the growing corporate structure of society (Dewey, 1962). In the 1950s, W. H. Whyte expressed concern that 'organization man' would lose his individual characteristics and adapt his personality to fit the bureaucratic organizational environment (Whyte, 1956) – a paradoxical reversal of the previous and subsequent view that the capitalist corporation has been weakened by the organizational recalcitrance of individualism. The implication of David Riesman's essays on individualism was that the modern individual is increasingly dependent upon public evaluation and social inspection in a society where the urban context of organization man rendered individuality increasingly unlikely (Riesman, 1954). To some extent these inquiries went back to the view of Alexis de Tocqueville (1835), that the levelling impact of democratic American culture resulted in a crushing conformity to central institutions, where individual opinion and autonomy had little role to play. Other writers have taken up this theme, that the false community of public life in modern societies results in an artificial set of affectual relations between people, which are couched in the language of intimacy but which in fact deaden and stultify individuality (Sennett, 1974). These perspectives on the social space of modern societies often derive their inspiration from the work of Rousseau, who thought that the social pressures of modern society would corrupt the authenticity of the individual (Berman, 1971). Although much inspiration has been derived from writers such as de Tocqueville and Rousseau, we appear to need a more modern framework for the analysis of the problem of individualism and individuation which does not rest parasitically upon these classical sources.

We should also recognize that these new conceptualizations of the individual also reflect very important changes of mood and orientation to modern society: namely, they represent a fundamental shift towards a more pessimistic and nihilistic viewpoint. The shift from rugged individualism to the emphasis on the embattled dissenting individual in a bureaucratic world also represents a shift from optimism to pessimism. The rugged individual of competitive capitalism expressed the view that the individual could impose some sort of order and direction on society and history, whereas the doubting and crisis-ridden individual of the administered society reflects a much more decisively negative and pessimistic view of the individual in society and the future prospects of a social order based upon centralized control. The widely heralded disappearance of the subject in modern structuralist thought would be one indicator of this shift, as would the debate on the so-called narcissistic personality of the modern time (Lasch, 1980). A wide variety of pressures seems therefore to bear down upon the modern individual: centralized bureaucratic regulation, the exposed and anonymous environment of towns and suburbs, modern technology, the loss of a protective family or kinship environment, and the growing scale and complexity of modern economic and political relations.

It is normally held that classical individualism in the liberal tradition was essentially optimistic and positive as a critique of existing traditions and a celebration of the freedom of the economic individual in the market place. Individualism from Hobbes to Locke had an expansionary and confident view of human achievements and potentialities (Sabine, 1964). This confident individualism had a

145

number of dimensions. It was closely associated with the rationalist tradition, which saw human beings emerging out of the dark age of magic and superstition and the rational individual as a new force who would shape society to enhance liberal values. It enshrined rational procedures and atheistic optimism. Optimistic individualism also embraced an empiricist epistemology, which broadly proclaimed that what can be seen and experienced exists. Empiricism and rationalism formed an emancipatory creed. In the English context, adherence to Bacon's programme of science was seen to be part of the liberation of the individual from the trammels of conventional assumptions. In the political sphere the new individualism was associated with the confident belief that constitutionalism would guarantee the autonomy and freedom of the individual against tyranny. This political confidence was expressed primarily in the doctrine of checks and balances, which grew out of the English political experience. Finally, in economic arrangements, it was assumed that the struggle of individual wills on the market place would lead ultimately and inevitably to economic accumulation and that the so-called Invisible Hand would resolve any unfortunate conflicts in society that emerged from this competitive struggle. Although this characterization summarizes the consensus over the character of seventeenth and eighteenth century individualism, it must be noted that Sheldon Wolin (1961) has argued that even classical liberalism was suffused with anxiety, lacking confidence in economic growth and believing that pain was more likely than pleasure. Wolin's views in this area are interesting, but distinctly in a minority. Even anxious man in the eighteenth century does not come near the level of nihilism and neuroticism that characterize the twentieth century.

In the second half of the nineteenth century we can see a gradual change in the constitution of liberal individualism, a change that heralded a more pessimistic view of the future of the individual. In *Utilitarianism*, J. S. Mill modified Bentham's moral theory, to show that self-interest as a criterion could not provide an adequate understanding of moral actions. Mill was unconvinced that the educational theories of his father and Bentham were capable in practice of producing a happy and self-confident individual. Mill clearly had great anxiety about the underlying theoretical structure of utilitarian individualism. He was equally anxious about the impact of mass democracy on the autonomy and authenticity of the individual, and thought that without safeguards the enfranchisement of the working class would undermine the liberty of the individual. Thus Mill brought into the British debate the same uncertainties about democracy that were present in the work of Alexis de Tocqueville. In the sociology of Herbert Spencer, we find the classical dilemma of defending a laissez-faire principle in a society where social regulation was becoming increasingly obvious. Although Spencer had confidently predicted a shift from militarism to industrialism, in which free market principles would be dominant, by the end of his life he lived in a society where there was a significant growth in the scale of the professional civil service, the development of compulsory primary education, the origins of a welfare state, the beginnings of working-class trade unionism and finally an increasing dominance of the state in the economy. In addition, Britain was involved in the scramble for overseas colonies, which necessitated re-armament and was associated with a new nationalism and militarism (Peel, 1971).

On the Continent, there were also developments which pointed towards a departure from the normal canons of science based upon rationalism and empiricism. The emergence of Freudian psychoanalysis emphasized the crucial role of the unconscious and irrational forces in human mental activity. In his interpretation of dreams, Sigmund Freud rediscovered a dimension of human activity that had been largely neglected by the traditional forms of science. Although Freud still adhered to a conventional neurological perspective, which emphasized a natural science model of energy, Freud's theories and methods challenged traditional forms of rationalism. Freud's psychoanalytical approach should be put alongside a number of other developments by writers such as Adler and Jung, who also gave a greater emphasis to imagination, sexuality and mythology in human life. In Britain, the work of Havelock Ellis helped to transform attitudes towards sexual behaviour at a popular level, with consequences which were to some extent compatible with the Freudian tradition (Grosskurth, 1980). All these models of human behaviour in various ways indicated a new awareness of the irrational or at least the non-rational forces that governed human life. We can detect similar cultural forces working through art and music, which express the same awareness that the old model of rationality was not wholly adequate to grasp human existence, especially those features of human existence characterized by the imagination, by feeling and sentiment. For example, in poetry, in the movement that may be broadly called the new symbolism, there was a growing awareness of the importance of myth, of imagination, of symbol in human experience (Bowra, 1959).

From about 1870, European sociology also attempted to come to terms with the new issues that dominated Freudian psychology and symbolic poetry, namely the role of the irrational in the life of the individual and the place of mythology in the organization of society as a whole. The central tradition of French sociology had been its commitment to a rational science of society, based upon an empiricist model of man. Writers such as Comte and Saint-Simon were confident in proclaiming the positive benefits of the new science of sociology, and their commitment to a model of rational individuals had been inherited by subsequent generations of sociologists. It is widely agreed that Pareto probably represented the high-water-mark of this confidence in rational science, empirical methods and the centrality of reason and self-interest (Parsons, 1937). In his classic study of European sociology in the 1890s, Stuart Hughes has argued, however, that confidence in the positivist framework, and with it a confidence in the rational self-interest of the individual, began to break down under the impact of Croce, Sorel, Bergson and Freud (Hughes, 1959). The main theorists of sociology in the 1890s were thus brought to a new confrontation with the problem of the irrational in human life, the impact of group structures on the individual, the role of ideology and mythology, and the survival of religion in an apparently secular and industrial culture. This move towards an appreciation of group and social forces on the individual, combined with an evaluation of the importance of religion and mythology, was represented by Durkheim's special interest in totemism and religion, by Weber's enquiries into the role of religion in capitalism and science, and by the role of ideal forces in history in the work of Troeltsch and Croce.

Privacy and the Individual

Privacy is typically associated with individualism in the modern world, and is seen as the natural social space within which the individual can be cultivated, free of constant interference from the wider society. The meaning of privacy, however, has changed considerably over time. In the ancient world, privacy was associated with privation and deprivation, being the domestic world of women and removed from the rational and fulfilling world of public activity. The citizen of ancient civilization did not look towards the private as an elevating and ennobling social space, but saw it rather as an undermining and diminution of genuine, rational social relations (Arendt, 1959; Lukes, 1973). It is in contemporary Western industrial society that privacy is elevated to a desirable moral condition, and is regarded as essential for self-development. While privacy in modern society is seen to be threatened by the intervention of the state via new technologies of surveillance and communication, it is important to bear in mind that there was much greater invasion of privacy in many pre-modern societies. In his study of colonial America, Flaherty (1972) reminds us that in puritanical New England there was extensive and regular surveillance of the population and private life was systematically scrutinized in order to rid the community of personal evil. The Puritan Fathers exercised a patriarchal control over society, interfering with all features of domestic life. Within this perspective, we can argue that surveillance of individuals has now moved from localized surveillance by intimates and equals to centralized investigation by anonymous superiors. Thus, in colonial times, control in America was on a local face-to-face basis, while the detailed surveillance of modern systems is the product of a variety of changes but in particular the growth of welfare states and advances in technology relating to the storage of information (Shils, 1975).

The capacity for storing information and for monitoring the behaviour of citizens made possible by new technology is often thought to be a serious threat to democracy and individual freedom (Westin, 1967). The growth of data banks and other systems of information storage is perceived to be incompatible with genuine individuality (Kaplan, 1970). There has been considerable debate and anxiety within the social sciences about the involvement of social scientists in the study of large populations under the auspices of the state (Barnes, 1979; Bulmer, 1979). The components of this new surveillance of the individual are usefully outlined in *The Politics of Privacy* (Rule *et al.*, 1980). In advanced industrial societies there has been a great increase in the registration and certification of vital events by the use of census and surveys. This involves the full registration of births, deaths and marriages, as well as other features of human mortality and morbidity. Secondly, there

149

has been an extensive development of the passport as a crucial personal document which, with the birth and death certificate, identifies an individual. With the development of individual motorized transport has come the driver's licence, which may also act as an identity card. In America, there are approximately one hundred and thirty-seven million licensed drivers and the driver's licence provides a suitable system of monitoring this large population. Recent developments in consumerism, the consumer credit-card and the growth of credit unions, have also greatly extended investigation into individual creditworthiness by monitoring individual debt. There has been an extensive development of public and private systems of insurance, which also require investigation of individual health and worthiness. Another interesting development in the American context is the expansion of the Federal Bureau of Investigation, which started in 1908 and now maintains the fingerprint records of some sixty-three million people. As well as the development of consumerism, insurance and credit-cards, we can note another important development in personal record-keeping through the growth of income tax registration. We might also consider the growth of the social security system as a further form of individual documentation. The net effect of all of these cross-linking systems is the growth of a systematic, anonymous and effective system of surveillance.

The response to these developments in social science and in literature is typically negative and apprehensive. Data banks and information systems are seen to be a feature of political centralization and potential authoritarianism, whereby the individual can no longer escape from the control of the state. Sinister alliances are alleged between the police, welfare agencies, commercial companies offering consumer credit and the general apparatus of the state, whereby the individual is left with virtually no protection from inquiry and scrutiny. The illegitimate use of electronic surveillance devices has further added to public anxiety about individual autonomy and freedom in a mass democracy. These changes in the nature of the relationship between the state and the individual would appear to bear out and confirm Weber's diagnosis that we have entered the iron cage of bureaucratic domination. However, the situation is more contradictory and more paradoxical than this simple analysis would suggest. The growth of bureaucratic regulation of the individual must also be seen in part as the outcome of a struggle for social rights on the part of citizens who seek to protect themselves from the inequalities emerging from the market place. Thus the pressure for social rights, which leads to the quest for equal treatment and the equal treatment of citizens, is one reason for the growth of census material and social survey investigations. The pressures towards the growth of an information society are usefully summarized by Edward Shils (1975) in his essay 'Privacy and power', where he notes that the transformation of modern society and the need for greater information on human populations have emerged out of the increased aspirations of the citizenry, the development of more effective administrative capacities, the improvement of the economic basis of society, a new conception of authority and the relationship between the state and the individual and, finally, the disappearance of the traditional liberal state, which did not intervene in the economy. There is something of a contradictory relationship, therefore, between the classical notion of the private individual and the growth of citizenship rights through popular struggles in the development of Western democracy.

We should also briefly note another apparently contradictory pressure. We have argued that modern society can represent an invasion of the area within which people are free to act: an invasion of private rights. There is also a sense in which it can be argued that modern capitalist societies *create* a private sphere into which people can withdraw, a private sphere consisting essentially of the family and ultimately of the self and subjectivity. There is no essential contradiction here, but rather two moments of the same process. There is a progressive erosion of the area of liberty and a corresponding retreat into what private world is left.

So far, we have argued that modern society may *de facto* represent a limitation of the scope of individual subjects. Capitalism no longer works through the individual subject. There is, in a related process, greater intervention by the state and greater bureaucratic domination, which results in greater supervision of subjects, decreased privacy yet increased withdrawal into a private family world. That this is a process full of paradox and contradiction we have already noted. We see that the very process that we have called the Discovery of the Individual not only gives importance to individuals, it also makes it meaningful to tell individuals apart, to identify them, to register them and ultimately to control them; the uniqueness of the individual is his or her subordination. At the most fundamental level, the importance, and even dignity, of individuals is conveyed by giving them names, but the custom of unique names gives the state a powerful means of control. We propose to call the process of control by individual identification *individuation*. We have noted that the growth of the state apparatus may derive from those very pressures that originally produced individual citizenship. It is to this latter issue that we now turn.

Democracy, Individuation and the Citizen

We have seen that the Weberian criticism of capitalism leads to a particularly pessimistic view of the outcome of the bureaucratic tendencies inside rational capitalism. Weber's pessimistic view of capitalism was encapsulated in the notion of an iron cage, which bound the individual to a life of mediocre uniformity. For Weber, the individualistic aspects of capitalism were overwhelmed ultimately by the effects of bureaucracy, which led to individuation. However, other perspectives on capitalism tend to lead to equally pessimistic and uniform conclusions. For example, most Marxist criticisms of capitalism emphasize the effects of rational factory management on the individual through the notion of Taylorism, which brings about an equally uniform standardization of the person. In addition, Marxism also emphasizes the role of dominant ideologies in incorporating the working class and the role of consumerism and the mass media in domesticating the individual in a capitalist environment. For Marxism, everything appears to point towards compliance to the system. Similarly, in structuralist criticisms of contemporary capitalism, there is the notion that the dominant discourses of capitalism bring about an equally uniform standardization of individuals and their subordination to the dominant processes of capitalist systems. Many trends in Western thought, therefore, point towards fairly consensual conclusions: namely, that capitalism and individualism are incompatible and that capitalism in combination with bureaucracy produces an individuation of persons.

Our previous work has pointed to the improbability of total working-class incorporation inside capitalism, an argument which could be extended to suggest that, paradoxically, capitalism creates simultaneously conditions for subordination and conditions for opposition. For example, in so far as capitalism requires an educated working class (however minimal that education may be) it also creates a situation where workers can read oppositional literature. Rather than seeing bureaucracy as uniformly a system of domination through surveillance, we might see bureaucratic regulation of populations as the unintended outcome of popular struggle for equality and social rights. In short, individuation may not be necessarily the consequence of bureaucratic surveillance but an unintended feature of the search for equity as an outcome of struggles for general rights of citizenship.

Marx was critical of the notion of social rights because he assumed that such rights simply disguised the real exploitation of people in a capitalist system. For him, the worker was free to be exploited and equal only in the sense of being equally exposed to market forces. This view of bourgeois rights has been especially influential in left-wing traditions, which see these rights of citizens as merely reformism, permitting capitalism to continue functioning as an exploitative system. This view of citizenship rules out successful struggles inside capitalism for a more equitable distribution of resources. This interpretation precludes by definition any possible change in capitalism that would be advantageous to the worker. There are strong arguments for suggesting that citizenship is potentially incompatible with capitalist accumulation, for to deny this possibility would be to ignore struggles and opposition inside capitalism. Marx, by contrast, saw the benefits of reformism. He regarded the factory legislation of the nineteenth century as a definite triumph of the working class against exploitation, in that it limited the freedom of the employer to extract labour from workers in an uninhibited way.

More recent theories of citizenship have addressed themselves specifically to this question of social rights in relation to class inequality. As we have noted in Chapter 4, T. H. Marshall divided citizenship rights into three elements: namely, civil, political and social. These three elements of citizenship correspond to three orders of institution: the courts of justice, parliament and the welfare system. Within a historical framework, civil elements of citizenship were developed before the nineteenth century and it was only as the outcome of social class struggles that social rights emerged significantly towards the end of the nineteenth century. Marshall was perfectly aware that the possession of formal rights of citizenship, namely, the bourgeois liberties and rights of the private

153

person, was relatively insignificant as a check on capitalist control and exploitation of the worker. The social rights developed in the twentieth century far exceed such limited freedoms, however, and cannot be disregarded as unimportant or as mere reformism which changes little. Marshall correctly pointed to the contradiction of class and citizenship within democratic capitalist formations: he argued that there was a contradiction between the inequalities of class relations, which emerged directly from the capitalist economy, and citizenship, which arose out of a popular struggle against the inequalities of the market place. There are good theoretical and political reasons for regarding the relationship between citizenship and class as an open-ended struggle, which on occasions may lead to an enhancement of individual rights and under other circumstances to a diminution of welfare and other entitlements, as Marshall himself recognized. In the modern period, this struggle takes the form of an economic conflict between the principles outlined by Keynes and those adopted more recently by monetarists. Thus, the economic downturn of the 1980s has produced an erosion of rights previously achieved in the postwar period. Much of the debate about citizenship, therefore, is closely tied up with debates about inflation, political institutions, and the possibility of change inside capitalism which is of a beneficial and progressive nature (Hirsch and Goldthorpe, 1978).

At this stage we are less concerned with the debate about citizenship and more interested in the paradoxical relationship between the individual and individuation. Pessimistic theories of capitalism tend to see individuation as the inevitable outcome of either capitalist requirements *per se* or capitalism and bureaucracy in combination. However, we can also see individuation as the outcome of pressures for equity and equal access to resources in the light of the struggle for citizenship rights against capitalism. The requirement to treat all citizens equally, irrespective of their particular and peculiar features, leads towards individuation. Rather than seeing passports, insurance numbers, consumer credit-cards and other features of regimentation as inevitably forms of surveillance and domination, we can see such standardization of persons in a more positive light: namely, as unavoidable consequences of the requirement to treat people equally. It was for this reason that Weber saw there was little to choose between socialism and late capitalism: there was in both a commitment, however formal, to a universalistic notion of egalitarian rights.

154

The tendency towards universalism, away from particularism, is clearly characteristic of modern Western societies. Talcott Parsons (1963) saw this in part as a product of the Christian tradition, while Marx and his followers saw it as part of the revolutionary nature of the capitalist mode of production. In this section we have suggested that popular struggles for social rights also tend to promote universalistic standards of social welfare. These in turn give rise to the need for a centralized bureaucratic control and regulation of such rights. These processes of centralized regulation of rights tend to push society towards an individuation of persons on the basis of bureaucratic standards and regulations, which are seen to be somewhat in opposition to individualism. We should see such processes as essentially double-edged and paradoxical, since individuation means both freedom from particular constraints but also greater opportunities for surveillance and control on the part of a centralized state. Individuation, by enhancing the rights of the individual, leads to greater surveillance and control of large populations.

Contemporary Culture and Discourses of the Individual

Discourses of the individual change in reaction to the changes in the place given to the individual in Western societies. There are three, closely connected elements in this reaction. First, the loss of dominance of any one discourse makes possible the development of a plurality of discourses, competing with one another but without any powerful social purchase. Secondly, individual discourses are now oppositional. While, in the nineteenth century, individualism appeared to be a confident and secure discourse, in the twentieth century it has become oppositional, even wingeing. Last, in part as a result of a common opposition to the degradation of the individual, discourses that previously were easily separable become fused; they form discursive alliances. To illustrate these points, we now look at the discourses of individualism and individuality in the twentieth century.

Individualism in Popular Culture

As many have pointed out, individualism is characteristic of many popular fictions. Several otherwise rather different genres (for example, science fiction, thrillers and westerns) are organized around the activities of an individualistic hero. In the western, a common plot shows the hero riding into town or into the homestead. He is alone, unattached and apparently has no roots, for he is a wanderer and we do not know where he has come from and, indeed, that does not matter particularly for the course of the plot. The society into which he comes is under threat from the activities of a villain, or more usually, of a group of villains. This threat could stem from the greed of a local landowner who wishes to force small farmers off their land (as in *Shane*) or, perhaps, from the desire for revenge on the part of a group of outlaws who want to terrorize a township (as in *High Noon*). Whatever the nature or source of the threat, the main point is that the members of society, townspeople or homesteaders, are unable to deal with it themselves; however apparently determined some individuals are, in the end they are supine and weak. Collective organization is shown not to work. The society may try to organize to protect itself at the beginning, but this collective form of self-defence soon collapses before the force exercised by the villains. Society's protection is seen to lie, not in collective self-defence, but in employing the talents of an individualistic hero who is willing to take on the numerically superior villains with some (rather minimal) support from the members. After many vicissitudes, the hero wins in his struggle with the villains, not by arbitrary or unplanned action but by the rational use of superior skill and cunning and by the capacity to take swift, independent action. After the struggle is over, the hero can either lose the unattached quality, so important to the construction of individualistic heroism, perhaps by marrying the schoolmarm and being absorbed into society, or can reassert his essential autonomy by returning to the unknown wilds whence he came in the first place.

The triangular relationship of society–villain–hero is characteristic of many forms of popular culture and there are several different ways of demonstrating the individualism of the hero. For example, in many adventure stories or thrillers, the hero is not only counterposed to a villain, he is also shown acting individualistically with respect to a bureaucracy, which is seen as necessarily repressive of individual qualities. Sometimes bureaucracy and villainy are one. James Bond, for example, is an individualistic hero in that he is unattached emotionally and free to act, and imposes his will on the world (on a very large scale). His capacity for independent action is contrasted with the villain, who is crushingly bureaucratic, attempting to achieve his ends by means of an enormous organization and meticulous planning. The relationship between individualism and bureaucracy is counterpointed and modified by Bond's relationship with his own organization and his immediate superior, M. Bond is frequently seen as the determined individualist within the organization. He breaks rules, is flamboyant when the norm is dignified reserve, makes jokes about others' obedience to bureaucratic rules, and frequently behaves childishly, almost as if the constraints of formal behaviour were too much. Yet, at the same time, Bond is also definitely within an organization. He is licensed to kill and his adventures are set in motion by his being given a task by the bureaucracy. Bond's starting point is bureaucratically defined, even if he is then free to use his initiative.

In general, then, both genres of popular fiction celebrate individualism via the activities of a hero who operates in a world where people apparently are unable to act for themselves. These stories are more like tales, and specifically fairy tales, being arranged as a series of oppositions of qualities or characters. In the Bond stories, for example, the narrative structure can be seen partly in terms of oppositions between Bond and villain, initiative and bureaucracy, Bond and M. In westerns, there are structuring oppositions between the hero and society, society and villain and villain and hero. The aggregate of these oppositions creates an individualistic hero and the relative crudity of the tales makes the individualism particularly obvious. To take these points further we now turn to a more detailed account of individualism in science fiction.

Individualism in Science Fiction

One of the most common plots in science fiction revolves around a hero who is instrumental in altering the existing social arrangements and substituting new and better ones. These existing arrangements are characterized as repressive, denying individuality and suppressing human freedom. They are, in fact, repressive in many different ways. Straightforward physical force may be used by the rulers to dominate the ruled, or there may be more subtle manipulations, like the subliminal advertising of Pohl and Kornbluth's *The Space Merchants* (1965). Indeed so sensitive may some writers be in this area that, in novels set in our time, they call attention to allegedly repressive features of the normal functioning of the machinery of the state. The hero of Heinlein's *Glory Road* (1969), for example, actively resents income tax, policemen, parking regulations and traffic lights. Again a Martian hero fears world government because it is 'too easy for it to turn monolithic, for individualists to kill individualism without knowing it. Why not seven or eight federations corresponding to the major civilizations, under a world recognizing their right to be different?' (Pangborn, 1966, p. 47).

Related to this external oppression is a kind of self-inflicted internal oppression. For example, the 'unenlightened masses' may voluntarily stunt their individuality in order to escape to some more satisfying fantasy world. The forces of custom and tradition may also inhibit the independence of the individual. In Pohl and Kornbluth's *Wolfbane* (1960), Citizens are bound by convention, Wolves are individualists: 'It was not proper for one Citizen to advantage himself at the expense of another; Wolves did that. It was proper for a Citizen to accept what he had, not to strive for more . . . to accommodate himself, with the minimum of strain and awkwardness to whatever his life happened to be' (Pohl and Kornbluth, 1960, pp. 21–2). In this novel, as in many others, it is the ability to free themselves from the bounds of convention that enables heroes to succeed in the struggle. One of the favourite targets of science-fiction writers is the conforming society, where to be different is to be evil: 'all the irrational bigots swarming on this cock-eyed world would invariably jump to the conclusion that any one radically different from themselves must be bad' (Russell, 1963, p. 85).

Society in science fiction is not only seen as repressive, it is also rigidly stratified. Generally, there is a small privileged elite, and the hierarchy has the tone of a feudal aristocracy. The rigidity, and the assignment of everybody to a fixed social position, may be further underpinned by a religious ritual, designed to inspire the masses with fear. Indeed the obedience to any *system* of belief is often seen as the very antithesis of individualism. The wandering hero of *Davy* wonders 'whether over there the spooky religion of communism may not have slugged it out with its older brother Christianity in the ruins. Whichever won, the human individual must be the loser' (Pangborn, 1969, p. 56).

Just as the masses are somnolent and repressed, so the elite is essentially decadent. The masses may be incapable of independent action and initiative because they are drugged and unfree, but the aristocracy are similarly incapable because their privileged status allows them to wallow in luxury and avoid the struggle for survival.

So, the hero operates in a society that is repressive, somnolent, manipulative, rigidly stratified, decadent and static. His task is, by exercising his own individual talents, to break through the rigid confines of the society to establish an alternative. Science-fiction writers, however, are always set a problem in having to explain where their heroes come from (Kelley, 1968). A common solution is to picture the hero initially as much like any other member of the society, sharing the values of his fellow-men and being as undistinctive as they, although he may be a person with considerable concealed talents of one kind or another, which will prove useful in the coming struggle. Some incident then occurs which awakens him to the truth of the society around him and to a sense of the mission which he, as an individual, must perform. This incident can be some accident like a spaceship's failure to rescue the hero or, more frequently, it takes the form of contact with a conspiracy against the existing order. Now, this conception of the hero as originally indistinguishable from any other member of the society gives plausibility to the notion of an individualistic revolt, because it looks possible that *any* person could, given the right circumstances, begin to realize the repressive nature of his society and act accordingly. Having been awoken, the hero's task is easy: he simply transforms the world about him. The social change involved, though it is conceived as a fairly startling *moral* change, is not often seen as structural, and the hero does not have the aid of a revolutionary army, for society is pictured essentially as a series of commanding heights, which only need to be captured to give automatic political power.

The hero, then, celebrates the virtues of the individual in a society of sullen conformists. He is the exceptional individual who stands apart from the common herd. In fact, in order to emphasize the way in which the hero is set against the mass, and that he is first and foremost an individual and only secondarily a member of a moral community, some writers are prepared to make the hero almost an immoral person. Gully Foyle, for example (Bester, 1967), is prepared to lie, cheat, steal and rape in the single-minded pursuit of his objective. Again, Amis (1963) notes the interest displayed by science-fiction writers in 'the deviant'. Indeed we might have thought that the strongest way to emphasize individualism, in contrast to conformity, would be to stress the *irrational*, random aspects of human character. The stamp of individualism would then be the unpredictable, unplanned outburst of anger or spontaneous generosity, in much the same way as Genet makes his central characters stand out by depicting them, in terms of conventional morality at least, as evil and immoral men. There is some warrant for such a suggestion in the science-fiction literature, since there is a tendency to stress the essentially emotional nature of human beings as compared with soulless aliens or mechanical robots. However, as Kelley (1968) has pointed out, science fiction does not typically emphasize the irrational sources of human behaviour. Quite the contrary: heroes, though obviously full of stock human emotions and responses, set about their tasks in a calm, rational and planned way, and it is usually superior cunning rather than overwhelming force that achieves their goals. The sort of individualism that is being insisted upon, then, consists of what is essentially *rationally* planned action.

The use of a plot that turns on heroism in a repressive society is one way of demonstrating individualism. There are others. For example, some stories do not necessarily show the hero as radically altering society, but instead portray his solving some particular problem which threatens to destroy the society. Thus, a number of novels are concerned with the 'alien menace'. Wade Harper in *Three to Conquer* (Russell, 1963) is an exceptional individual because he is telepathic, and his talent is essential for the detection of aliens who have invaded the Earth. Almost singlehandedly he overcomes the invasion but, significantly, one of the most difficult problems in doing so is to penetrate the rigid bureaucracy that runs the society and which, perhaps understandably, fears the uncontrollable gift of telepathy. This makes Harper rather wilful in 'asserting the freedom of the individual at the moment when it is likeliest to become disputed' (Russell, 1963, p. 99). This tendency extended in Heinlein's *Glory Road* (1969), to the extent that the hero is content only when he is performing heroic deeds and finds himself continually restless living in a society that allows no room for individual adventure. Others recognize his condition – 'wherever you go, you will make yourself felt, you won't be one of the herd' (Heinlein, 1969, p. 180) – and one of his heroic colleagues sets the matter out plainly: 'But a democractic form of government is okay, as long as it doesn't work. Any social organization does well enough if it isn't rigid. The framework doesn't matter as long as there is enough looseness to permit that one man in a multitude to display his genius' (p. 233). In a different way, other stories contrast the individualism, not of a hero, but of the human race as a whole, with alien beings. Hive-creatures or robots behave either *collectively* or entirely *predictably*, and in the conflict between them and humankind, it is the capacity of human beings to act independently of each other and to act unpredictably that finally counts (see, for example, Heinlein, 1970; Laumer, 1967).

We have suggested so far that science-fiction novels exhibit, by a wide variety of devices, on the one hand a dislike of social arrangements that reduce the possibility of individual initiative and, on the other, an assertion of the possibilities of individual action, and rational action at that. One of the ways that the dislike of certain social arrangements is often shown is by a caricature of a rigid and static society, and the possibilities of individual initiative are demonstrated by examining the hero, who starts out just as conformist as the rest of the society. In our view, the central aim of the novels is to say something about the necessity for rationally ordered individual action. To do this the novelist has to provide a backdrop of a society which in some way represses the individual. In other words, the novels do not describe a 'future nightmare'; they are not pessimistic novels whose purpose is only to describe some thoroughly undesirable, but possible, future societies in the way that Orwell's *1984* does. Undoubtedly the repressive societies of the kind that we have described are seen as undesirable, but they really function as *devices* to enable the novelist to picture his hero struggling against adversity. They give the hero some way of demonstrating his individualism.

In sum, the important point is that science fiction portrays an individualism that is essentially active and involved in the world. In addition some of the novelists' more theoretical musings stress the importance of human freedom. For example, the autonomy of men may be contrasted with the manner in which chess pieces are moved in a determined way: 'you have reduced your citizens to the status of pawns and attempted to direct their actions and even their thinking as though they were pieces of carven wood . . . I have come to say that a man is not a pawn, and if you try to make a man into a pawn, you must expect him sooner or later to turn on you and spit in your eye' (Brunner, 1965, p. 285). Not only is it a case of there being an irreducible element of autonomy in the human constitution, there is also a responsibility never to forget it: 'Anyone is guilty who has so far renounced his right to think and act rationally that someone else can press his buttons and make him dance' (Brunner, 1965, p. 307). This autonomy is reinforced in some novels by an emphasis on the essentially emotional nature of human beings as opposed to the mechanical obedience of hive creatures or machines. Notions of negative liberty are often expressed via proposals to restrict the area of political authority. One sequence of novels, for example, is all about the importance of individual citizens carrying arms as protection against arbitrary political power, and the organization responsible for selling the guns has as its slogan: 'The right to buy weapons is the right to be free' (Van Vogt, 1970, p. 19).

In contrast to these aggressively individualistic novels, there is also a group of science-fiction novels that express an essentially passive individual viewpoint, with an emphasis on private withdrawal from the world and, at its extremes, the cultivation of the uniqueness of the individual personality, free from the constraints of active participation in men's affairs. These novels – an example is Ballard's *The Drowned World* (1965) – do have heroes or, more accurately, they do have central characters. As in some of the stories discussed above, these characters inhabit a world that is being transformed, but the crucial difference is that they have very little part in engineering the transformation. They are essentially passive observers in a world made strange by some dramatic act of nature. The central character, then, is merely used to tell the story; he is as much affected by the changes as everyone else. His problem lies not in manipulating the environment, but in adapting to it. So, although there are some formal similarities with more 'individualist' novels, there is no ideology of an active individualism at work. The world-view that is being presented is that of persons who cannot control the events that have shattered the familiar world.

In sum, the individualism of the bulk of science fiction is the 'aggressive self assertion of individuals freed from an externally given framework of authority' (Lukes, 1973, p. 23), the lessening of the area in which society has legitimate claims against the individual, and the necessity for individual enterprise.

An important feature of the individualism contained within all forms of popular culture is that its emotional tone is oppositional, not triumphant. The world and its tradition, custom, bureaucracy and political repression are against the hero, who may well succeed but whose success is uniformly unconvincing. James Bond's feats of ingenuity and initiative are on an enormous and totally improbable scale, and it is often difficult to see how the audience can successfully suspend disbelief. The world, in sum, is no longer full of opportunities to be exploited by the exercise of individualism; it is instead a dark and threatening place in which the hero struggles against adversity.

Individuality and 'High' Culture

Although this book is primarily about the relationship of individualism to capitalism, we ought to make some very brief comments about the place of discourses of *individuality* in modern societies. Our argument is that the functional relationship between capitalist social relations, on the one hand, and discourses of individualism, on the other, has become very much weakened. The result is that individualism loses its position of discursive dominance. *Relatively* speaking, other discourses of the individual increasingly make their appearance. There is in Berger's telling phrase a 'pluralization of life worlds'. One such discourse is that of individuality, the central points of which are the uniqueness of the individual, the importance of self-development and a notion of positive liberty (see Chapter 3 for a fuller exposition).

Our suggestion is that, in modern Western societies, the pluralization of discourses of the individual is not socially random. We have already tried to show how *popular* cultural forms are characterized by individualism. Individuality, on the other hand, is rather more present in 'high' culture. Again, we have to stress that we do not want to over-emphasize the substantive differences between the two. Of course there are elements of both discourses of the individual in both popular and high culture.

Like individualism, the discourse of individuality in the 'high' culture of this century is a mixture of darkness and light. On the one hand, it is characterized by a feeling of the threats posed to the autonomy and creative powers of the individual, who may well be prevented from realizing his or her selfhood by the social pressure of modern society. On the other hand, it celebrates the individual's uniqueness and inner life and even his or her eccentricity. In sum, individuality, like individualism, is marked by an oppositional and threatened emotional tone, combined with an insistence on the importance of certain individual qualities.

The dark side of modern society emerges in a number of ways. Most notably, modern culture is felt to lack authenticity; it is shallow, vapid, and fails to reflect and develop the inner life of the individual. Furthermore, it imposes false values of materialism, which divert people from the pursuit of more worthy, deeper goals. The point is well put by one of the manifestos of Expressionism:

> This is the vital point – that man should find himself again . . . It is the inhuman attempt of our time to force this loss upon him against his own nature. We would turn him into a mere instrument; he has become the tool of his own work, and he has no more sense since he serves the machine. It has stolen him away from his soul . . . Expressionism is the symbol of the unknown in us in which we confide, hoping that it will save us. It is the token of the imprisoned spirit that endeavours to break out of the dungeon – a tocsin of alarm given out by all panic-stricken souls.
>
> (Bahr, 1920, p. 165)

One of the possible consequences of this point of view, as also with early nineteenth-century Romanticism (see Chapter 3), is the artist's absorption into self as a means of restoring authenticity and individuality. As R. Hughes (1980) writes of Munch: 'Munch embodied the nature of Expressionism and lived it out before it was named. It may be summarized thus: insecurity and unease become so strong that the artist has no choice but to recoil upon himself, treating that self as the one secure point in an otherwise hostile universe' (p. 281). Much the same point is made by Walter Benjamin (1968) in his famous essay on 'The work of art in the age of mechanical reproduction'. Benjamin argues that the mechanical reproduction of a work of art, a characteristic of contemporary societies, always depreciates the quality of the object; it takes away the uniqueness and authenticity of the experience: 'Even the most perfect reproduction of a work of art is lacking in one element: its presence in time and space, its unique existence at the place where it happens to be . . . The presence of the original is the prerequisite to the concept of authenticity' (1968, p. 20).

The modern world, therefore, robs individual experience of its authenticity; individuals cannot see themselves as unique and possessed of an inner life that can find adequate expression. This is partly a question of freedom, for the empty modern world is also a bureaucratized place. Identities are given by numbers, as we pointed out in Chapter 2. Individuals cannot realize their powers, because of the inexplicable and capricious activities of officialdom. In the novels of Kafka, for example, or in Orwell's *1984*, it is everyday life that is interfered with. The central characters of these books are not individualistic heroes in the sense that they wish to transform the world. In their dark world even their everyday inner life becomes impossible. It is a depersonalized, numbered world. As Kaplan (1970) says, 'So it is that many of us today feel that we have been robbed, are constantly being robbed, of our most precious essence, our innermost being as the particular human beings which we are. We are treated as identified individuals, but not as persons with identities' (p. 5).

If many modern writers, artists or intellectuals feel that individuality in the sense in which we have defined it earlier is being stifled, there are also several ways in which they can simultaneously assert its possibility or desirability. For example, the presentation of eccentricity in some English fiction is one such assertion. The eccentric individuals in the novels of Waugh, Wodehouse and Powell have carved out some niche in which they are free to pursue their own interests – or follies. Eccentricity is individuality. Again, more theoretically, the 'mass-society' theorists classically posed the problem of mass society destroying individuality. Ortega y Gasset, for example, enjoined us to remember that 'living is precisely the inexorable necessity to make oneself determinate, to enter into an exclusive destiny, to accept it – that is, to resolve to be it. We have, whether we like it or not, to realize our "personage", our vocation, our vital program, our "entelechy" – there is no lack of names for the terrible reality which is our authentic I (ego)' (quoted in Dubos, 1970, p. 154).

We should stress again that one very important thing about these assertions of individuality is that they do not represent engagements with the world as does the individualism of popular culture; they are instead demonstrations of the uniqueness of self. Indeed, a more logical development of individuality is a withdrawal from the world into self. This may be one way to understand the narcissism that many writers have found to be characteristic of modern culture; an exclusive preoccupation with self is one extreme version of the discourse of individuality.

Our arguments about the place of individuality in modern culture have some similarities with Bell's account in *The Cultural Contra-*

dictions of Capitalism (1979). He argues that, in the early stages of capitalism, culture and economy fitted together. The capitalist economy depended on a culture that emphasized hard work and its rewards, the postponement of satisfactions, the Protestant sanctification of work and functional rationality. However, there have been profound changes in cultures, which have resulted in economy and culture splitting apart. Instead of a continuing and supportive relationship between them, they may actually become contradictory. These cultural changes move in two main directions, to modernism in 'high' culture and hedonism in the sphere of consumption. Bell sees modernism as a very influential movement, extending well beyond serious artists to what he calls the cultural mass. The movement emphasizes movement and flux, but it also stresses the crucial importance of authentic experience and the uniqueness of the self. Hedonism is also to do with the centrality of the self in that it stimulates the involvement in individual experience and the satisfaction of desires. Modern individuals live with an ethic of consumption, which encourages spending and enjoying not working and spending. Underlying modern culture is what we have called individuality. As Bell says: 'in the modern consciousness, there is not a common being but a *self*, and the concern of this self is with its individual *authenticity*, its unique, irreducible character free of the contrivances and conventions, the masks and hypocrisies, the distortion of the self by society' (Bell, 1979, p. 19).

We have argued that individuality is one of a number of discourses responding to changes in the position of the individual in modern society. There is a variety of responses precisely because no one discourse of the individual has pre-eminence. As we have stressed, discourses are not only engaged in struggles with one another, they can also form alliances. So it is with individualism and individuality in the modern period. There is a certain fusion in the discourses, in which people may freely move between both discourses in accounting for the position of the individual in modern society. For example, in the 1960s, American academics were much exercised by this problem and collections of articles were published in which writers simultaneously praised the individualism of the free market and the individuality of free expression (for instance, Morley, 1958, and Kaplan, 1970). Despite this occasional fusion, however, the discourses are still separable and have, as we have tried to show, different social bases. Why they have different social bases, why individualism is characteristic of popular culture and individuality of 'high' culture, is a question that lies outside the scope of the present study.

Summary

Social theory has commonly postulated a relationship between individualism and capitalism. There is the implicit assumption that, because British and American capitalism appear to be individualistic, capitalism *per se* requires an individualistic culture. More specifically, it is assumed that the capitalist mode of production requires private property, egoism and a legal system that protects the autonomy of the private individual. Against these assumptions, this chapter has established five main points. First, an examination of Japanese capitalism shows that rapid capitalist development is possible in a cultural context where individualism is little developed. Japanese Confucian values and capitalism have proved completely compatible. Second, 'rugged' individualism is no longer appropriate to the more collectivist character of contemporary capitalism and is increasingly incompatible with the bureaucratic structures of production and industrial control. We identified a number of the consequences of individualism, which promote instablity and inefficiency in contemporary American capitalism. Third, there is the rise of a more collective discourse, which is associated with the state. The paradox is that surveillance has been associated with the expansion of citizenship. The popular demand for welfare and the extension of social equality arising out of the political advancement of the working class in late capitalism creates a new bureaucracy, which is part of a centralized system of social control based on the detailed individuation of persons. Fourth, discourses of the individual have acquired a distinctively oppositional tone. Individualistic beliefs have lost their self-confidence and there is a distinctive shift in the mood of individualism from optimism to pessimism. The relatively confident liberalism of ascendant capitalism has given way to new anxieties and uncertainties about the future of liberal culture and of the autonomous individual. The egoism of individuals is no longer seen as threatening to the social order; instead, the bureaucratic social realm threatens the independent individual. Last, the loss of discursive dominance of individualism means that a plurality of more equally competing discourses is possible. Indeed, in a common antipathy to the perceived menace of collectivism, a kind of discursive alliance is possible between formerly separate discourses of the individual. There is also an intriguing separation of these discourses into different social bases. Individualism is characteristic of popular culture, while individuality is more characteristic of 'high' culture.

6

The Dominance of Discourse?

In the first five chapters of this book, we have presented the strands of our argument about the relationship of individualism to capitalism. In this chapter, we locate our position on the relationship of the two phenomena in a wider debate about the connection between discourses and society. As a result, this chapter is less concerned with empirical and historical issues; it outlines a theoretical programme rather than stating definitive and substantive conclusions.

Behind the issue of individualism and capitalism lies the perennial sociological problem of the relationship between knowledge and society. This inescapably involves consideration of the Marxist injunction to look at the economy. We are interested in whether, and how, certain discourses steer the economy and how, in turn, the economy influences the form and content of these discourses. More directly, we have to answer two closely related questions; namely, 'Is discourse autonomous of the economy?', and 'Is the relationship between discourse and economy contingent or necessary?'.

Classical Marxism never held that the economy uniquely *determined* forms of discourse. Marx and Engels argued that discourse could be relatively autonomous of the economy and have its own laws of development. Engels said that not all kinds of discourse were equally determined by the economy: 'The further the particular sphere we are investigating is removed from the economic sphere and approaches that of pure abstract ideology, the more shall we find it exhibiting accidents . . . in its development, the more will its course run in a zig-zag' (Engels, 1955, p. 466). The forms taken by

169

art or literature, for example, might be less closely related to the economy than would political or economic theories. More radically, Marx and Engels also argued that discourses, far from being economically determined, would themselves influence the character or constitution of the economy. In *Capital*, for example, Marx went to considerable lengths to demonstrate the independent importance of beliefs on the conduct of capital. He argued that there was no reason inherent in the nature of capital why the working day should be limited: 'apart from extremely elastic bounds, the nature of the exchange of commodities itself imposes no limit to the working day, no limit to surplus labour' (Marx, 1970, p. 234). The length of the working day was set by factors outside the strictly economic, largely by beliefs about the physical or moral harm that would result from long working hours, which were eventually expressed both in legislation and the personnel practices of enterprises. Marx claimed that the legislation limiting the working day was only won after a struggle between opposing social groups with opposing systems of belief. The discursive struggle over the length of the working day, therefore, contributed to the determination of an important feature of the capitalist economy, namely, the volume of surplus labour. However, Marx and Engels are materialists, so the autonomy of discourse is a constrained autonomy. As Engels has said quite bluntly, 'The economic movement finally asserts itself as necessary'. Discourse is only *relatively* autonomous.

The relative autonomy of discourse has been a conclusion accepted and even emphasized by subsequent commentators on the work of Marx and Engels (see Abercrombie, Hill and Turner, 1980), and is one we share, as will be obvious from earlier chapters. More recently, the independence and importance of discourse has been much stressed by Althusser and those influenced by him. This discovery, of the importance of discourse, is the discovery that discourse cannot be reduced to economy. Writers of a variety of theoretical persuasions have so extended the position as to argue that economies cannot exist without particular discourses; *particular* discourses are necessary to *particular* economies.

It will be clear from the earlier chapters that we do not believe there is any *necessary* connection or significant elective affinity between discourses and social structure and, more particularly, between individualism and capitalism. Nor do we accept the counter argument, fashionable among New Right liberals, that capitalism is necessary for individualism:

> A necessary condition for individual freedom is the organization of the bulk of economic activity through private enterprises operating in a free market – a form of organization I shall refer to as competitive capitalism.
>
> (M. Friedman, 1958, p. 168)

Rather, the connection is contingent, a point we develop in the rest of this chapter. Polemically, therefore, we argue for both autonomy and contingency in the relationship between discourse and society. As slogans, however, these lack substance. We also need to know what are the limits of autonomy and contingency to be able to say anything at all of *general* import about the relationship between discourse and economy.

We have claimed that, whatever were the views of the individual in antiquity, in early medieval Europe discourses that stressed the importance of the individual began to develop noticeably in the twelfth century. We have called attention to a variety of ways in which this process manifested itself, from more individualized painting of the face to the significance of religious confessions for the development of the individual. The Catholic confessional was particularly important in the development of a concept of the autonomous moral individual in Western culture and it was within the confessional that the notion of a moral conscience within the individual became fully articulated. As the confessional developed, there was less emphasis on the ritual purification of the individual by absolution and a greater emphasis on individual moral development under the control of an inner court of conscience. Although parallels to confession may be discovered in other cultures, it was in the Christian West that this special institution developed as the vehicle for the development of the moral individual. The prominence of the confessional meant that external torture of the body was less significant than internal moral conscience for the development of truth and moral culture. This Discovery of the Individual is, however, very *general*; it is simply a question of putting emphasis on individuals rather than collectivities of various kinds. The generation of this general discourse of the individual was autonomous of the economy, and we have called attention to various causal factors that contributed to this social development. For example, the church fostered the notion of the individual with its emphasis on individual salvation. The impact of Christianity in Europe also promoted a de-tribalization of society, because the church gave special emphasis to faith as the basis of communal membership. Following Weber, we have also noted the importance of the autonomous city and the Western legal tradition as two conditions for the emergence of the autonomous self.

The Discovery of the Individual is a primitive and undifferentiated notion, in the sense that it can develop into more specific ways of treating the individual. There are, in other words, a number of different ways of treating the individual as important; different specific discourses may pick out different specific qualities as belonging inherently to individuals, while they all agree on the general principle that individuals are important. We have identified four different ways, four different specific discourses, in which the individual becomes important, all of which develop out of the primitive, undifferentiated Discovery of the Individual. There are, of course, other logical possibilities for the development of the primitive discourse. There are also other substantive possibilities. All social and political theories have to formulate some theory of the individual, *especially* in an intellectual context which assumes that individuals count. We have not, for example, considered early nineteenth-century European conservatism in our discussion of specific discourses. Yet this political and social philosophy does have a conception of the individual, even if it effectively celebrates the significance of particular collectivities, natural law and the importance of organic and moral solidarity.

We have suggested in earlier chapters that the generation of the Discovery of the Individual and of the more specific discourses of the individual are autonomous of the economy, even if they may later come to have economic effects, as is the case with individualism. Indeed, we have often presented these changes in discourse as intellectual processes, as matters of debate and argument in an intellectual community. We have seen them as shaped by discursive struggle. This form of presentation and the insistence on autonomy indicate that discourse does have its own laws of motion, but it does not mean that discursive processes operate in a social vacuum; discourses do not change by some mysterious process peculiar to the mind or spirit. Social processes are not irrelevant to intellectual movements, as is sometimes implied by historians of ideas. Such historians may display little interest in explanations of any kind, in showing why it is that people should hold one set of ideas rather than another or in explaining why some ideas persist while others do not. A good deal of contemporary sociology of culture – that influenced by Foucault – also isolates discourse from society. It is clear that Foucault did not intend his work to be simply one more contribution to the sociology of knowledge and, in *The Archaeology of Knowledge* (1969), he also went to some lengths to argue that his approach was not a 'history of ideas' perspective. The consequence of his epistemology is that it is difficult to establish the relationship between discourse and extra-discursive structures. He rejected the idea of simple causal relations, and as a result his analysis of discourse suggests that discourses are autonomous and self-generating. He provides no recognizable historical or sociological analysis for the emergence of new epistemes; nor does he provide any suggestion on how we should analyse transitions and ruptures in discourses.

We cannot, however, separate discourse from society. Discourse is neither beyond causation nor is it determined by factors locked in the 'mental' realm. Discourses are *socially* organized, as is the intellectual community. Clearly, many social processes are involved. The emphasis on multiple causality and multi-dimensional levels of explanation derives from Weber's contribution to the sociology of knowledge, when he argued in the Protestant Ethic thesis for the validity of taking a variety of perspectives on the same social phenomenon. For example, Weber saw the rise of scientific discourse to be associated with Protestant rationalism, with the autonomy of an intellectual class, with the development of scientific associations (such as the Royal Society), and with the specific economic needs of a trading society for navigation and basic mathematics. Within the Chinese context, the emergence of science was associated with a very different range of structural determinants, such as the need for the state to regulate waterways. For us, the special interest of the variety of social processes cited by Weber is the association he draws between discourses and social groups that are struggling for dominance. This is also the concern of the classical sociology of knowledge formulated by Mannheim.

We have illustrated these points in our account of the relationship between the general discourse that we have called the Discovery of the Individual and the specific discourses, one of which is individualism. The specific discourses compete with one another when the intellectual communities and social groups with which they are associated conflict in the struggle for dominance. In this light, individualism, when it legitimates dissent by emphasizing the rights of the individual, can be related to a struggle by certain social groups against absolute monarchy. We showed in Chapter 4 how individualism had its origins in a struggle for power between the monarchy and propertied groups that lasted for half a century. It became a theory of the political rights of the propertied against the traditional rights of sovereigns. As long as they went unchallenged, the rights of kings remained largely implicit and taken-for-granted assumptions. The effect of competition from aspirants to power with a novel discourse of rights was to promote in response an explicit statement and justification of monarchical rights. In the early nineteenth century, there were several competing discourses of the individual, three of which we have described as socialism, individuality and individualism. Behind this discursive competition was a conflict between social groups. Mannheim described this process in his account of conservative thought in early nineteenth-century Germany, one element of which is what we have called individuality.

So far, we have called attention to the way in which discourses are socially organized. Of particular interest is the question of the discursive struggle, which can be related to the conflicts between social groups and their associated intellectual communities. The generation, change and conflict of discourses is socially organized, if only in the limited sense that proponents are organized as communities of intellectuals – specialists in the production and dissemination of discourses of whatever kind. These communities have their own social structure, social rules and customs, hierarchies, and patterns of training or apprenticeship, which affect the manner in which discourses are produced and deployed. However, it is difficult to see these discourses as being simply *reducible* to social processes, because we clearly have to take seriously the procedures of intellectual argument and debate. We have already pointed out that the various specific discourses of the individual take part of their meaning from opposing each other. Proponents of individuality, for example, develop theories of the proper role of individuals, at least partly in contrast to the view of the individual provided in individualism. We cannot ignore the fact that there is an intellectual competition between specific discourses. Furthermore, just as the specific discourses developed out of the general Discovery of the Individual, so also that general discourse provides a background of shared understandings to the discursive competition. In other words, disputants have to have some common ground to provide the basis for their dispute; intellectual debate of this kind is a question of appealing to a common vocabulary and set of concepts, which each party tries to appropriate to its own debating ends. In the conflict between individualism and individuality, this common ground is provided by the Discovery of the Individual. Any model of the relationship between discourse and society, therefore, must make provision for rational communication. The outcome of a discursive struggle is not settled merely by social forces, not the least because not all discourses are attached to social forces. The formulation of a theory of rational communication and its relationship to social forces is outside the scope of this book. However, it has always been a concern of the sociology of knowledge and, of course, of Jürgen Habermas. Many earlier formulations presented the problem of truth and rationality, and their relationship to social determination, in a rather static manner. What is now required is a model of rational communication that is dynamic and presents a satisfactory account of both the origin and *change* of discourses. Two further requirements of such a model would be a conception of rationality broader than the merely formal, and an ability to handle *systems* of concepts – discourses – rather than single propositions.

Stephen Toulmin (1972) provides an account of this kind, though not for a sociological purpose. He argues for an evolutionary theory of the development of 'populations of concepts'. Such populations, or discourses in our terms, change through the interaction of factors that generate discourses with factors that select discourses, where both are processes of rational communication. Toulmin's proposal trades specifically on a Darwinian metaphor. There is a mechanism that produces a pool of variation within a population of concepts, from which some concepts are selected because they have specific advantages in the struggle with other concepts. As Toulmin says, 'The development of these conceptual populations will be characterized . . . as reflecting a balance between factors of two kinds: innovative factors, responsible for the appearance of variations in the population concerned, and selective ones, which modify it by perpetuating certain favoured variants' (Toulmin, 1972, p. 134). To avoid being carried away by the Darwinian metaphor, it is worth

175

emphasizing again that the processes of conceptual innovation, struggle, selection and change are all processes of rational communication. Throughout this book, we have emphasized the sociological significance of the struggle between discourses for dominance. One advantage of an evolutionary scheme for the development of conceptual systems by means of rational communication is that it both gives a central place to conceptual conflict and struggle and provides a way of establishing the *outcomes* of such struggles.

Social organization and rational communication are, then, analytically separate, and any sociological account of discourse has to give some place to the latter. However, in any substantive analysis of the relationship between discourses and society the two are fused together. We wish to argue that discursive struggles are socially organized. At the minimal level, the participants in such struggles are themselves organized as communities of intellectuals. Social organization can also refer to larger-scale collectivities such as social groups and classes. So discourses may be socially organized in a variety of ways. A modified evolutionary model might also be appropriate for describing this process of attachment. Discourses originate, conflict, change and develop in the ways described above, involving small-scale social organization and rational communication. Some discourses become attached to more substantial and powerful social forces; they are not only influenced by that attachment but themselves become more powerful and influential thereby. Rational communication has a substantial role to play in deciding the outcomes of conflicts between discourses. When discourses and powerful social forces become functionally related, rational communication becomes of less moment, though it is still present (a case for Habermas's systematically distorted communication). We now want to illustrate these suggestions by reviewing what we have said in the earlier parts of this book about the relationship between individualism and capitalism.

Discourse and Economy

Our argument about discourse and economy is that their relationship constitutes what we shall call a functional circle. Although, as we have already insisted, both discourse and economy are relatively autonomous of each other and they have no *necessary* connection, they also have a functional relationship; both discourse and economy function in the internal workings of the other. There is nothing methodologically inappropriate or teleological about this scheme, provided that we can specify the creation of the circle independently of the relationship between economy and discourse. The circle works simply as a chain of cause and effect, as long as some explanation of its creation is provided by reference to factors outside the circle. In our analysis, this explanation is provided by the relatively autonomous nature of both discourse and economy. We have already suggested that there are changes in discourse generated by the internal, socially organized mechanisms of discourse itself. Discourses can change their direction, new discourses can arise, and there can be substantial conflicts between discourses. These changes and conflicts are socially organized; they are associated with social forces. However, discursive conflict and debate is not only a matter of social organization; debate has a certain rationality and discourses can emerge triumphant partly by means of their more successful appeal to commonly agreed principles of morals and logic. The important point is that, by means of these processes, a discourse emerges as dominant, and attains a wider currency in society. This, we have argued, is what happened with individualism, which in Britain emerged as a dominant, specific discourse of the individual out of the Discovery of the Individual. Dominant discourses, or those rising to dominance, affect the way that people think and act. This is particularly the case with those social groups (notably social classes) that are most open to influence because they are most affected by the mechanism of dissemination of particular discourses. In turn, any economic practice that is dominant, or is rising to dominance, is affected by a dominant discourse. Discourse and economy relate to one another *via the fact of their social dominance*. Clearly, any final relationship of this kind has small beginnings. Over a considerable period of time, discourse and economy come to have a closer and closer relationship. Discourses will affect the form taken by the economy (of which more below). The economy, in its dominance and via the power of social classes and other social groups, will further confirm a discourse, to which it has become appropriate, in a position of discursive dominance. Other discourses, because they are not associated with dominant economic practices and hence carry lesser social clout, will fade by comparison. Thus, a functional circle is created whereby discourse and economy fit one another and have *over time* acquired an affinity for each other that is based on their earlier reactions.

The functional relationship of discourse and economy, specifically individualism and capitalism, once it has been established by their common positions of dominance, generates an affinity between them. At this point, the processes of change in the discourse/ economy relationship are not unlike the mechanism of conceptual evolution proposed by Toulmin (1972). Furthermore, the style of our argument is similar to that proposed by Weber in *The Protestant Ethic and the Spirit of Capitalism*. Weber argued that capitalism and Protestantism came to have an affinity, which partly explained the appearance of capitalism in the Protestant West. As I. M. Zeitlin neatly puts it, 'There was such great congruence between the two, that they mutually reinforced each other to produce a methodical devotion to work and business activity and thus to a vigorous development of capitalism' (Zeitlin, 1968, p. 124). For example, Calvinism, that ascetic form of Protestantism, had a doctrine of predestination. The faithful could not influence their eventual destination, but they could receive a sign that they were predestined for heaven. One such sign was success and good works in an earthly calling. Not unsurprisingly, Calvinists found this doctrine a psychological pressure to strive after success and to organize their conduct rationally in pursuit of that aim. This rationalization of conduct and striving for success were important constituents of the spirit of capitalism. Weber argued that capitalism and Protestantism mutually supported each other in apparently much the same way as we suggest that individualism and capitalism form a functional circle. However, the critical difference is that we do not believe that individualism and capitalism had any *initial* affinity; such affinity as there is develops as a result of the growing power of capitalist organization and the discursive dominance of individualism. This belief is consistent with the principle that discourses and society are not in any way necessarily connected; their relationships are contingent.

Weber, as we have noted, further argued that the Protestant Ethic was only relevant to capitalism in its early stages. Once that economic system became established, it would function by itself. 'The capitalistic economy of the present day is an immense cosmos into which the individual is born and which presents itself to him . . . as an unalterable order of things in which he must live. It forces the

178

individual, in so far as he is involved in the system of market relationships, to conform to capitalistic rules of action' (Weber, 1930, p. 21). In late capitalism, individual economic motivation does not require the sustenance of the Protestant Ethic. Similarly, we have argued that the functional circle of individualism and capitalism has come unstuck in late capitalism. In general, the relations between discourse and economy are not invariant or necessary. As the functional circle of discourse and economy is set up by autonomous movements in discourses of the individual and in economic structures, so also can it be undone.

In Chapter 6 we described the various changes within individualism and the social organization of the capitalist economy that have broken the relationship between individualism and capitalism in the West. These points raise the possibility of a relationship between a collective discourse and a collective capitalism. Following T. H. Marshall (1977), we suggest that there was an expansion of citizenship as a consequence of political struggle. With the reform acts of the nineteenth century, private property rights became increasingly less important to the franchise. The notion of the citizen became more abstract and general and less tied to particularistic characteristics such as property or gender. Corresponding to the notion of the abstract citizen as a political agent, there was the development of new political discourses such as trade unionism or Chartism. These discursive struggles eventually produced a more articulate and coherent alternative to traditional liberalism. In particular, various groups of intellectuals came to provide an emphasis on social equality and common citizenship in contrast to the focus on individual uniqueness characteristic of individualism. These different discourses (socialism, utopianism, Fabianism) shared a common theme – the moral value of equality and the significance of collective values. A variety of discourses with very different presuppositions and objectives in fact shared a common underlying commitment to certain collective values, such as working-class solidarity, the community, the village or the people. The discursive dominance of individualism is significantly challenged by collectivism of various sorts.

The emergence of welfare citizenship could only become effective if it was accompanied by the growth of a state bureaucracy capable of enforcing these rights in practice. Welfare citizenship entailed the development of centralized agencies to deliver and enforce these new 'privileges' of social membership. Although the welfare state is in part the expression of successful struggle by subordinate groups, these welfare agencies also brought about a new and extended pattern of surveillance and control. This paradoxical growth of welfare institutions is what we mean by the Foucault Paradox. The rights of citizenship were associated with 'panopticism' as an original technique of social control through administration and surveillance. The collective discourses of social rights were part of a more detailed order of urban control, which was made possible by knowledge (criminology, penology, demography) and by institutions (the asylum, factory, penitentiary). The growth of social statistics, social medicine and social science provides a clear index of these changes. These discursive and political struggles were enhanced under conditions of mass warfare. The Crimean and the Boer wars were important in the development of social medicine and social statistics because there was the need to monitor large groups of men. Warfare creates conditions favourable for the expansion of state intervention in civil society. The First World War was particularly significant in this respect because of conscription. As we have indicated, collective discourses of this kind threaten the pre-eminence of individualism, a fact that did not pass unnoticed by nineteenth-century social theorists. For example, Mill and de Tocqueville were anxious that the autonomy of the individual would be overwhelmed by a collectively organized mass that dominated political institutions.

In earlier chapters, we have described the emergence of a more collective form of capitalism, the growth of the corporation, of institutional investment, bureaucratic management, the separation of ownership and control, and the concentration and centralization of capital. Late capitalism functions with an economic subject – the corporation – that is neither an individual nor simply reducible to individual persons. Moreover, the growth of the bureaucratic mode of internal organization characteristic of the modern corporation means that the personal qualities traditionally associated with individualism, such as self-seeking and independent behaviour, are no longer particularly appropriate for rational capital accumulation, if they ever were.

The development of collective discourses out of political/discursive struggle and the evolution of collective forms of capitalist organization are parallel, autonomous developments. As with the earlier association of capitalism and individualism, however, there is the potential for the creation of a functional circle of collective discourse and collective capitalism based on their common dominance.

With the link with capitalist economic practices broken, individualism is deprived of one of the main supports for the continuation of its position of discursive dominance. The result is that the discursive structure of contemporary British and American society has a more pluralistic character, at least as far as discourses of the individual are concerned, as the constraint of the functional relationship with capitalism is broken. Other discourses of the individual, previously repressed by individualism, can now emerge and develop freely. The implication of these points is, once again, that there is no necessary connection between discourse and economy.

We have argued that capitalism does not have any ideological or discursive conditions of existence. There are no requirements of this kind that *must* be met for capitalism to flourish, although, as we have suggested, capitalism may take certain forms because of the influence of particular discourses. This is not to say that capitalism as an economic system does not have requirements of *any* kind. Two of these requirements are of particular interest in the analysis of individualistic discourses that we have presented in this book. First, capitalism has to be provided with a mechanism that ensures continuity and, in particular, that ensures the accumulation of capital over time. Secondly, capitalism is an essentially revolutionary system that requires continuous novelty, the continuous replacement of the old by the new. Marx, of course, identified both of these in talking of accumulation as the Law and the Prophets, and of the capitalist bourgeoisie as continually revolutionizing the means of production. In certain circumstances, however, the two requirements are contradictory. Constant novelty may actually impede the orderly accumulation of capital.

This point relates to the antithesis between collective and individualistic discourses in an interesting way. Collective discourses do make for continuity of capitalist relations. In an obvious sense, for example, families permit the accumulation of capital within one unit of ownership. Capital accumulated by one individual can easily be passed on to descendants, ensuring continuity. This was our argument in *The Dominant Ideology Thesis*. Similarly, other collective entities, such as the state, the corporation and the church, can actively encourage the orderly transmission of units of capital across generations. Collective entities of this kind last longer than individuals. Individualism, similarly, may encourage originality and novelty. In a sense, individualism is subversive of all stable social relationships. In that all individuals are expected to follow their own stars and have a right to pursue their own desires, nothing is safe or sacred. An endless quest for the new is the result. The contradictory requirements of capital – accumulation and novelty – in this way may be reproduced at the discursive level in the tension between collective and individualistic discourses. Although we have talked throughout this book about the discursive dominance of individualism and about the historically recent importance of collective discourses, this dominance is always contradictory because capitalism could not survive unless it were. Hence, we have drawn attention to the way that individualism in early capitalism is qualified by the significance of the family, and discourses of the collective in late capitalism are qualified by the continued salience of discourses of individualism and individuality.

We have discussed the relationship of discourse and economy, individualism and capitalism, as constituting functional circles. We have not, however, paid much attention to the causal mechanisms that connect the elements within the circle. How do discourses and economic practices relate, and specifically what are the mechanisms that connect individualism with capitalist economic practices?

There is, of course, a line of argument which suggests either that discourses and practices are conceptually inseparable, or that the concept of discourse should be defined in such a way that beliefs and practices are inseparable. Our position is that there has to be an analytical separation of discourses and practices. We have to allow for the possibility that discourses and practices are not related at all or are even contradictory. For example, because the discourse of individualism is dominant does not *necessarily* mean that people engage in individualistic economic practice (Abercrombie, 1980; Abercrombie, Hill and Turner, 1980).

One traditional way of dealing with the relationship between discourse and economic practice is via the concept of motivation. The suggestion is that discourses provide actors with the appropriate motivations to engage in given economic practices. Within the sociology of industrialization there is the well-established argument that the motivation of individual achievement was crucial in the development of entreprenuership, and that entreprenuership was in turn a major feature in the emergence of industrial economic societies. This emphasis on individual achievement is often traced back to Weber's account of the purported relationship between the Protestant calling and the development of capitalist society. In more recent analyses, this emphasis on achievement motivation has been associated with McClelland's work, which was discussed in Chapter 4. In McClelland's theory, both individualism and capitalist development are effects of entreprenuerial activity, which in turn is the outcome of certain changes in the patterns of socialization of children within the family. These arguments suggest, in effect, that discourses work through the motivations of members of certain social classes who happen, for whatever reason, to be particularly open to the influence of those discourses. Arguments about motivation may explain part of the relationship between individualism and capitalism. However, they provide neither a necessary nor a sufficient condition for that explanation. There are other ways in which individualism and capitalism relate to one another that are not dependent on motivation. For example there is the familiar argument of Weber and Marx that a capitalist economy will constrain individuals to behave appropriately, regardless of their beliefs and motives, if they are to survive economically.

Our view is that discourses interact with economic practices chiefly, though not only, via the constitution of the economic subject. All modes of production have to define the appropriate economic subject, that is, what kinds of economic subjects can act and how they are to act, technically and morally. One of the ways in which economic subjects are defined is in relation to property, that is, as socially recognized possessors of socially sanctioned rights concerning the use of productive property. Control over the disposition of property is an important element in the relationship between discourse and economy, because discourses typically have economic effects through those members of social classes that control property – it is these classes that are most 'open' to discourses. Dominant classes, or those classes rising to dominance, are more likely both to control property *and* to be closest to the mechanisms by which discourses are transmitted in society. From the point of view of the way that discourses 'steer' the economy, therefore, the effects of discourses on subordinate classes is of much less importance, an issue extensively discussed in *The Dominant Ideology Thesis*. Thus discourses form the economic subject, partly by defining control over the use of property. Our analysis of early capitalism showed a continuing tension between different conceptions of economic subjects and their associated property rights. On the one hand, the discursive dominance of individualism signified the individual person as an economic subject. The common law had embedded within it a philosophy that gave control over property to individuals. On the other hand, the continuing social significance of the idea of the family and the actual organization of economic units along familial lines demonstrated the countervailing force of families as subjects. Literary evidence and social practices show that family considerations were expected often to take precedence over individuals within the property-owning classes. The modification of the legal device of the trust reflected this concern. This clearly gives discourses an important role in the constitution of the economy. Discourses may neither create nor sustain an economy, *but they do give it a certain shape by constituting the economic subject in a particular way.*

The manner in which discourse constitutes the economic subject is then one side of the functional circle of discourse and economy. As we have already said, the other side is the effect of the economy on discourse. A dominant economy and dominant social classes can reinforce the power of any discourse with which they have developed an association. The emphasis on the *possessive* individual was one example of this influence.

Earlier in this chapter, we suggested that individualism and capitalism initially became associated with one another because, independently of each other, both acquired positions of social dominance. They have become intertwined not because of any constitutional affinity, but because they were both socially prominent. This was a long process by which individualism and capitalism, through mutual influence, *acquired* an affinity for each other. Specifically, individualism and capitalism fitted together when the economic subject was defined as the individual. As we have shown already, individual economic subjects are not at all necessary to capitalism. In different dominant discursive structures the economic subject is socially constituted in a different way, as in Japan. Individualism, first in Britain and then in America, therefore *directed capitalism into a certain mould*; it formed capitalism largely as an *individualistic* economic system. Our definition of individualism also implies that discourse not only constitutes economic subjects as individuals, but further defines certain qualities of individuals, who are restless, self-seeking, and intent on rationally organized interventions in the world. The important issue here is the conception of autonomous individuals as self-directing, being free from traditional restraints and conventional culture. These autonomous individuals are directed by their own conscience rather than by the dictates of traditional culture and the restraints of hierarchical structures. Furthermore, they are ethically committed to transforming the world in the name of a rational plan.

One implication of our arguments about the functional relationship between individualism and capitalism should be stressed. In our view, the important question is the functional relationship between discourse and economy and how it works, and *not* which came first. Critics of both Marx's and Weber's views of the origins of capitalism have suggested that what mars these accounts are difficulties of temporal and causal priority. This is the familiar problem of periodization. In our view, such criticisms are of minor importance. Since economy and discourse are relatively autonomous and so are not necessarily related in any way, it does not matter which came first. Doubtless some capitalist economic practices (in the land market, for example) and traces of individualistic discourse can be found as early as the twelfth century. However, for us, the crucial issue is the way that individualism and capitalism come together in the seventeenth and eighteenth centuries, because of their joint social prominence, and the manner in which individualism in the West has constrained the form that a developed capitalist economy takes.

Discourse, Everyday Life, and the Dominant Ideology Thesis

Discourse can be said to have three moments: creation, transmission and appropriation. Each of these is a social process, but they do not necessarily fit together very well and the degree of fit can vary considerably. For our purposes, in considering the relationship of discourses to the economy, we have concentrated on intellectualized discourses. Although this is not a topic that we have explored in any detail, such a concentration would focus attention on the role of intellectuals and their relationship to other, economically active social groups in the creation of discourse. The crucial feature of intellectuals and intellectualism is the emphasis on rationalization and the development of systematic, coherent discourse in opposition to ad hoc and emotionally tainted modes of thought. In Weber's sociology, the process of intellectualization was one important feature of the master trend of rationalism whereby the everyday world was subordinated to the requirements of logically consistent thought. The more autonomous the intellectual stratum the more systematic its thought becomes, because intellectuals are not dependent upon the economic power or direction of immediate patrons. One illustration of this argument would be Weber's view of legal intellectuals who, from a university basis, developed rational constitutional law as a logically consistent system. By contrast, legal intellectuals who are employed directly by clients tend to develop a pragmatic approach to law, which is based upon case work rather than upon logical lines of deductive reasoning. An exclusive concentration on intellectual production for the analysis of discourse *in general* would, of course, be very misleading. As many writers have pointed out, most notably Gramsci, there are many sites and social mechanisms for the production of discourses with social effects. Such a view has informed a common critique of the classical tradition in the sociology of knowledge, which is accused of an exclusive concentration on the theoretical, abstract discourses of intellectuals to the neglect of the discourses of everyday life. Discourses operate at many different levels, each with its own means of discursive production.

Our argument in *The Dominant Ideology Thesis* has similar implications. There, we argued that many sociological analyses of belief, ideology or discourse gave priority to the production of these forms and tended to take their transmission and appropriation for granted. We argued that not only do subordinate classes act as a site for the creation of often dissenting discourses, but also that examination of the machinery of transmission shows that dominant classes are much more likely than subordinate classes to be affected by dominant discourses. This is not to exclude the possibility that dominant discourses will have effects on subordinate classes. However, as we argued in that book, these effects will be secondary.

Creation, transmission and appropriation are, in other words, relatively independent social processes, whose relationships vary from society to society and time to time.

Our present argument about individualism and capitalism concentrates on intellectualized discourses, serious speech acts as Foucault called them, and we have not considered the perhaps different discourses of the individual prevalent in the everyday world. We have done so deliberately for the reasons already given, namely, that the effect of discourses of any kind on the economy is through propertied classes that are most affected by the machinery of discursive transmission. In Chapter 4, we indicated that individualism shapes developing capitalism into a certain form through the economic practices of the members of certain social classes. Clearly, there are problems both of theory and method in establishing the relationship between discourse and economic practice, some of which we have referred to in earlier chapters. Theoretically, there is a difficulty of specifying the mechanism, whether of motivation or interpellation, that connects discourse and practice. Though once capitalism is established as the dominant economic form, this difficulty is less significant. Methodologically, especially when dealing with materials that are not contemporary, we may be able to identify discourses in various ways, but it is difficult to find out how discourses are manifest in specific practices.

The methodological problem is not simply a consequence of the fact that the original materials may not survive or the oral record is incomplete. Neither is it simply the fact that the tradition of the dominant class, as a literate tradition, survives better than the tradition of subordinate groups. The difficulty is that researchers are often too content with an explanation that shows merely parallel lines of development or plausible connections. For example, with respect to liberal individualism there is a seemingly plausible connection between the content of liberal doctrine, with its emphasis on political rights and contracts, and the structural requirements of a free economic market. Historical explanation of these relationships between liberal ideology and economic practice are typically arguments by way of analogy. Liberal individualism, of course, was always contradictory, since it expressed both the specific class interests of property owners and was also available as a doctrine for the radical critique of existing traditional rights, including these class interests. Another problem is that researchers are often content merely to show the presence of a belief without demonstrating its specific relation to given social structures. It is not enough, therefore, simply to show that a certain epoch gave a special emphasis to the individual; it is necessary to show that specific discourses of the individual had a direct function with respect to the development of political and economic structures. Sociological theory often attempts to resolve these problems merely by assertion, so the primary research difficulty is to translate these theoretical assumptions into research procedures that allow the effects of discourse actually to be demonstrated.

In this book, we have attempted to advance an argument consistent with that contained in our earlier work. One final issue in this respect should be mentioned. We have argued that individualism became appropriate to British capitalism in its early stages because it constructed the individual as the economic subject. As capitalism developed in the late nineteenth and twentieth centuries, individualism became less relevant, losing its position of dominance and leaving a plurality of discourses of the individual. In both the present book and our earlier work (Abercrombie, Hill and Turner, 1980, 1983), therefore, we have stressed the very great differences between capitalism in its original and in its developed form, the plurality of discourses in late capitalism, and the possibility that late capitalism can tolerate a wide range of discourses. None of this holds out any certainties for the future; it is perfectly possible for a discourse emphasizing collective rights to attain some social dominance and to define a collective economic subject for capitalism.

Conclusion

In this study we have argued that all societies have some theoretical conception of the individual. This is true even when the conception suggests that the collective is more important than the individual. We have outlined a process, which we have called the Discovery of the Individual. This process involves an emphasis on the difference between individuals and the importance of individuals. We have illustrated this development by analyses of novels, confessions, diaries and portraits. While all societies have some theory of the individual, the Discovery of the Individual was a process unique to Western culture. The Discovery of the Individual was a long-run development that took place over many centuries. During this period the emphasis on the individual became generalized, influencing many areas of culture and social relationships.

The Discovery of the Individual has had contradictory consequences. As individuals become more separate and different, they are more recognizably unique. In turn, uniqueness and identity are closely connected and the identification of individuals makes their control that much easier. We have called this the Foucault Paradox.

The Discovery refers to very general properties of individuals. That is, the process of differentiation does not pick out specific characteristics of persons for emphasis. There are, however, more specific discourses of the individual, which do place an emphasis on particular qualities as important. We have chosen four such discourses for discussion: individualism, individuality, anarchism and socialism. In the same context, we have also discussed the social constitution of the human agent as an individual.

The Discovery is the background discourse out of which the specific doctrine of individualism emerged. Although the conventional position is that individualism and capitalism are necessarily conjoined, we have shown that they developed separately. We endorse the view that capitalism developed in England as a conse-

189

quence of the transformation of agriculture in the early modern period. This transformation of the countryside had no necessary relationship to ideology. Individualism developed separately and as a result of distinctive causes. Individualism has a separate historical logic. Our position is that individualism as a doctrine is a consequence of discursive struggles. This discursive development was the outcome of intellectual conflicts, competition between groups and classes, and of institutional changes. It is in the arena of such conflicts that Habermas's notions of rationality and communicative competence are especially important. However, we have also noted that political struggle was an essential feature of the emerging dominance of individualism as a general discourse. In particular, individualism was mobilized in the seventeenth century as a legitimation of dissent. In sum, individualism became dominant as a result of discursive and political struggles. There was an undercurrent to the discursive dominance of individualism in the often contrary discourse of the family. The family can cut across individualism but at the same time acts as an institution permitting capital accumulation. Unrestrained individualism might well make family life impossible and, indeed, extreme individualism is subversive of almost all social arrangements.

Individualism and capitalism develop independently and separately. But in the seventeenth century they came to be related to one another. This relationship was not one based initially on an elective affinity; nor was it a functional relationship in origin, although we argue that it became one later. They related because they both became dominant social forms. Individualism shapes capitalism in a particular mould, in that is provides a particular type of economic subject, namely, the individual and individual property ownership. Capitalism influences individualism by confirming its discursive dominance and emphasizing the possessive aspects of individualistic theory. Individualism and capitalism are contingently related. We do not argue that capitalism causes individualism or vice versa. Furthermore, the capitalist mode of production does not have any necessary ideological conditions of existence.

We demonstrate this theoretical and empirical position by a series of case studies. We draw particular attention to the differences between Japan and the USA. These examples show that capitalism has developed with a variety of cultural systems.

In the modern period, the functional circle of capitalism and individualism gradually falls apart. This is the result of changes both in discourse and in capitalism. Collective discourses, arising partly out of the political struggles of the working class and other subordinate groups, become more prominent and powerful. The dominance of individualism has been weakened as a consequence of political and discursive struggle. For example, the commitment to equality of opportunity has challenged beliefs in the relatively unrestricted rights of individuals. The increasing importance of collective discourses is most obvious in the growing intervention by the state in social and economic life. The emphasis on the rights of the public citizen partly replaces the traditional stress on the rights of the private citizen. At the same time as individualism loses its position of discursive dominance, capitalism also acquires a more collective character. The crucial features of this are the development of the modern corporation and the replacement of individual ownership with corporate ownership. Capitalism begins to acquire a collective economic subject. There is thus the potential of a *new* functional circle of collective discourse and collective capitalism, formed in much the same kind of way as individualism and capitalism in the seventeenth and eighteenth centuries. This is a recent development in modern capitalism and varies in extent and pace among different societies.

Individualism thus loses its position of discursive dominance, both because it is no longer so closely associated with capitalism and because of the political and discursive strength of rival collective discourses. In such a situation a plurality of discourses of the individual flourishes, individuality in high culture and individualism in popular culture. There is no dominant ideology in modern capitalist societies.

References

Abercrombie, N. (1980), *Class, Structure and Knowledge: Problems in the Sociology of Knowledge* (Oxford: Blackwell)

Abercrombie, N., Hill, S., and **Turner, B. S.** (1980), *The Dominant Ideology Thesis* (London: Allen & Unwin).

Abercrombie, N., Hill, S., and **Turner, B. S.** (1983), 'Determinacy and indeterminacy in the theory of ideology', *New Left Review*, vol. 142, pp. 55–66.

Allegro, J. M. (1964), *The Dead Sea Scrolls: A Reappraisal* (Harmondsworth: Penguin).

Allegro, J. M. (1968), *The Discoveries in the Judean Desert* (Oxford: Oxford University Press).

Althusser, L. (1970), *Reading Capital* (London: New Left Books).

Amis, K. (1963), *New Maps of Hell* (London: New English Library).

Anderson, P. (1974), *Lineages of the Absolutist State* (London: New Left Books).

Arendt, H. (1959), *The Human Condition* (Garden City, NY: Anchor Books).

Bahr, H. (1920), 'Expression', reprinted in F. Frascina, and C. Harrison, (eds) (1982), op. cit., pp. 165–9.

Bakunin, M. (1950), *Marxism, Freedom, and the State* (New York: Freedom Press).

Ballard, J. G. (1965), *The Drowned World* (Harmondsworth: Penguin).

Barnes, E. A. (1979), *Who Should Know What? Social Science, Privacy and Ethics* (Harmondsworth: Penguin).

Beckett, J. V. (1977), 'English landownership in the later seventeenth and eighteenth centuries: the debate and the problems', *Economic History Review*, 2nd series, vol. 30, pp. 567–81.

Bell, D. (1974), *The Coming of Post-Industrial Society* (London: Heinemann).

Bell, D. (1979), *The Cultural Contradictions of Capitalism*, 2nd edn (London: Heinemann).

Bellah, R. N. (1964), 'Religious evolution', *American Sociological Review*, vol. 29, pp. 358–74.

Benjamin, W. (1968), 'The work of art in the age of mechanical reproduction', in F. Frascina and C. Harrison (eds) (1982), op. cit., pp. 217–20.

Berger, J. (1980), *About Looking* (London: Writers and Readers Cooperative).

Berger, B., Berger, P. L., and Kellner, H. (1973), *The Homeless Mind* (Harmondsworth: Penguin).

Berle, A. A., and Means, G. C. (1932), *The Modern Corporation and Private Property* (New York: Macmillan).

Berlin, I. (1969), *Four Essays on Liberty* (Oxford: Oxford University Press).

Berman, M. (1971), *The Politics of Authenticity, Radical Individualism and the Emergence of Modern Society* (London: Allen & Unwin).

Berman, M. (1983), *All That Is Solid Melts into Air* (London: Verso).

Bester, A. (1967), *Tiger! Tiger!* (Harmondsworth: Penguin).

Blunt, A. (1962), *Artistic Theory in Italy* (Oxford: Oxford University Press).

Bonfield, L. (1983), *Marriage Settlements, 1601–1740* (Cambridge: Cambridge University Press).

Bowra, C. M. (1959), *The Heritage of Symbolism* (London: Macmillan).

Boxer, C. (1965), *The Dutch Sea-Borne Empire* (Harmondsworth: Penguin).

Bradley, K., and Hill, S. (1983), '"After Japan": the quality circle transplant and productive efficiency', *British Journal of Industrial Relations*, vol. 21, pp. 291–311.

Bronowski, J. (1982), 'Leonardo da Vinci', in J. H. Plumb (ed.), *The Pelican Book of the Renaissance* (Harmondsworth: Penguin).

Brubaker, R. (1984), *The Limits of Rationality: An Essay on the Social and Moral Thought of Max Weber* (London: Allen & Unwin).

Brunner, J. (1965), *The Squares of the City* (Harmondsworth: Penguin).

Bulmer, M. (ed.) (1979), *Census, Surveys and Privacy* (New York: Holmes and Meier).

Burckhardt, J. (1958), *The Civilization of the Renaissance in Italy* (London: Harper and Row).

Burnham, J. (1941), *The Managerial Revolution* (Harmondsworth: Penguin).

Carter, A. (1971), *The Political Theory of Anarchism* (London: Routledge and Kegan Paul).

Chenu, M-D. (1969), *L'Éveil de la Conscience dans la Civilisation Médiévale* (Montreal: Institut d'Etudes Médiévales).

Clark, R. (1979), *The Japanese Company* (London: Yale University Press).

Cochran, T. C. (1985), *Challenges to American Values* (New York: Oxford University Press).

Cole, R. E. (1979), *Work, Mobility and Participation* (Berkeley, Calif.: University of California Press).

Coleman, D. C. (1977), *The Economy of England 1450–1750* (Oxford: Oxford University Press).

Connell, R. W., and Irving, T. H. (1980), *Class Structure in Australian History, Documents, Narrative and Argument* (Melbourne: Longman Cheshire).

Corrigan, P. (1977), 'Feudal relics or capitalist monuments? Notes on the sociology of unfree labour', *Sociology*, vol. 11, pp. 435–63.

Denoon, D. (1983), *Settler Capitalism: The Dynamics of Dependent Development in the Southern Hemisphere* (Oxford: Clarendon Press).

de Tocqueville, A. (1835), *Democracy in America* (Glasgow: Collins, 1968).

Devane, R. S. (1977), *The Failure of Individualism* (London: Greenwood Press).

Dewey, J. (1962), *Individualism Old and New* (New York: Capricorn Books).

Dore, R. P. (1964), 'Education: Japan', in R. E. Ward and D. A. Rustow (eds), *Political Modernization in Japan and Turkey* (Princeton, NJ: Princeton University Press), pp. 176–204.

Dore, R. P. (1973), *British Factory – Japanese Factory* (London: Allen & Unwin).

Douglas, M. (ed.) (1970), *Witchcraft Confessions and Accusations* (London: Macmillan).

Draper, J. W. (1871), *History of the American Civil War* (New York: Longman).

Dubois, A. B. (1938), *The English Business Company after the Bubble Act* (New York: The Commonwealth Fund).

Dubos, R. (1970), 'Biological determinants of individuality', in A. Kaplan (ed.), op. cit., pp. 148–159.

Dupont-Sommer, A. (1961), *The Essene Writings from Qumran* (Oxford: Oxford University Press).

Durkheim, E. (1893), *The Division of Labor in Society* (Glencoe: Free Press, 1960).

Durkheim, E. (1912), *The Elementary Forms of the Religious Life* (London: Allen & Unwin, 1954)

Durkheim, E. (1969), 'Individualism and the intellectuals', translated by S. and J. Lukes in *Political Studies*, vol. 17, pp. 19–30 (originally published in *La Revue Bleue*, 1898).

Edwards, R. (1979), *Contested Terrain* (London: Heinemann).

Elias, N. (1978), *The Civilizing Process: The History of Manners* (Oxford: Blackwell).

Elias, N. (1982), *State Formation and Civilization* (Oxford: Blackwell).

Elias, N. (1983), *The Court Society* (Oxford: Blackwell).

Engels, F. (1955), 'Letter to Starkenburg', in K. Marx and F. Engels, *Selected Correspondence* (Moscow: Progress Publishers).

Evans, E. J. (1983), *The Forging of the Modern State: Early Industrial Britain, 1783–1870* (London: Longman).

Finch, R. (1966), *The Sixth Sense: Individualism in French Poetry 1686–1760* (Toronto: University of Toronto Press).

Flaherty, D. (1972), *Privacy in Colonial New England* (Charlottesville, V.: University Press of Virginia).

Foster, J. (1974), *Class Struggle and the Industrial Revolution* (London: Weidenfeld and Nicolson).

Foucault, M. (1969), *The Archaeology of Knowledge* (London: Tavistock).

Foucault, M. (1979a), *Discipline and Punish: The Birth of the Prison* (Harmondsworth: Penguin).

Foucault, M. (1979b), *The History of Sexuality: Vol. 1, An Introduction* (Harmondsworth: Penguin).

Fox-Genovese, E., and Genovese, E. D. (1983), *Fruits of Merchant Capital* (New York: Oxford University Press).

Frascina, F., and Harrison, C. (eds) (1982), *Modern Art and Modernism* (London: Harper and Row).

Francis, A. (1980), 'Families, firms and finance capital', *Sociology*, vol. 14, pp. 1–27.

Friedman, M. (1958), 'Capitalism and freedom', in F. Morley (ed.), op. cit., pp. 168–82.

Frisby, D. (1981), *Sociological Impressionism: A Re-assessment of Georg Simmel's Social Theory* (London: Heinemann).

Frisby, D. (1984), *Georg Simmel* (London: Tavistock).

Furst, R. (1969), *Romanticism in Perspective* (London: Macmillan).

Gilsenan, M. (1973), *Saint and Sufi in Modern Egypt* (Oxford: Oxford University Press).

Goffman, E. (1956), *The Presentation of Self in Everyday Life* (Garden City, NY: Doubleday).

Goffman, E. (1961), *Encounters* (Indianapolis: Bobbs-Merrill).

Goffman, E. (1967), *Interaction Ritual* (Chicago: Aldine).

Goldmann, L. (1973), *The Philosophy of the Enlightenment, the Christian Burgess and the Enlightenment* (London: Routledge and Kegan Paul).

Goldmann, L. (1975), *Towards a Sociology of the Novel* (London: Tavistock).

Gombrich, E. H. (1982), *The Story of Art* (London: Phaidon) (originally published in 1950).

Goody, J. (1983), *The Development of the Family and Marriage in Europe* (Cambridge: Cambridge University Press).

Grosskurth, P. (1980), *Havelock Ellis: Stranger in the World* (London: Allen Lane).

Gungwu, W. (ed.) (1975), *Self and Biography: Essays on the Individual and Society in Asia* (Sydney: Sydney University Press).

Habbakuk, H. J. (1939–40), 'English landownership, 1680–1740', *Economic History Review*, vol. 10, pp. 2–17.

Habbakuk, H. J. (1950), 'Marriage settlements in the eighteenth century', *Transactions of the Royal Historical Society*, 4th series, vol. 32, pp. 15–30.

Hagen, E. F. (1962), *On the Theory of Social Change* (Homewood, Ill.: Dorsey).

Hallam, H. E. (1975), 'The medieval social picture', in E. Kamenka and R. S. Neale (eds), *Capitalism, Feudalism and Beyond* (London: Edward Arnold), pp. 28–49.

Harrington, J. (1656), *The Commonwealth of Oceana* (Heidelberg: Winter; ed. S. B. Liljegren, 1924).

Hauser, A. (1962), *The Social History of Art* (London: Routledge and Kegan Paul).

Hayek, F. A. (1967), 'The corporation in a democratic society: in whose interest might it and will it be run?', in F. A. Hayek (ed.), *Studies in Philosophy, Politics and Economics* (London: Routledge and Kegan Paul), pp. 300–12.

Heinlein, R. (1969), *Glory Road* (London: New English Library).

Heinlein, R. (1970), *Starship Troopers* (London: New English Library).

Heller, A. (1978), *Renaissance Man* (London: Routledge and Kegan Paul).

Hepworth, M., and **Turner, B. S.** (1982), *Confession, Studies in Deviance and Religion* (London: Routledge and Kegan Paul).

Hexter, J. H. (1961), *Reappraisals in History* (London: Longman).

Hill, C. (1969), *Reformation to Industrial Revolution* (Harmondsworth: Penguin).

Hill, C. (1980), 'A bourgeois revolution?', in J. G. A. Pocock (ed.), *Three British Revolutions, 1941, 1688, 1776* (Princeton, NJ: Princeton University Press), pp. 109–39.

Hill, S. (1981), *Competition and Control at Work* (London: Heinemann. Cambridge, Mass.: MIT Press).

Hilton, R. H. (1975), *The English Peasantry in the Later Middle Ages* (Oxford: Oxford University Press).

Hinnells, J. R. (1975), *Mithraic Studies*, 2 Vols (Manchester: Manchester University Press).

Hinnells, J. R. (1981), *Zoroastrianism and the Parsis* (London: Ward Lock Educational).

Hirsch, F., and **Goldthorpe, J. H.** (eds) (1978), *The Political Economy of Inflation* (London: Martin Robertson).

Holton, R. J. (1985), *The Transition from Feudalism to Capitalism* (London: Macmillan).

Honeyman, K. (1982), *Origins of Enterprise: Business Leadership in Industrial Revolution* (Manchester: Manchester University Press).

Howe, A. (1984), *The Cotton Masters 1830–1860* (Oxford: Clarendon Press).

Howell, C. (1983), *Land, Family and Inheritance in Transition: Kibworth Harcourt 1280–1700* (Cambridge: Cambridge University Press).

Huff, T. E. (ed.) (1981), *On the Roads to Modernity, Conscience, Science and Civilisations: Selected Writings by Benjamin Nelson* (Totowa, NJ: Rowman and Littlefield).

Hughes, H. S. (1959), *Consciousness and Society: The Re-orientation of European Social Thought, 1890–1930* (London: Macgibbon and Kee).

Hughes, R. (1980), *The Shock of the New* (London: BBC Publications).

Inkeles, A., and Smith, D. H. (1974), *Becoming Modern: Individual Change in Six Developing Countries* (London: Heinemann).

Jay, M. (1984), *Adorno* (London: Fontana).

Johnson, C. (1982), *MITI and the Japanese Miracle: The Growth of Industrial Policy, 1925–75* (Stanford, Calif.: Stanford University Press).

Jones, A. (1979), 'Caddington, Kensworth and Dunstable in 1297', *Economic History Review*, 2nd series, vol. 32, pp. 316–27.

Kaplan, A. (ed.) (1970), *Individuality and the New Society* (Seattle, Wash.: University of Washington Press).

Kelley, G. (1968), 'Ideology in some modern science-fiction novels', *Journal of Popular Culture*, vol. 1, pp. 91–113.

King, E. P. (1973), *Peterborough Abbey 1086–1310: A Study in the Land Market* (Cambridge: Cambridge University Press).

Kocka, J. (1978), 'Entrepreneurs and managers in German industrialization', in P. Mathias and M. M. Postan (eds), *The Cambridge Economic History of Europe*, Vol. VII, Part 1 (Cambridge: Cambridge University Press), pp. 492–589.

Koschman, J. V. (1978), 'Introduction: soft rule and expressive protest', in J. V. Koschman (ed.), *Authority and the Individual in Japan* (Tokyo: University of Tokyo Press), pp. 1–30.

Ladurie, E. Le Roy (1980), *Montaillou* (Harmondsworth: Penguin).

Lasch, G. (1980), *The Culture of Narcissism* (London: Sphere).

Laslett, P. (1983), 'Family and household as work group and kin group: areas of traditional Europe compared', in R. Wall (ed.), *Family Forms in Historic Europe* (Cambridge: Cambridge University Press), pp. 513–63.

Laumer, K. (1967), *A Plague of Demons* (Harmondsworth: Penguin).

Lee, J. J. (1978), 'Labour in German industrialization', in P. Mathias and M. M. Postan (eds), *The Cambridge Economic History of Europe*, Vol. VII, Part 1 (Cambridge: Cambridge University Press), pp. 442–91.

Lehmann, J-P. (1982), *The Roots of Modern Japan* (London: Macmillan).

Lerner, D. (1958), *The Passing of Traditional Society: Modernizing the Middle East* (New York: Free Press).

197

Lewis, C. S. (1936), *The Allegory of Love* (London: Oxford University Press).

Lewis, I. M. (1971), *Ecstatic Religion: An Anthropological Study of Spirit Possession and Shamanism* (Harmondsworth: Penguin).

Locke, J. (1690), *Two Treaties of Government* (Cambridge: Cambridge University Press; ed. P. Laslett, 1960).

Lukács, G. (1971), *The Theory of the Novel* (London: Merlin Press).

Lukes, S. (1973), *Individualism* (Oxford: Blackwell).

McLellan, D. (ed.) (1971), *Marx's Grundrisse* (London: Macmillan).

McClelland, D. C. (1961), *The Achieving Society* (New York: Van Nostrand).

Macfarlane, A. (1978), *The Origins of English Individualism* (Oxford: Blackwell).

Macpherson, C. B. (1962), *The Political Theory of Possessive Individualism* (Oxford: Oxford University Press).

Macpherson, C. B. (1975), 'Capitalism and the changing concept of property', in E. Kamenka and R. S. Neale (eds), *Capitalism, Feudalism and Beyond* (London: Edward Arnold), pp. 104–24.

Mannheim, K. (1953), 'Conservative thought', in K. Mannheim (ed.), *Essays in Sociology and Social Psychology* (London: Routledge and Kegan Paul)

Manning, B. (1976), *The English People and the English Revolution, 1640–1649* (London: Heinemann).

Marshall, G. (1982), *In Search of the Spirit of Capitalism* (London: Hutchinson).

Marshall, T. H. (1977), *Class, Citizenship and Social Development* (Chicago and London: University of Chicago Press).

Marx, K. (1970), *Capital*, Vol. I (London: Lawrence and Wishart) (originally published in 1887).

Marx, K. (1973), *Grundrisse* (Harmondsworth, Penguin).

Marx, K. (1974), *Capital*, Vol., III (London: Lawrence and Wishart) (originally published in 1894).

Marx, K., and Engels, F. (1970), *Selected Works* (London: Lawrence and Wishart).

Masao, T. (1968), *Modern Japanese Economy since 1868* (London: Japan Cultural Society).

Miller, D. (1976), *Social Justice* (Oxford: Oxford University Press).

Moore, B. (1968), *Social Origins of Dictatorship and Democracy: Lord and the Peasant in the Making of the Modern World* (London: Allen Lane).

Morishima, M. (1983), *Why Has Japan 'Succeeded'?* (Cambridge: Cambridge University Press).

Morley, F. (ed.) (1958), *Essays on Individuality* (Philadelphia: University of Pennsylvania Press).

Morris, C. (1972), *The Discovery of the Individual 1050–1200* (London: SPCK).

Neale, R. S. (1975), ' "The bourgeoisie, historically, has played a most revolutionary part" ' in E. Kamenka and R. S. Neale (eds), *Feudalism, Capitalism and Beyond* (London: Edward Arnold), pp. 84–102.

New York Stock Exchange (1985), *Fact Book, 1985* (New York: NYSE).

Nozick, R. (1974), *Anarchy, State and Utopia* (Oxford: Blackwell).

Ouchi, W. G. (1981), *Theory Z* (New York: Avon).

Pangborn, E. (1966), *Mirror for Observers* (Harmondsworth: Penguin).

Pangborn, E. (1969), *Davy* (Harmondsworth: Penguin).

Parekh, B. (1982), *Marx's Theory of Ideology* (London: Croom Helm).

Parsons, T. (1937), *The Structure of Social Action* (Glencoe, Ill: Free Press).

Parsons, T. (1963), 'Christianity and modern industrial society', in E. Tiryakian (ed.), *Sociological Theory, Values and Sociocultural Change* (New York: Free Press) pp. 33–70.

Parsons, T., and Smelser, N. J. (1956), *Economy and Society: A Study in the Integration of Economic and Social Theory* (London: Routledge and Kegan Paul.

Pashukanis, E. B. (1978), *Law and Marxism: A General Theory* (London: Ink Links).

Peel, J. D. Y. (1971), *Herbert Spencer* (London: Heinemann).

Perkin, H. J. (1968), 'The social causes of the British industrial revolution', *Transactions of the Royal Historical Society*, 5th series, vol. 18, pp. 123–44.

Phythian-Adams, C. (1979), *Desolation of a City: Coventry and the Urban Crisis of the Late Middle Ages* (Cambridge: Cambridge University Press).

Plumb, J. H. (ed.) (1982), *The Pelican Book of the Renaissance* (Harmondsworth: Penguin).

Pocock, J. G. A. (1975), *The Machiavellian Moment* (Princeton, NJ: Princeton University Press).

Pocock, J. G. A. (1980), 'Introduction', in J. G. A. Pocock (ed.), *Three British Revolutions, 1641, 1688, 1776* (Princeton, NJ: Princeton University Press), pp. 3–20.

Poggi, G. (1983), *Calvinism and the Capitalist Spirit* (London: Macmillan).

Pohl, F., and Kornbluth, C. M. (1960) *Wolfbane* (London: Gollancz).

Pohl, F., and Kornbluth, C. M. (1965), *The Space Merchants* (Harmondsworth: Penguin).

Pollard, S. (1978), 'Labour in Great Britain', in P. Mathias and M. M. Postan (eds), *The Cambridge Economic History of Europe*, Vol. VII, Part 1 (Cambridge: Cambridge University Press), pp. 97–179.

Postan, M. M. (1973), *Essays in Medieval Agriculture and General Problems of the Medieval Economy* (Cambridge: Cambridge University Press).

Potter, D. M. (1965), 'American individualism in the 20th century', in G. Mills (ed.), op. cit., pp. 92–112.

Poulantzas, N. (1973), *Political Power and Social Classes* (London: New Left Books and Sheed & Ward).

Prais, S. J. (1981), *The Evolution of Giant Firms in Britain*, 2nd impression (Cambridge: Cambridge University Press).

Rasmussen, K., (1931), *The Netsilik Eskimos: Social Life and Spiritual Culture* (Copenhagen: Nordisk-Vorlag).

Rex, J. (1971), 'The plural society: the South African case', *Race*, vol. 12, pp. 401–13.

Reynolds, S. (1984), *Kingdoms and Communities in Western Europe, 900–1300* (Oxford: Clarendon Press).

Riesman, D. (1954), *The Lonely Crowd* (New Haven, Conn.: Yale University Press).

Robertson, D. W. (1980), *Essays in Medieval Culture* (Princeton, NJ: Princeton University Press).

Robertson, R. (1982), 'Parsons on the evolutionary significance of American religions', *Sociological Analysis*, vol. 43, pp. 307–26.

Roth, G., and Schluchter, W. (1979), *Max Weber's Vision of History, Ethics and Methods* (Berkeley, Calif.: University of California).

Rule, J., McAdam, D., Stearns, L., and Uglo, D. (1980), *The Politics of Privacy* (New York: Mentor Books).

Russell, E. F. (1963), *Three to Conquer* (Harmondsworth: Penguin).

Sabine, G. H. (1964), *A History of Political Theory* (London: Harrap).

Samuelson, P. A. (1965), 'Modern economic realities and individualism', in G. Mills (ed.), op. cit., pp. 51–71.

Saxonhouse, G. R. (1976), 'Country girls and communication among competitors in the Japanese cotton spinning industry', in H. Patrick (ed.), *Japanese Industrialization and Its Social Consequences* (Berkeley, Calif.: University of California Press), pp. 97–126.

Schenk, H. G. (1966), *The Mind of the European Romantics* (London: Constable).

Schochet, G. J. (1975), *Patriarchalism in Political Thought* (Oxford: Oxford University Press).

Scott, J. (1979), *Corporations, Classes and Capitalism* (London: Hutchinson).

Sennett, R. (1974), *The Fall of Public Man* (Cambridge: Cambridge University Press).

Sethi, S. P., Namiki, N., and Swanson, C. L. (1984), *The False Promise of the Japanese Miracle* (London: Pitman).

Shils, E. (1975), *Center and Periphery: Essays in Macro Sociology* (Chicago and London: University of Chicago Press).

Simmel, G. (1950), 'Individual and society in eighteenth and nineteenth century views of life: an example of philosophical sociology', in

K. H. Wolff (ed.), *The Sociology of Georg Simmel* (New York: Free Press)).

Simmel, G. (1978), *The Philosophy of Money* (London: Routledge and Kegan Paul.

Smith, A. (1776), *An Inquiry into the Nature and Causes of the Wealth of Nations* (London: Methuen, 1950).

Smith, G. L. (1973), *Religion and Trade in New Netherland, Dutch Origins and American Development* (Ithaca and London: Cornell University Press).

Smith, R. J. (1983), *Japanese Society: Tradition, Self, and the Social Order* (Cambridge: Cambridge University Press).

Snell, K. D. M. (1985), *Annals of the Labouring Poor: Social Change and Agrarian England, 1660–1900* (Cambridge: Cambridge University Press).

Spearitt, P., and Walker, D. (eds) (1979), *Australian Popular Culture* (Sydney: Allen & Unwin).

Steven, R. (1983), *Classes in Contemporary Japan* (Cambridge: Cambridge University Press).

Stirner, M. (1907), *The Ego and His Own* (London: Constable) (originally published 1844).

Stock Exchange (n.d.), *The Stock Exchange Survey of Share Ownership* (London: The Stock Exchange).

Stone, L. (1979), *The Family, Sex and Marriage in England 1500–1800* (Harmondsworth: Penguin).

Stone, L. (1980), 'The results of the English revolutions of the seventeenth century', in J. G. A. Pocock (ed.), *Three British Revolutions, 1641, 1688, 1776* (Princeton, NJ: Princeton University Press), pp. 23–108.

Sumiya, M., and Taira, K. (eds) (1979), *An Outline of Japanese Economic History 1603–1940* (Tokyo: University of Tokyo Press).

Swart, K. W. (1962), 'Individualism in the mid-nineteenth century (1826–60)', *Journal of the History of Ideas*, vol. 23, pp. 77–90.

Taira, K. (1978), 'Factory labour and the industrial revolution in Japan', in P. Mathias and M. M. Postan (eds), *The Cambridge Economic History of Europe*, Vol. VII, Part 2 (Cambridge: Cambridge University Press), pp. 166–214.

Tawney, R. H. (1941), 'The rise of the gentry', *Economic History Review*, vol. 11, pp. 1–38.

Taylor, C. (1979), 'Atomism', in A. Kontos (ed.), *Powers, Possessions, and Freedom* (Toronto: University of Toronto Press), pp. 39–62.

Therborn, G. (1980), *The Ideology of Power and the Power of Ideology* (London: New Left Books).

Tomlinson, A. (1974), *The Medieval Face* (London: The National Portrait Gallery).

Toulmin, S. (1972), *Human Understanding*, Vol. 1 (Oxford: Oxford University Press).

Trinkaus, C., and **Oberman, H. A.** (eds) (1974), *The Pursuit of Holiness in Late Medieval and Renaissance Religion* (Leiden: E. J. Brill).

Troeltsch, E. (1912), *The Social Teaching of the Christian Churches* (New York: Macmillan, 1931).

Turner, B. S. (1981), *For Weber, Essays on the Sociology of Fate* (London: Routledge and Kegan Paul).

Turner, B. S. (1984), *The Body and Society: Explorations in Social Theory* (Oxford: Blackwell).

Turner, F. J. (1920), *The Frontier in American History* (New York: Henry Holt, 1937).

Ullman, W. (1961), *Principles of Government and Politics in the Middle Ages* (London: Methuen).

Ullman, W. (1967), *The Individual and Society in the Middle Ages* (London: Methuen).

Utton, M. A. (1979), *Diversification and Competition* (Cambridge: Cambridge University Press).

Utton, M. A. (1982), *The Political Economy of Big Business* (Oxford: Martin Robertson).

Van Vogt, A. E. (1970), *The Weapon Shops of Isher* (London: New English Library).

Watt, I. (1957), *The Rise of the Novel* (London: Chatto and Windus).

Weber, Marianne (1975), *Max Weber: A Biography* (New York: Wiley).

Weber, M. (1930), *The Protestant Ethic and the Spirit of Capitalism* (London: Allen & Unwin) (originally published in 1904–5).

Weber, M. (1958), *The City* (Glencoe: Free Press).

Weber, M. (1961), *General Economic History* (New York: Collier).

Weintraub, K. J. (1978), *The Value of the Individual, Self and Circumstance in Autobiography* (Chicago and London: The University of Chicago Press).

Wells, H. G. (1914), *New Worlds for Old* (London: Constable).

Westin, A. F. (1967), *Privacy and Freedom* (London: Bodley Head).

Whyte, W. H. (1956), *The Organization Man* (New York: Simon and Schuster).

Williams, R. (1976), *Key Words* (London: Fontana/Croom Helm).

Wolin, S. S. (1961), *Politics and Vision, Continuity and Innovation in Western Political Thought* (London: Allen & Unwin).

Wolpe, H. (1972), 'Capitalism and cheap labour power in South Africa', *Economy and Society*, Vol. 1, pp. 425–56.

Yamamura, K. (1978), 'Entrepreneurship, ownership, and management in Japan', in P. Mathias and M. M. Postan (eds), *The Cambridge Economic History of Europe*, Vol. VII, Part 2 (Cambridge: University Press), pp. 215–64.

References

Zeitlin, I. M. (1968), *Ideology in the Development of Sociological Theory* (Englewood Cliffs, NJ: Prentice-Hall).

Zeitlin, M. (1974), 'Corporate ownership and control: the large corporation and the capitalist class', *American Journal of Sociology*, vol. 79, pp. 1073–1119.

Zeitlin, M. (1978), 'Who Owns America?', *The Progressive*, vol. 42, pp. 14–21.

ADDENDUM

The following references were omitted from the list provided at the end of the volume (pages 192–203).

Berger, P. L. (1969), *The Social Reality of Religion* (London: Faber and Faber).

Dore, R. P. (1983), 'Goodwill and the spirit of market capitalism', *British Journal of Sociology*, vol. 34, pp. 459–82.

Durkheim, E. (1977), *The Evolution of Educational Thought* (London: Routledge and Kegan Paul).

Lenski, G. (1961), *The Religious Factor* (New York: Doubleday, Anchor Books).

Mill, J. S. (1946), *On Liberty* (Oxford: Blackwell; ed. R. B. McCallum).

Miller, D. (1967), *Individualism* (Austin, Tex.: University of Texas Press).

Mills, G. (ed.) (1965), *Innocence and Power: Individualism in 20th Century America* (Austin, Tex.: University of Texas Press).

Tillich, P. (1952), *The Courage to Be* (New Haven, Conn.: Yale University Press).

Weber, M. (1968), *Economy and Society* (Totowa, NJ: Bedminster).

Erratum

The references to the work of Michel Foucault on pages 43 and 56 should be to Foucault (1979b) rather than Foucault (1976).

Index

204